Praise for Off the Beaten Trail

"This is a brave, beautiful book. Most of us experience periods of doubt and discontent at some point in our lives, and the way we respond to those seasons can chart the course for the rest of our lives. Jake made a bold choice to question everything. The lessons of his search, told here in Off the Beaten Trail, can help you when you arrive at your next set of crossroads."

-CHRIS GUILLEBEAU

NYT bestselling author of *The $100 Startup* and *The Happiness of Pursuit*

"I hated to see Off the Beaten Trail end. I wanted more. Jake Heilbrunn may be a young man but no one but an old soul could write a book that contains so much inspiration and wisdom."

-PAUL COLEMAN, PSY.D.

Author of *Finding Peace When Your Heart Is in Pieces*

"Jake Heilbrunn's journey of self discovery gives hope to all who are willing to risk the unknown in the pursuit of finding oneself and one's passion. His wisdom belies his youth and his message speaks to all of us who seek clarity and purpose in our lives."

-WALTER GREEN

Author of *THIS Is the MOMENT!* ..How One man's Yearlong Journey Captured the Power of Extraordinary Gratitude.

D0188030

Off the Beaten Trail

A Young Man's Soul-Searching Journey through Central America

JAKE HEILBRUNN

First Edition

ISBN: 978-0-9977612-0-7

True Path Publishing
122 15th Street
PO Box 473
Del Mar, CA 92014
www.JakeHeilbrunn.com

Editor: Madalyn Stone
Cover photo: Trevor Capozza
Cover Design: 1106 Design
Interior Design: Jay Polmar

Table of Contents

Introduction

A little voice in my head gnawed at me for months, whispering a vision that was exciting and fascinating, yet seemingly unrealistic and impossible. At the time, I was anxiety-ridden and depressed, breaking out in hives and rashes almost daily. This voice persisted to call out to me until the day I finally mustered the courage to answer it. Little did I know that by answering this calling, I would embark on the journey of a lifetime—one I'm still on—and my life would radically change.

This is the true story of my decision to break off from an unfulfilling path and pave a new one. It is a story of self-discovery that describes the inner workings of the human mind, the universal struggles that we all face and insights about how I moved past them. While at college and in Central America, I kept a journal where I documented my thoughts and experiences, enabling me to share with you my emotions and encounters in vivid detail. I had the idea of writing this book before I left on my travels. That idea turned into a purpose—a mission I was called to answer—as I progressed on my journey and realized that personal fulfillment stems from the process of following your own true path.

We each have a personal calling, a path in life that speaks to us. The tragedy is that many of us never answer the call, or are unaware that it even exists. Many things – fear, the possibility of failure, "what ifs," external expectations and pressures, self-limiting beliefs – prevent us from living a life in pursuit of our dreams. And yet, for many of us, simply knowing this truth does not enable us to summon the courage to answer our calling and take action. That's why I wrote this book.

By sharing my story, I hope you will acknowledge your own and realize that you can take your life in any direction. My journey is a testament to the fact that there are limitless ways to live our lives, and when we follow our intuition, the universe guides us down a path that is nothing short of our wildest dreams.

"It's important that we share our experiences with other people. Your story will heal you and your story will heal somebody else. When you tell your story, you free yourself and give other people permission to acknowledge their own story." - Iyanla Vanzant

This book is dedicated to my dad.

And to anyone who is going through a rough time and may feel on the edge of taking a leap of faith.

Prologue

March 19, 2015

Sitting at Gate 55A, I felt at peace. It seemed strange how serene I was considering the present circumstance. I was drawn to the faces of the people around me, pondering what their lives were like, what they were thinking, where they were going, and what drew them to this moment in time.

I was waiting to board a one-way flight to Guatemala with just a backpack. I barely spoke any Spanish. I had no phone. I had never traveled alone before. I was going by myself to a third world country where I was going to board a bus and embark on a nine-hour trip to a rural, northern town. Part of me felt like I was walking into a disaster. But the other part assured me that true courage is stepping past your fears in pursuit of your wildest dreams even if you don't know exactly how you will get there. I chose to focus on the latter.

It's comical how unpredictable life is. There is absolutely no way in hell I would have believed someone if they told me a year ago that I would be where I was in this moment. But reality speaks the ultimate truth. And there I was, an ambitious and maybe slightly naive eighteen-year-old kid whose curiosity led him to journey on a completely unknown and uncommon path. Excitement, eagerness, and trepidation all stirred through my body and mind. But I was resolute. Outwardly, what I was doing could be perceived as ludicrous. Yet, despite my feelings of consternation, I felt wholeheartedly that this decision was going to lead me in the right direction, even if I didn't know where that was.

Of course, experience is such a personal commodity, and it is ultimately up to the individual to attribute meaning to one's own life experiences. It is actually irrelevant whether or not others agree with your interpretation. As life coach Tony Robbins says, "Nothing in life has any meaning except the meaning you give it. So make sure that you consciously choose the meanings that are most in alignment with the destiny you've chosen for yourself."

When I embraced this realization and disregarded my fears, I felt overwhelmingly tranquil. The events that had transpired in my life had led me to this moment. And I couldn't help but reflect on the last seven months and how I ended up here...

CHAPTER 1

Are You Satisfied with the Life You're Living?

August 2014

*"Life is like a box of chocolates. You never know
what you're gonna get."*
—Forrest Gump

It all started in August 2014, three days after I arrived in Ohio to attend Ohio State University. I noticed some bumps on my thighs. Red, itchy, and extremely irritating bumps. I didn't know what they were, but their presence was impossible to ignore. They grew in number, and the stinging itchiness that accompanied them only continued to get worse. Before long, I waddled almost everywhere I went, as even the touch of my shorts on these bumps was extremely aggravating. I felt like a duck. I would have liked to say I felt like a lion entering college roaring with confidence. But no, I felt like an uncomfortable, weak, and insecure little waddling duck.

Great, I thought. *A speed bump that I will just need to get over, and then my skin will be fine, and in no time, things will be great!* But I had no idea what I was in for. For the entire semester—almost daily—I awoke to new hives and rashes on my body. Even if it were a single hive, I was afraid of it breaking out into a big rash because that's how my worst skin problems developed. This fear made me severely anxious.

I was convinced something in my new environment was causing these problems; a toxin or chemical that I was exposed to disagreed with me. *All I need is to get back home to San Diego and I will be fine. Screw Ohio for causing these problems.* I had not envisioned anything like this happening to me. Why me, of all people? *Why can't someone else get this?*

Unfortunately, the rashes and hives didn't subside. Not only were these rashes aesthetically unappealing, but they were awfully uncomfortable. I literally did not feel comfortable in my own skin. My negative thoughts and anger only made the situation worse. My skin problems seemed to drain all of my self-esteem. I felt insecure and self-conscious. I had no confidence. I dreaded going out because I felt so uncomfortable, both physically and mentally. But worst of all, I began to hate myself.

By the end of my first semester, I had also lost all confidence in the medical system. Immunologists, allergists, and dermatologists had recommended so many different pills and creams, yet nothing worked. I had been tested for just about everything. I had had video camera tubes stuck up my butt and down my throat; I had peed in diagnostic jars and pooped in test tubes; I had spit in test cups; I had been patch-tested for thirty-six allergens all over my back; I had taken skin-prick tests and blood tests; I had blown in a diagnostic paper bag for three hours; and I had gone through skin biopsies. The doctors eventually diagnosed me with chronic urticaria (chronic hives), another way of saying, "We have no idea what the hell is causing your problem, but hives and rashes are a result of it." I felt as if this condition was preventing me from living the life I wanted—a life of happiness. And it was—but only because I let it happen.

I didn't choose to be optimistic about my condition. I didn't choose to stop complaining about my problem. And I definitely didn't choose to allow myself to be happy—in my eyes, I couldn't be happy as long as my skin was like this. My brain decided that as long as I had this condition, my life would suck and I would be miserable.

* * * * *

When winter break finally rolled around, I was beyond relieved. *Perfect, leaving Ohio is just what I need. When I'm back in San Diego, my skin will return to normal!* But being back home didn't seem to change anything. My mom, with her background in nutrition, had been saying for a long time that she thought my skin issues were related to my gut.

So I went to see a holistic doctor who put me on a strict diet to avoid gluten and other potentially harmful foods. The doctor explained to me, "We must solve the root of the problem." He said that the skin ultimately reacts to what is either being put in or on the body. It made a lot of sense to me that what I was eating could be a culprit. I started a new diet on January 1st. It seemed appropriate with the New Year—hopefully, a new beginning as well. My skin started to clear very slowly, but the stinging and itching did not quickly subside.

While home, I thought a lot about not going back to school. As a senior in high school, I had considered taking a year off before college to explore other options and maybe even travel abroad. I didn't understand why these thoughts kept entering my head. It seemed that everyone else I talked to had his or her plan set: going straight to college. I didn't want to feel like the odd man out, choosing a path that could be seen as foolish or easy. I was scared that departing from the common course could leave me behind in the rat race to success. Yet, the idea of traveling or volunteering abroad kept drifting into my head. When I thought about it, I felt both excited and afraid of the unknown. I pushed those thoughts away. I thought that my mind was just conjuring up unrealistic ideas about a path in life that didn't exist—or at least only existed for a special few.

The struggles I had at college led me to see the world in a new light. I began to question the "why" in everything. *Why am I even in school right now? I don't have the faintest idea of what I want to do the rest of my life, and here I am spending thousands of dollars to copy and paste what my professor tells me to in order to attain a "number" (grade point average) that helps distinguish my worthiness as compared with another student's "number" so we can all be employed by people who value and compare these "numbers." Perfect logic. Why are we making graphs every day in economics class? The professor has not once explained to us the significance of the graphs or any economic terms. I want to learn about things that relate to my everyday life and the world around me. Why just graphs?!? And even if my skin problems were to magically disappear, what then?*

It seemed pointless to slave away at uninspiring classwork five days a week, cramming information into my mind only for it to be dumped out and forgotten after the test. After an unfulfilling five days, the *weekend* arrived—the happy ending to an unsatisfying week. I joined the masses and partied until I couldn't remember what happened, killing brain cells that I had worked so hard to develop during the week before. I had been "living for the weekend" since my sophomore year in high school. I was done. I wanted a life where I could wake up every day excited to add value to the world. I wanted a life where I looked forward to Mondays, eager to follow my passions. I wanted a life where I wanted to work on the weekends because it fulfilled me and made a difference in the lives of others.

Beyond just questioning aspects of my everyday life, I began to explore deeper philosophical matters that had no answer. *What is the purpose of life? Why is it that not one person can give me a legitimate answer as to why we are all here?* At eighteen years old, I felt alone. It seemed as if no one else my age had even the slightest interest in the deep philosophical concepts I pondered daily. I thought that everyone else was concerned with their exams, the party coming up on Friday, football, or what they were going to eat for lunch. I didn't blame them because I am sure if it had not been for my unhappiness, I wouldn't have been so deeply concerned with these questions. I knew that my past experiences and present circumstances influenced my thoughts. Here I was trying to contemplate how the human race was created and for what purpose. Why are we here?

Because I was unsure of what I wanted to do for the rest of my life, I began to question my friends and peers about what they were studying.

"Hey, Ryan, what are you studying?"

"Mechanical engineering."

"Oh, wow, that sounds interesting. Why?"

"Because a mechanical engineering degree can lead to a job that pays a ton of money. And I like math, so I figured, why not?"

"Hey, Cole, what are you studying?"

"Accounting."

"Nice, man. Why accounting?"

"A job in accounting is stable and makes solid money. My sister is an accountant and got a great job right out of school with high pay."

I asked so many people these questions and got the same response almost every time. Of course, every now and then the person I asked was deeply interested and passionate about what he or she was actually studying. But more often than not, the responses were all directed at one thing: money. *Is everyone actually in it for all the same reason? Money?* I understand that money is important and necessary. But how is that the main driving factor for so many people here? Will making lots of money actually ensure happiness? Will pursuing a 9-5 job every day for the next forty years bring fulfillment even when no passion exists for the job? Maybe I'm the one who is looking at this wrong and should be focusing more on the money?

People get a job so they can afford to have a life—the ability to buy food, shelter, clothing, and so on. The type of job they seek appears to be determined by the amount of money they hope to earn and little to do with what they really care about. They spend all their time at a job they hate and end up having no time to live the life they're working so hard for. The logic didn't add up in my mind.

I grew up in a well-to-do suburb in southern California where material things are an integral part of life. Everyone is concerned about getting a college degree straight after high school. There is no time to mess around. You start working immediately after college graduation and then retire when you have enough money saved up. This is the dogma I grew up with that seemed to ensure "success": a big house, a nice car, and a job title that looks and sounds like you're raking in tons of cash. These were the things that were supposed to ensure happiness. At least, this is what my community raised me to believe.

But I also knew that I had a different perspective about money. My dad had had what many wanted: an Ivy League degree, a high-paying job, a nice car, and a fine house. He majored in literature, which he felt passionate about. However, because of others' expectations, he ended up going to medical school after graduating from college. It was a much safer choice than pursuing a career as a writer. My dad had no real interest in medicine but felt inclined to follow the course that had been prescribed for him. A stable, high-paying job with a big, well-known company was the goal that everyone wanted, or so it seemed. But after years of receiving a high-paying salary at a job he hated, my dad ran out of fuel.

When I was eleven, I came home from school and learned that my dad had quit his job. He ran out of fuel because the fuel he was running on was not his own. My dad has what is called a *major depressive disorder,* a condition involving changes in the brain's chemistry that adversely affected him in many aspects of his life. I remember when he didn't get out of bed for a month, but I didn't think much of it at the time. I didn't know my dad was depressed, and I didn't know that his condition could literally disable him. The years passed, and my dad still did not work. I hated to see my father unhappy. He had lost his zest for life in many ways. I know he is an insightful person with a real spark for learning new things. He is a caring, responsible, and outstanding father. He is also extremely creative and an amazing writer. I couldn't believe how this incredible man had become so submerged in this condition. And I couldn't help but fear that I might fall into a similar trap.

Part of the reason I went to Ohio State was to experience something different. When I told people I was from San Diego, I got the same response every time: "Ew, why Ohio?" They would ask this with their heads slightly tilted and eyes sinking back, totally confused.

I would talk about my love for sports, the school's pride, its renowned business school, prestigious alumni network, the scholarships and financial packages I had been awarded, and my yearning to experience a new place with people who came from a different area than where I had grown up. I was usually met with a response something along the lines of, "Oh, that makes sense—I guess." I wasn't sure if the person really understood my words or was still confused by my decision but nodded in agreement anyway.

Although Ohio was definitely different from San Diego, I realized that what I was searching for, what I desired, was something *drastically* different. I wanted to experience a world completely different from what I knew.

I began toying with the idea of taking a semester off and traveling abroad. The thought stirred within my belly, creating a warm feeling that this was "right," and at the same time, causing a release of adrenaline that produced a sense of exhilaration and anticipation. I felt as if I were about to sky dive or bungee jump, to take that indescribable leap of faith. But I was just sitting at my desk imagining myself trekking through unknown lands in places so far away and tremendously different from anything I had ever experienced. I got lost in this vision until I had to shake myself awake to the unfulfilling reality of my life.

I mean, after all, college was hyped-up to be the "best four years of your life," filled with crazy parties and outrageous fun. At least, that's what I had pictured going in because that's what everyone portrayed it to be. I had it all planned out. I would thrive in my classes, join various clubs to help boost my resume, and get ripped at the gym every day. The stars would align for me in college as they had in high school. But I didn't realize that things don't always play out as you think they will.

Despite my dreams and the significant doubts I had about what I was doing, at the end of the holiday break, I decided to return to school for my second semester.

And oh boy, was that a mistake.

*"Open your eyes, look within. Are you satisfied
with the life you're living?"*
—Bob Marley

CHAPTER 2

Hiding from the Truth

January 12, 2015

"If you fuel your journey on the opinions of others,
you are going to run out of gas."

—Dr. Steve Maraboli

My first day back for my second semester at Ohio State happened to be the day of the College Football National Championship. And Ohio State was in it. This was the first college football playoff in history, and the hype for this game was astounding. College football in Ohio is a *big* deal. Everywhere, people were covered in scarlet and gray from head to toe, beaming with pride. There was an electric buzz in the air as everyone at school had an attachment, a love, for Ohio State. Everyone, it seemed, except me.

It's not that I had anything against the football team. I had enjoyed watching all of the games that year. But because my hives and resulting unhappiness and anxiety started when I came to Ohio, I didn't have the most positive association with the school. I knew academics were not the cause for my anxiety. I did well my first semester, even making the Dean's List. In addition, I liked my roommate and had made several friends. So I knew something else was going on.

But beyond just coming back to Ohio, I wondered if there were other, more significant reasons why I didn't want to return. *What if going to college in general is not right for me? What if my anxiety and depression are due to a mismatch between my current and desired reality? What if the life I'm living is not for me at all?*

I remember asking so many people how their holiday break was and if they were excited to be back. The typical response was usually something along the lines of, "Yeah, break was nice. But I am so ready to be back!" I felt my spirit wither briefly each time I heard this. *Why am I the only one absolutely dreading coming back here? Is there something wrong with me?*

I went through the motions robotically that first day of the semester. As the day wore on, I began to feel short of breath with a knot tightening in my throat. Tears threatened, and I suppressed the urge to cry, frustrated as to why I couldn't identify the source of this awful anxiety. Oddly, my new professors and classes seemed much more interesting than the ones from the previous semester. Finally done with my classes for the day, I slumped into the chair in my dorm room, feeling trapped. The cold, contoured surface of the chair sent a chill up my spine. I didn't want to be here. It was actually a beautiful and comfortable dorm room. Yet I hated being back in this room, which felt more like a prison to me. It brought up all the memories of my aggravating skin issues and also the feelings that went with them: anxiety, stress, insecurity, and unhappiness. Those four words haunted me daily as I now had a deeper appreciation for what they actually meant.

As the day rolled on, darkness slowly settled in over campus. My roommate, Max, and I headed over to a fraternity house that was hosting a watch party for "The Game." Bright, scarlet Ohio State football uniforms flooded my vision as we approached High Street, the main drag off campus that was lined with bars and restaurants. Horns were blasting from cars. Chants and loud shouts were howled from bars. People walking by called out, "*O-H...I-O!*" a renowned slogan known by everyone at Ohio State. There was an invigorating energy in the air that seemed to be fueling everyone around me. But I felt uneasy and filled with apprehension. As we approached the fraternity house, I tried to relax. *You've got this Jake*, I tried to reassure myself.

It's difficult to explain why I was so nervous. I liked watching the football team play and got along well with many members of the fraternity. But mentally I felt like a ticking time bomb just waiting to go off. I felt so insecure just being myself. I lacked the confidence I once had, and this empty replacement, this hollowness, was immensely disconcerting. My skin condition definitely exacerbated my anxiety, but something told me that the root of my feelings lay elsewhere. Digging deeper, I began to realize that my stress and anxiety stemmed from a misalignment within myself—a disconnect between my dreams and passions and what I was actually doing. Being back at school was not what I truly desired, studying business had no appeal for me, and college in general was not where I wanted to be. I felt like a fish out of water.

After greeting all of the guys at the fraternity, I took refuge in a metal fold-up chair in front of the large flat screen TV where the game was going to be shown. I actually felt slightly relieved after talking with the guys. I reminded myself that, just like me, they were people and had their own issues. We could just shoot the shit and watch football. *I actually might enjoy this*, I assured myself. *This is not going to be so bad after all.*

"Hey, Jake, you want a beer?" one of the guys kindly offered.

"Thanks, but I have to pass. I can't have gluten anymore. It gives me skin problems," I said, attempting to sound relaxed.

"Oh, that sucks. Well, no worries, man. Just let me know if I can get you anything," he replied.

Just like that, my state of comfort vanished. Looking around, everyone else was drinking beer. I didn't like being the odd man out. Because I was already so uncomfortable being myself, standing out filled me with dread—despite the fact that I was being treated well, just like any of the other guys. I was new to this gluten-free diet, and being gluten intolerant struck me as a sort of weakness. Plus, I was so used to alcohol fueling me with confidence that being exuberant and outgoing while sober seemed an impossible task.

The game finally started and the atmosphere was frenzied. There were about sixty guys crammed into the room hooting and hollering.

I found myself stuck in an internal battle: part of me was enjoying the electric atmosphere, the gripping football game, and being around a group of carefree guys. At times, I found myself cheering loudly, genuinely interested in the championship game. However, part of me wanted to escape. I wanted to escape from this room and escape from Ohio. I felt a tremendous sense of imbalance. Everything having to do with Ohio State was adding to my anxiety. What made it so unnerving was that it was generalized anxiety. I wasn't anxious over an upcoming test or anything in particular. I had no idea why I was feeling the way I did. A piece of me actually wanted Ohio State to lose the game. I was angry with myself for even thinking this thought. I tried to figure out why on earth I would want this outcome. And then it hit me.

I didn't want to have to mask my lack of excitement for Ohio State if they won. I didn't want to fake celebrating with fifty thousand other students at Ohio State. I didn't want to pretend to have an overwhelming love for a school that I actually wanted nothing to do with. I was afraid of lying to myself again and afraid of the tense knot in my stomach that was becoming ever-present.

A loud roar disrupted my thoughts. Ohio State had just scored again and now had a two-touchdown lead. I joined in the ruckus, screaming my head off along with the others in the room, giving high fives to the guys next to me. I pushed away my previous thoughts as quickly as they'd come, at least for the moment.

The seconds ticked away and the final whistle blew. "Ohio State is the undisputed national champion!" the commentator proudly declared.

People swarmed the streets and fireworks boomed in the sky. I joined the mass of students flooding the central quad on campus. It was surreal. I watched as people climbed up thirty-foot trees, proclaiming their love for Ohio State. I listened to the roar of thousands of students shouting and chanting.

After participating in this mass celebration, I headed back to the fraternity house with Max where the festivities were expected to continue all night. We arrived to hear music blasting and people still screaming. Big bottles of liquor were being passed around like free candy on Halloween. When a bottle reached my hands, I hesitated for a second. I knew that there was probably gluten in the bottle and that I shouldn't drink it. I didn't even want to get drunk. Yet everyone else was so immersed in celebrating, and I wanted to be a part of it. I ignored the voice in my head, leaned back, and tilted the bottle up. The liquor flowed down, burning my throat as I took large swigs. I had done this so many times before, but this time I found the taste putrid. I justified to myself that my actions were reasonable. We just won the first ever National Championship playoff game. This is a once-in-a-lifetime occurrence. *Screw your skin problems for this one night. Just do it and have fun like everyone else. Stop worrying so much.*

I felt a warm rush in my forehead. My desire for control started to fade, and I began to enjoy the looseness in my mind and body. I tried dancing for a while but just wasn't feeling it. The party was nothing special. What my mind had hyped up to be a night like never before was actually just the opposite—a night like any other. The pounding music and strobe lights started giving me a headache. Again, I felt the urge to leave this place. Annoyed at the fuzziness that my brain was trapped in, I wanted to regain a sense of full control. I began drilling into myself about how much of an idiot I was for drinking. *You're going to regret this in the morning when you wake up, hung over with hives, as you trudge across an icy campus to your 8 a.m. class.* I tried dismissing these awful thoughts. The rest of the night felt like a daze. The next thing I knew, I found myself in my room, climbing up to bed. I was out within seconds.

"The most important kind of freedom is to be what you really are. You trade in your reality for a role. You give up your ability to feel, and in exchange, put on a mask."

—Jim Morrison

CHAPTER 3

The Biggest Risk is Not Taking Any Risk at All

January 13, 2015

"In moments of uncertainty, when you must choose between two paths, allowing yourself to be overcome by either the fear of failure or the dimly lit light of possibility, immerse yourself in the life you would be most proud to live."

—Adam Braun

"*Beep, beep, beep, beep...*" my alarm clock obnoxiously sounded. I turned over and shut it off. It was 7:00 a.m. I had come to hate the sound of my alarm. My head pounded and my stomach rumbled. My eyes were open now. I gazed at the ceiling, lying like a plank. I felt paralyzed. I didn't want to move.

After what seemed like hours but was really only minutes, I sat up and grabbed my phone. I was shocked to see tons of notifications on my screen. Curious, I swiped the screen and tapped on my messages icon.

"Congratulations, Jake, what an awesome game!"

"Dude, you must be so happy! I can't believe Ohio State won!"

"Congrats on the game, my man! Don't kill yourself celebrating tonight!"

"Wow, what a game! I would do anything to be in your shoes celebrating tonight. Enjoy it!"

I felt this wave of remorse sear through my body. It was as if a dagger had punctured me. My friends and family had texted me, congratulating me on the game. They were all thrilled for me. They were all happy for me. And I was not. I actually felt sick.

I swiped to check my Instagram, which was also giving me notifications. I remembered that I had posted a picture of the crazy stampede of people in the central quad. My picture had 172 "likes." Friends commented on the photo as well as congratulating me. Usually, I would have been thrilled about this, but it actually made me more upset. I realized in this moment how superficial social media could be. I had posted a single picture, captured a single moment in time from the perspective I chose. That single image showed that I was celebrating with everyone else and how great it was to be at Ohio State.

In reality, I was miserable. I hated the fact that I was portraying myself as happy and loving my life. I was depressed and anxiety-ridden. I wanted to express that side of me openly. I felt like I was lying to myself and everyone else. *I'm depressed and unhappy! I feel like a growing mass of anxiety.* I wanted to scream these thoughts, these realities out to the world. But on social media, users generally put out their "best selves." It's like a competition; the person who can portray his or her life as "happiest" and "perfect" and get the most "likes" wins. This whole "like" concept also seemed ridiculous to me. I was basing my satisfaction and validating my self-esteem on the number of "likes" I received with my own pictures. I almost wanted to laugh at how ridiculous the whole social media construct was. But I realized I was a slave to it and had been for a long time. I was done with it now. I was ready to break free.

Getting out of bed seemed like an enormous task. I managed to lift myself up, climb down from my top bunk, and trudge to the bathroom. My head swirled and thumped painfully. I brushed my teeth, took a steady stance and peered at my reflection in the mirror. It was difficult to keep staring. I couldn't look myself in the eye for very long. The person in the mirror was not who I wanted to be, and this realization stung me deeply.

I knew I was in a fragile emotional state. The idea of going through another day of classes made me shudder. I felt this dense ball rolling up in the back of my throat. This tightening sensation was no longer a foreign feeling; it usually happened when I was on the verge of tears or when I was feeling overly anxious, followed by my mouth, tongue, and throat becoming paralyzed. The day ahead seemed like an enormous, dark mountain. I began brainstorming my options.

I decided to call Julia, a career counselor at the University whom I trusted implicitly. Months ago, I had gone to talk with her about possible career paths. However, the "career counseling" visits essentially turned into therapy sessions where I could freely reveal my thoughts. I was comfortable around Julia and could tell her things that I couldn't express to anyone else. I went to see her five times during my first semester. She made me feel secure and safe. I had broken down in her office on two occasions. Her sensitive and compassionate nature granted me the opportunity and space to do so. Her office was a place of refuge, a place for me to release all my tension and emotions.

Her secretary informed me that someone had just canceled a 9:00 a.m. appointment. It was the only opening in her schedule for the entire day, and it was mine if I wanted it. I gladly took it, thinking that this was meant to be. I needed this appointment.

I skipped class, something I had never done, and headed toward her office. She greeted me with a warm smile, and her presence calmed me immediately. She had strawberry-blonde hair, which complemented her pale complexion. Her light-blue eyes appeared to radiate empathy and understanding. I smiled and said hello.

For the first few minutes, we exchanged details about our holiday breaks. Julia was familiar with my desire to travel and understood where I was mentally. Every time I had previously brought up this subject, she always did a remarkable job of laying out the pros and cons. She helped me understand my fears in a way that made so much sense, and I often felt foolish at having had those fears in the first place. I explained my situation to her.

"I'm really struggling and have no desire to be back here. Something inside is warning me that this isn't right. My gut is telling me that I should leave school and go travel abroad. I get this warm, joyful feeling just thinking about it. But then my mind interjects. It tells me that no one else is doing that. It tells me that this decision will leave me behind, or put me on a bad path, or that I will become a huge failure."

Julia nodded her head, absorbing my predicament. She responded, "So, is that the worst thing that will happen? Really think about why this path sounds so fearful. What is the worst thing that could happen?"

My mind began to turn its wheels. I already knew that the choice of leaving school to travel brought about fears of the "what ifs" and unknowns. But now, I started to really contemplate the worst thing that could actually happen. Of course, I could die. But just before school let out for break, a twenty-one-year-old student had been killed in a car accident while just walking in the city. I knew that death could strike at any moment. It wasn't death that I feared. What I feared most was dying knowing that I hadn't truly lived a life pursuing my dreams. I dug deeper and hit the bull's eye. I realized my fears extrapolated to a point where I believed that steering off the path I was on—the path of "safety and security"—would result in my becoming unemployable, a beggar, and someone who would never amount to anything. These fears—an intangible construct of my imagination—loomed so large in my mind that they immobilized me from taking action. In the world of psychology, there is a word for this thought process—*catastrophizing*.

Realistically, these "worst fears" would probably not happen. I knew that my diligent work ethic would always be my fallback. Plus, I was fortunate enough to have a family who would always help me get back on my feet. Not following my heart, when the only real excuse I had was fear, would be more than a shame. To die with a dream inside of me, one that I never even tried to pursue, seemed to be the real tragedy that I had to avoid.

I explained this to Julia, almost laughing. My mind conjured up such ridiculous possibilities that when I heard myself say them aloud, I couldn't help but laugh. Julia smiled, glad to know I was now seeing my thoughts for what they were: thoughts.

After a few moments of silence, Julia looked me in the eye and raised a question that I will never forget: "You keep focusing on the worst thing that could possibly happen. What is the *best* thing that could happen?"

I sat there silently, my mind now moving at a mile a minute. I saw myself living in a rural town in some third-world country. I saw myself trekking through mystical landscapes. I saw myself meeting people from all over the world. I saw myself coming back from this experience with the power to make a difference in my community, society, and the world, and perhaps even writing a book.

I beamed at Julia. "I'm going to travel," I proudly announced.

A smile formed on Julia's face. I knew she was happy for me because I had finally made my decision.

I had often been frustrated that Julia never steered me toward a particular answer. She always helped me understand all the options open to me but never offered even the slightest inclination of what choice I should make. Now that I had made my decision, I felt confident that it was my decision and no one else's. How could Julia, or anyone else, truly know what was best for me? They had no idea how I grew up or what experiences I went through or what thoughts went through my head. They are not me and never will be. Only I could make this decision.

Other people can offer advice and wisdom to help clarify certain matters. But only you can know the truth that comes from within you— and recognizing that truth is often the most difficult aspect of moving forward in the "right" direction. Experience is the ultimate test. Someone else's words will mean nothing to you until you've gone through an experience where you can testify to that wisdom. When it comes to major life decisions, the best decisions come from within. I am forever thankful to Julia for helping *me* choose my own path.

I walked back to my dorm with a new sense of calm. I walked slowly, examining the bare trees, the frosty street, and the brick buildings. I observed the people who passed by, noticing their pace and facial expressions. I felt free. I was still in Ohio, yet a leash was finally broken off from around my neck.

I called my parents and explained the situation. We had been communicating back and forth, so my decision didn't seem totally out of the blue. They were nonetheless surprised but happy to know I was coming home. They both knew that I was not in a good place mentally and that being at school was not easing the situation for me. Because I acted early, I could get all of my money refunded for the semester. Plus, they were reassured when I told them that the leave of absence still meant I was enrolled in the university. I could return to school in the fall. However, deep down, I knew I would not be returning. I decided to keep this part to myself. They didn't need to know that yet.

After securing my finances and notifying the school, I packed my bags and headed for the airport the next day.

One of the airport TSA employees asked me where I was heading and why.

"I'm taking a leave of absence from school to travel. I'm heading home and will figure out more details then."

The TSA worker looked mortified as she warned, "Oooh, honey, be careful. It's always risky to take a leave from school. Your poor parents must be pretty anxious."

Annoyed, I nodded and half-smiled at her as I walked past security to retrieve my bag. *What the hell does she know? Why can't she just mind her own business and keep her mouth shut? But what if she is right? What if I am making a huge mistake? What if this all turns out to be a disaster?* The self-confidence I had felt after leaving Julia's office seemed to drift away. *Why do I care so much about what other people think?* I was frustrated. I let this woman, whom I didn't even know, make me feel wrong and uncomfortable.

Again, I caught myself dreaming about being in a foreign land. I couldn't wait to escape these types of questions and reactions. I knew they were inevitable, and each time I was asked about what I was doing, I felt myself becoming overly defensive as if I were trying to justify my insanity.

"Truth lies within ourselves: it takes no rise from outward things, whatever you may believe. There is an inmost center in us all, where truth abides in fullness and to know rather consists in opening out a way whence the imprisoned splendor may escape than in effecting entry for light supposed to be without."
—Robert Browning

CHAPTER 4

Embracing Uncertainty

January 17, 2015

"Conditions are never perfect. 'Someday' is a disease that will take your dreams to the grave with you."

—Tim Ferris

Upon arriving home, I immediately began to research possibilities for my upcoming journey. I had $4,000 saved up from working over the last year. I figured that through volunteer work exchange and other means, I could make it stretch.

I looked at many volunteering programs but was frustrated with my search results. Many of them were very short-term, expensive, and highly structured. I wanted no time constraints, as I didn't know how long I wanted to travel. I didn't have much money and wasn't about to pay $1,000 for one week. And most important, I didn't want structure. I craved personal freedom and wanted to take in stride what the world threw at me. I needed to escape the confines of a system. I needed a challenge, to test the world and see how the Universe really worked.

I had read many inspirational books that talked about people's ability to create their desired reality through positive, focused intentions. Authors like Jack Canfield and Tony Robbins explained how a change in attitude could change your entire world. I wanted to believe this was true. But I didn't have any experiences in my own life that led me to believe this. I knew I had to test this theory for myself.

After hours of research, I found a site called Workaway that links hosts and volunteers from all over the world. Essentially, I could work a few hours a day in return for food and a place to sleep. There were thousands of hosts all over the world who offered work options ranging from farming and teaching English to working in a hostel or an eco-community. I was overjoyed at my discovery. It was perfect. It would allow me to volunteer without paying much. Plus, I could find the cultural experience I was looking for. I just needed to figure out where I wanted to go.

The pieces of the puzzle did not fall into place as easily as I had thought they would. Yes, I had found this incredible volunteering site. However, that was only a small step. I was still having some problems figuring things out. There were a couple of bad days in the process, one in particular.

My skin was flaring in another one of those stinging, painful episodes. I woke up completely doubting myself and wondered if backpacking alone in some third-world country was the dumbest idea ever. I felt like a failure, some loser who couldn't handle college. I tossed my phone on the couch, hopped in my car, and drove off. I didn't know where I was going; I just drove. I felt myself shaking. I was driving, almost hoping someone would crash into me. I was scared by my own thoughts— half of them rational, the other half insane. My hands were practically cemented to the steering wheel, gripping it so tightly that I thought they would remain there permanently.

Thankfully, I shook myself out of this fragile state long enough to make it to a 7-11 in Pacific Beach. I got out of the car, feeling my face burn from the stinging rash that had erupted from its once smooth surface. The medicinal cream I had applied earlier that morning was dripping down my cheeks. I looked into the mirror to see how crazy and uneasy I looked. I was feeling agitated and worthless and jittery at the same time. I walked into the 7-11 and asked the clerk for a pack of cigarettes.

"What kind?" he muttered monotonously.

"Uh, the blue ones," I responded with a false confidence as if I knew what I was talking about. I had smoked a cigarette maybe four times in my life, not taking more than a couple of puffs. "Yeah, those ones," I announced as he grabbed the pack from the shelf. "And a lighter, too, please."

"Those ones are the shit," the man behind me croaked out creepily. He had a wriggly, bobbing, gray beard and edgy eyes that melted into his wrinkled, sun-leathered skin. By the term "the shit," I didn't know if he meant that the cigarettes I chose were awful or the best. I simply nodded to him, mustering a quarter of a smile, and walked out just as confused as I had been walking in.

I made my way toward the boardwalk, pulled out a cigarette, and lit up as if I were in some Hollywood movie. I inhaled, coughed almost instantly, and felt like an idiot. I choked momentarily and spat out onto the curb. I trudged slowly up and down the boardwalk, examining people's eyes, what they were wearing, whom they were with.

Before I knew it, I was halfway through the pack. Nauseous and dizzy, I dragged my legs toward the pier and plopped down on a wooden log that was shaded from the sun. A couple of homeless guys were sleeping under the pier about twenty feet away from where the crashing waves foamed up onto the shore.

I simultaneously felt numb and confused and full and empty. My lungs were burning as if I had swallowed a hot piece of charcoal, and I threw the remaining cigarettes into a trash can a few feet away from me. I felt queasy, the bile in my stomach threatening to fly up my throat and out of my mouth at a moment's notice.

I stared out into the horizon, angry at how beautiful a day it was. I tried to breathe but struggled. *Breathe. Just breathe.* I swallowed little gulps of air unevenly, feeling woozy and unsteady even as I sat on the wooden log. For a moment, I thought I was going to drift away. Part of me wanted to.

But the other part of me knew that this was not me. I felt as if someone were choking me, that dense ball of anxiety rolling up the back of my throat becoming thicker and thicker. I just sat there gazing endlessly at anything my eyes could zoom in on.

Finally, I picked myself up. I felt awful and wanted to go home. I sat in the car and let out a loud sigh. I made a promise to myself. Not again. Never again. I was finished with my pity party and my anger at life and my skin problems and everything else I was dealing with that paled in comparison to other people's problems. More importantly, I promised myself that this journey I was planning was going to happen. It had to happen. Nothing else made sense to me.

*　*　*　*　*

I spent hours on the phone with customer service people talking about many things: credit card information, travel insurance plans, weather patterns and vaccinations I might need if I decided to venture to a destination prone to disease. On top of this, I had to visit the doctor because my skin broke out in another painful, stinging episode. But despite all of the obstacles that kept arising, I was determined to overcome them. I knew why I was doing what I was doing. And because of this, I committed 100 percent that I would persevere through any and every bump in the road—not to mention on my skin. Not going on this journey was not an option.

Something was drawing me toward Central America. Learning Spanish and being immersed in the Latin culture, which included a love of soccer, appealed to me. Jake Ducey, author of the inspiring book, *Into the Wind,* started his journey in Guatemala. I had also watched a documentary on Guatemala that described what life was like living on a dollar a day in a third-world country. I couldn't ignore this pull I was feeling toward Guatemala.

"Whatever Your Skill Set May Be, the People of Petén Need Your Help."

This description of a Workaway profile immediately caught my eye. The profile described a town in rural Guatemala, off the beaten trail, called San Andres. There was a school in this small, poor town that needed all the help it could receive. I instantly sent an e-mail to the host explaining my desire to travel, my interest in volunteering in Petén, and my willingness to take on any job that would help make a difference. I suggested that I could teach English and soccer to children although I had absolutely no certified qualifications to teach English. I barely knew any Spanish. But I was willing to try with all my might.

A few days later, Mike, the host of the profile in Petén, e-mailed me back saying he would love for me to come and volunteer. After a few e-mail exchanges, I booked a one-way flight to Guatemala that departed from Los Angeles in a month. I figured that after volunteering in Petén, I would travel throughout Guatemala and other countries in Central America, seeing where the wind took me.

Pushing the enter key on my computer and purchasing my flight ticket was a surreal feeling. My decision to travel was solidified. This was it. I was turning my dream into a reality.

But I also began to think. *What if your skin gets drastically worse while you're away? What then? There are no doctors anywhere near you, let alone English-speaking ones. How are you going to get around? You don't even speak Spanish. What if...?* I shook myself and pushed these thoughts out of my head. There were some questions I really had to ask myself, but worrying about so many "what ifs" was not benefiting me.

I spent the next month diligently preparing for my trip. I researched backpacks at REI and found the perfect one. It was only 50 liters, much smaller than the other ones designed for backpacking. I didn't want a large or complicated bag to tempt me into packing more stuff than I needed. I read as much as I possibly could about backpacking in Guatemala. I read one article on solo travel that stated, "You will cry at one point—that part is inevitable." I wondered if that statement would be true for me.

I made sure to pack all the medication I needed for my skin in case of a major breakout. I purchased a tiny, cheap Kindle tablet so I could read as well as e-mail and communicate with my family and friends. I decided against bringing my phone. I didn't want to be consumed in social media and the constant urge to always be "connected." I craved personal, face-to-face interactions. My tablet only worked in areas where there was Wi-Fi, which was very limited in the town where I was going to live. I figured that would be enough for me. I went through important travel documents, my passport and immunization record, credit cards, and clothes for my trip. The month of preparation felt dreadfully slow at times, yet also frighteningly rapid.

The day of my flight finally arrived. I said good-bye to my dad and he looked at me with a huge smile across his face. "I'm so proud of you, Jake. It takes a lot of courage to do what you're doing." I hugged him one last time and walked outside where my mom was waiting in the car. My mom drove me from San Diego to the Los Angeles airport. On the way to the airport, we stopped by at my cousin's apartment. Three of my cousins ran a sticker store in Los Angeles called Sticker Planet. They generously gave me a bountiful amount of stickers which I could give to children on my journey. After thanking them, my mom and I continued to the airport.

My mom walked me toward the security checkpoint, which was as far as she could go. I hugged her good-bye, not knowing the next time I was going to see her. I saw her eyes becoming watery. I knew she was happy for me and trusted me to take care of myself. She was a free spirit in her own right and encouraged me to follow my heart. I let go from our embrace and looked into her eyes one last time. I gave her a smile of reassurance and silently waved good-bye. She knew that I was as ready as I could be. I hoisted up my bag onto my back. I turned and made my way toward security. I was on my own now.

"It is how we embrace the uncertainty in our lives that leads to the greatest transformation of our souls."
—Brandon A. Trean

CHAPTER 5

An Act of Kindness

March 19, 2015

"If one advances confidently in the direction of his dreams, and endeavors to live the life which he has imagined, he will meet with a success unexpected in common hours."

—Henry David Thoreau

After getting past security and finding my gate, I sat down and let out a sigh of relief. My stomach jittered with butterflies. While I waited for the boarding call, I began to focus on my next steps. This was a red-eye flight that was supposed to arrive around 6:30 a.m. I needed to get from the airport to the bus station and then buy a bus ticket to Santa Elena and from there take a taxi to San Andres. The bus ride was supposed to take nine hours. My thoughts whirled about the daunting tasks looming ahead and the possible dangers confronting me. If I faced any threatening encounters, I wouldn't be able to say much more than "hello" and "I need to use the bathroom." That could pose a problem. I tried to assure myself that as long as I paid attention to my surroundings and followed my intuition, I would be fine.

"If you are in Zone 1 of Flight 5864 to Guatemala City, you may now begin boarding." The voice of the airport gate announcer instantly caught my attention. As I rose from my seat, I watched as probably one hundred people rushed toward the boarding line. Almost in unison, the gentleman to my left rose from his seat as well. We both looked at the mass of people stampeding toward the line, glanced at each other, laughed, and sat back down.

"That line is not going anywhere," he said, still laughing. "Might as well relax here until it dwindles."

"Good point," I replied.

"What brings you to Guatemala?" the man questioned in a friendly, curious manner.

"I'm heading toward the Petén department in the North where I'll be teaching English and soccer to children." I knew he would be at least somewhat interested in my response because he was wearing a hat with the design of the national Guatemalan soccer team. I also said that I was planning to travel throughout Central America and explained what motivated me to do this.

"Wow, that is excellent, my friend. That sounds like it will be quite the adventure. How old are you?"

"Eighteen," I responded with a slightly deeper voice, attempting to sound older.

"Oh, my goodness, you are so young. You must be careful. How are you going to get to Petén?"

"I plan on taking a taxi to the bus station and then buying a ticket to San Andres from there."

"How's your Spanish?" he asked hopefully.

"It's pretty bad. I only know a few words." I felt embarrassed and almost stupid admitting this fact. *He probably thinks you're nuts.*

"Oh, wow. You must be careful. Never take a taxi that is not official. Guatemala can be dangerous." He was silent for a few seconds, thinking to himself. "My brother is picking me up when we arrive. I am sure he can give you a ride to the bus station."

"That would be incredible!" I exclaimed. I couldn't believe my luck.

"I'm Mynor, by the way."

"I'm Jake," I replied happily.

Mynor and I continued to talk for a while until we had to board the plane. He had moved from Guatemala to Los Angeles when he was eighteen in search of a better life for himself and his family. He could relate to my situation as he was once my age arriving in a distant land not knowing the native language. He told me about his job in the United States as a banker while his family was back in Guatemala. We talked about soccer as well. We were both deeply engaged in the latest matches and news. Soccer truly is a universal language, I reflected. I had never thought that playing soccer for fourteen years would help me in the way it was now.

The last call for our boarding zone was announced, and we made our way toward the plane. We parted for now, and I went to my assigned seat. It was a middle seat, and there were two elderly Guatemalan women sitting in the window and aisle seats. I squeezed in between them, a huge smile on my face.

"*Hola,*" I beamed, attempting to portray a positive aura.

"*Hola!*" they nodded back, returning my smile. It didn't take me long to figure out that they spoke no English.

Their clothes were gleaming with the most incredible variety of reds, yellows, greens, and blues; the fabric was woven with intricate patterns flowing both horizontally and vertically. I figured they must be related in some way to one of the indigenous tribes, which were known for their beautiful, elaborate clothing.

The plane grumbled and its engine roared. Gaining more and more speed, it finally lifted off the ground. I closed my eyes, feeling peaceful and content. I thought that sitting next to these women was the beginning of my cultural journey. I had a big day ahead, and I soaked in the calmness of the moment. My mind seemed to wind down as I relaxed and fell into a shallow sleep.

After hours of drifting in and out of a light sleep, I stared out the window to see the most beautiful sunrise I had ever witnessed. The sky was glowing with bright reds, oranges, greens and blues. It was as if the Guatemalan women's clothes were being reflected into the sky lighting up the earth in a rainbow of color. I took it as a sign that everything was going to work out. I drew energy from the vibrant sky and felt very much alive.

The plane began its descent, and we were soon on the ground in Guatemala City.

Upon exiting the plane, we were ushered toward Customs. I kept my eyes peeled for Mynor but couldn't find him. I approached Customs expecting to be bombarded with suspicious questions and a thorough bag search. To my surprise, I breezed past in seconds. I chuckled to myself as I pictured the author Harper Lee telling me, "Things are never as bad as they seem." Maybe she was right.

As I made my way toward baggage claim, I still couldn't spot Mynor. I figured he was still back in the Customs line. As I scanned each bag in search of my own, I felt a tap on my shoulder. I turned to see that it was Mynor, smiling.

We got our bags and proceeded toward the exit where Mynor's brother was waiting. The security at the airport would no longer provide protection. Mynor warned me, "Be alert at all times. Watch your bags and pay attention to people's faces and their body language. Use your sixth sense."

I listened intently, absorbing each word he said. We approached the sliding doors, and as they opened, I took a deep breath and immediately saw a crowd of people. I noticed their brown skin color, cowboy hats, and unfamiliar style of clothing—cultural differences that, albeit superficial, struck me instantly and emphasized the fact that I was now a stranger in a strange land. These people were anticipating the arrival of family and friends just as Mynor's brother was waiting for him. The gray, smoggy air emitted an unfamiliar stench. My nose twitched as I inhaled, and the air stung my eyes.

I followed Mynor closely, scanning in all directions and obeying his advice. We found his brother and he greeted us happily. He spoke no English, so he and Mynor communicated in Spanish, joyous in each other's company. Mynor informed his brother that I needed a ride to the bus station, which was a thirty-minute drive from the airport. "*No problema,*" he said. We piled into his small, gray car and set off into the city.

The glitz and glamour of Beverly Hills, which I had driven through the day before, seemed a universe away. State-of-the-art emporiums with shiny, clean glass windows displaying pricy cars and designer clothes had now morphed into cheaply built shops with mucky, tattered walls surrounded by barbed wire. The smooth boulevards surrounded by lush green grass and palm trees were now grimy streets and sidewalks filled with cracks. Sparkling, unblemished BMWs and Audis were now grumbling, aging pick-up trucks and motorbikes spewing excessive exhaust. Street vendors of all ages, selling everything from fruit and newspapers to handmade clothes and small gadgets, swarmed the streets. Kids, looking as young as six years old in tattered tank tops, rode in the backs of trucks. Men walking with goats on the side of the road weaved in and out of crowds of people who were consumed with their labor-intensive work.

I couldn't help but cringe throughout the entire drive. Driving here was madness compared with Los Angeles traffic. I felt like I was in a real-life game of Frogger. Cars and motorbikes zipped past each other, cutting in and out of lanes without the slightest signal. Avenues unexpectedly changed from three-way lanes to one-way streets. The constant honking horns and blaring stereos seemed like a soundtrack to a distorted musical. I saw a motorbike dart in between two cars mere seconds away from being crushed by an oncoming truck. I held my breath at every twist and turn as Mynor's brother drove aggressively yet assertively. He clearly knew the way of the road here and showed no signs of hesitation.

I let out a deep sigh of relief as we passed through the city. I realized how tense my body was when I noticed my fists tightly clamped and sweaty. Mynor was acting as the translator between his brother and me. He provided insight and information about the city, safety tips, and areas to avoid. I listened carefully as I absorbed the sights and sounds of this new world that I was now a part of.

We finally reached the bus station, and Mynor, his brother and I got out of the car. As I was preparing to thank Mynor and say good-bye to him, he marched up to the ticket office and signaled me to come over.

"I want to make sure you do not get ripped off. I talked with the ticket operator to ensure you pay the correct price. A bus ticket to Santa Elena costs 180 *quetzales* (about $23), and it will take about nine hours. There is a bus in one hour. Here is my e-mail. Do not hesitate to contact me if you run into any trouble." Mynor handed me a sticky note with his contact information.

"Thank you so much, Mynor. I cannot tell you how much I appreciate your help. You have done more for me than you will ever know." I offered him and his brother some cash to compensate for their time and gas, but they respectfully declined my offer.

"It was my pleasure. Take care of yourself and always be alert. I wish you a safe journey in Guatemala," Mynor responded.

I waved good-bye to Mynor and his brother as they took off. I was in awe of his kindness. Mynor anticipated that I might have trouble buying a ticket, as my Spanish was almost nonexistent. He went out of his way to take me to the bus station, oversee the purchase of my ticket, and provide me with invaluable advice. To him, it may not have been a big deal. I wondered if he would ever truly know how significant his actions were to me. Mynor gave me his kindness, something I will never forget.

"No act of kindness, no matter how small, is ever wasted."

—Aesop

CHAPTER 6

Stranded

March 20, 2015

"You can't always control the wind,
but you can control your sails."
—Tony Robbins

About three hours into the ride, the bus suddenly stopped. What I thought was just a temporary pause turned out to be just the opposite. I didn't yet understand Spanish and had no idea what was going on. I was the only white person on the bus, and I knew I stuck out because I felt many eyes intently fixed on me when I had boarded. After the bus had been stopped for twenty minutes, everyone got up and walked outside. I curiously followed, unaware of the situation.

Stepping off the bus, I inhaled the toasty air and saw waves of simmering heat rolling off the metal hood of the bus. We were on a single-lane road with nothing but trees, brush, and grassland on both sides. I looked ahead past the bus only to see other trucks, cars, and buses lined up for what looked like miles on end. I turned around and saw the same thing in the other direction. I figured there must be some roadblock or accident up ahead.

People were outside their vehicles sitting and standing on the side of the road. My mind took an optimistic path, and I reckoned the problem would be cleared up shortly and we would be back on the road in no time. Yet, after many hours passed, I had a feeling we were going to be there for a long while.

Oddly, everyone around me seemed perfectly calm. People chatted among themselves as if this were a common occurrence. There was no sense of fear, anxiety, worry, or anger about the current circumstance. The situation was what it was, and people didn't seem to be bothered by it—they just accepted it. I couldn't help but laugh, thinking about a situation like this in the United States. I imagined people freaking out and losing their tempers: "I have an appointment in twenty minutes!" "What's taking so long?" "Who's responsible for this?" "This is going to screw up my whole day." I pictured people talking angrily on their cell phones, frantically walking back and forth. I visualized people screaming at the bus driver and threatening to sue if they didn't get to their destinations on time.

I reflected on how the Guatemalans were reacting. They were unflustered and knew that there was nothing they could do about the situation. Instead of worrying about things outside of their control, they were content to focus on the moment at hand. Maybe they knew something that those of us back in the United States didn't. Their patience and sense of calm were admirable, and I tried to emulate their tranquility.

I grabbed *Unbroken*, a book I had brought with me, and began reading on the side of the road. I figured that the book, which chronicled the remarkable story of a World War II survivor, would inspire me to stay positive during my journey no matter what I faced. After reading for a little while, I found it hard to stay engaged in the book. Here I was, stuck in the middle of what felt like nowhere, on a rustic, one-way road. Plus, I was here to experience the culture, and this was a great opportunity to start. I wanted to strike up a conversation with someone but didn't know exactly how to do so. There were plenty of people on my bus; some looked my age and others much older. I kept thinking the language barrier would block me from communicating.

A thought suddenly clicked in my head, and I jumped up.

I hopped back on the bus and unzipped my backpack. I picked up my deflated soccer ball and small travel pump. I quickly filled up the ball with air and stepped back outside. I began juggling and kicking the ball up and down. I looked around and saw I had drawn the attention of some people near me on the side of the road. I passed the ball to one guy who was just a few feet away, and he appeared immediately intrigued. He took a couple of touches and passed it back. I flicked the ball up and continued to juggle and then kicked the ball back to the guy. He caught it on his thigh and kept it in the air with the precision of someone who clearly had played soccer before. After messing around with the ball for what felt like thirty minutes, we both sat down on the road as the heat was taking its toll and fatigue set in.

I looked at him and pointed to myself. "Jake," I annunciated clearly. He smiled in acknowledgment and responded, "Wilson," referring to himself with his index finger just as I had done. I nodded my head, smiling. Through body language and my broken, minimal Spanish, Wilson and I communicated. I learned that he was twenty-three years old and was heading back from the city to see his family. I put my hands up to my sides, palms facing up like one who doesn't understand, and pointed to the stopped truck and cars. He looked at me, grasping my question, and answered, "*accidente*." He put up his two fists and bumped them into each other, illustrating an auto accident with his hands. I bobbed my head in understanding.

The art of communication is incredible. Language is only a potential barrier that can be overcome in many ways. The many years I had played soccer, along with my knowledge of the game and its worldwide popularity, fueled this interaction with a total stranger. In countries rich and poor, war-torn and peaceful, soccer is a sport that brings people together. Wilson and I couldn't speak each other's language, but we both knew how to speak the language of soccer. And we did. I made a friend through the game I love, the game that transcends external differences.

Hours passed, and the sun began to set in the distance. Slowly, daylight was fading as darkness crept in. I began to worry if I was going to be stuck here the whole night. We had been sitting on the side of the road for eight hours and were surely not going to arrive until morning. *How can I contact Mike, the Workaway host? Will he think something happened to me? I don't want him waiting all night at the bus terminal.* I shook myself out of these thoughts. There was no point in worrying about what was beyond my control. I felt confident that it would all work out one way or another.

Way up ahead, I could see that the trucks and cars were beginning to move. "*Vamonos!*" the bus driver announced. I followed the others back onto the bus, relieved that we weren't going to be there overnight. It was pitch black outside, and the refuge of the bus was comforting. The engine rumbled, and the sound filled me with joy as if it were a person coming back to life. The bus pulled forward and on we went. I had barely slept the last twenty-four hours, and the day's heat had tired me out. I took a deep breath, let my body relax, and closed my eyes. I felt myself drifting away.

The next thing I knew, I heard noises and felt the bus come to a halt. I opened my eyes and saw people standing up preparing to get off the bus. I turned to Wilson. "Santa Elena?" I questioned, pointing outside. He nodded his head, and I shook his hand, saying good-bye. I slung my arms through the straps of my backpack and stepped off the bus.

There was a crowd of people waiting at the bus station. Immediately, someone approached me: "Taxi, taxi," he said. I considered my options. It was 3:00 a.m., and I had absolutely no way of contacting or finding Mike. Wi-Fi seemed to be rare among these parts. San Andres was about a twenty-minute ride away from the bus station. I decided to spend the night in a hotel and head over to San Andres in the morning.

The taxi driver took me to a hotel two minutes away. The building looked more like a deserted wooden shop than a hotel. There was no one there except for one man slumped over a desk, barely keeping his eyes open, who, I assumed, was working. At this point, I didn't know where else to go. I paid him and was escorted to my room. I thanked the man and shut the door. The paint was chipping off almost every wall in the room, and a thick layer of silt and dust covered the slim windows near the ceiling. The bed sheets were covered in stains, and the pillow was more like a lumpy loaf of bread than anything else. But I was exhausted and didn't care. I slid into bed and closed my eyes. I just wanted it to be morning.

"Going with the flow is responding to cues from the Universe. When you go with the flow, you're surfing Life force. It's about wakeful trust and total collaboration with what's showing up for you."

—Danielle LaPorte

CHAPTER 7

Unexpected Synchronicity

March 21, 2015

*"Once you put your attention, your thoughts, your energy,
your consciousness on a new intention, that's what you begin
manifesting into your life."*

—Wayne Dyer

I woke up early and hopped out of bed, anxious to get to San Andres. I zipped up my bag and raised it onto my back. I walked out of the hotel to be greeted by the bright sun. Squinting, I adjusted my face to the light's force. Not a single cloud dotted the clear, blue sky. I felt alive. It was a new day, and I was excited about traveling to San Andres and meeting Mike. But first, I had to figure out how to get there.

I walked into what felt like the town center where I saw a few men standing by small, three-wheeled vehicles called *tuk tuks*, which are the main method of taxi transportation in many parts of Guatemala. Essentially, they are mini-, three-wheeled cars, almost all of them painted a bright-red color. I approached the men and explained as best as I could that I needed to get to San Andres.

One man jumped up and exclaimed, *"Si, si, no problema!"* There was something about his demeanor that comforted me. I was well aware that I needed to be careful, and that there were some people out there who were going to try and rip me off. But this man had a soothing smile and an almost childish sincerity, which made my apprehension vanish. I climbed into the *tuk tuk* and the driver took off. The wind flew against my face, refreshing me and refueling my energy. I observed the landscapes we passed with the fascination of a young child. We traveled through gravel roads surrounded by glaring, green grasslands scattered with small shacks and huts. There were no skyscrapers looming, no cars honking, no people walking. I was enjoying the ride and taking in every detail my senses could possibly absorb.

We soon pulled up to a town, and my driver indicated this was San Andres. The most dazzling lake I have ever seen abutted the small town. It glowed with a crisp blue that almost matched the color of the sky. It was enormous, and if I hadn't known it was a lake, I might have thought it was an ocean or bay. The beauty of the lake sent an invigorating quiver of energy throughout my body. Something about being near a body of water—whether a lake, ocean, or river—always filled me with a sense of calm.

There were very few people around, and I suddenly remembered it was not even 9:00 a.m. on a Saturday morning. Mike had told me that in case he wasn't able to pick me up at the bus terminal, I should make my way to San Andres and ask locals where I could find "Mike the gringo." He had said that most people in the town knew who he was. We pulled up to a man walking along the street, and I asked if he knew Mike. He gazed at me as if not fully grasping the question and shook his head no. I figured that maybe he wasn't a local in town. Next, we pulled up to a stand where a woman was preparing tortillas on a sizzling, handmade circular stove. I asked her the same question. She shook her head no and focused her attention back on her tortillas. I felt confused and began to wonder if I was in the right place.

We kept driving, and as we turned down another street, I saw a man with white skin standing out like a full moon in the night sky. As we approached him, I was disappointed. I knew what Mike looked like from photos in the Workaway description, so I knew it wasn't him. But I figured that he might speak English, so I introduced myself.

"Hello, do you speak English?" I asked in a hopeful tone.

"Yes, I do," he replied. He was wearing a large straw hat that sheltered him from the beating sun. He had piercing, blue eyes and his face had few wrinkles. He looked to be in his fifties.

"Do you know of a man named Mike who lives here? I just arrived this morning, and I will be volunteering in this town for the next month or so. I have no phone and don't know how to contact Mike or where he lives."

The man scrunched his face together, scanning the sky to search for an answer. "No, I'm sorry. I actually don't live here. I live in a town called San Juan about a fifteen-minute *tuk tuk* ride away from here. I'm in San Andres because I need to buy supplies from the paper store, but it's not open yet." He chuckled. "Stores here sort of open whenever they feel like it."

"Oh, okay," I responded, somewhat let down. "I am sort of unsure what to do at this point. I was so relieved to find you as no one else here speaks English."

"Yes, you will not find people here who speak languages other than Spanish and Mayan. Tourists and travelers don't pass through these parts. I have to wait for the store to open anyway, so I would be glad to wait with you for a while. Do you like coffee?" he asked.

"Yes, I do," I replied. I considered his words carefully; his description matched my observations. This town was very different from any I had ever been in. I realized I would need to learn Spanish here to connect better with the locals.

"Would you like to join me for a cup?"

"Sure, that sounds great!" I responded enthusiastically. I had heard that some of the world's best coffee came from Central America. Plus, I felt an overwhelming comfort being with this man who spoke English. I couldn't believe how lucky I was to find him, especially after what he had just told me. *The world works in mysterious ways.* That stock bit of clichéd wording had passed through my mind frequently since I had started out on this journey. When we radiate positive energy and an open mind, the Universe responds accordingly. It answers our needs when we least expect it. The chances of my running into this man must have been so small that I couldn't help but wonder if this was just a coincidence.

I paid my *tuk tuk* driver and thanked him. I followed the man to a little street stand nearby. He ordered two cups of coffee, and we both sat down at a table.

"Thanks for the coffee. I'm Jake, by the way," I added.

"It's my pleasure. And I'm Peter. So what exactly brings you here?"

I explained my story, telling him about leaving school to explore Central America and my desire to volunteer and experience different ways of life.

"Wow, that's great," Peter, responded with widening eyes. "And to be doing this at your age is remarkable. The world needs kids to experience other cultures at a young age. It brings about a worldly understanding of people's differences."

"Thanks, and yes, I agree," I replied. "And how did you end up here?"

He chuckled, and then his voice took on a more serious tone. "I was a pilot in Germany for twenty years. I went in for an annual medical checkup and explained to the doctor that I was also having trouble with my vision. My doctor performed multiple tests and found a brain tumor that was two centimeters in size. I was informed that chemotherapy would give me my best chance at survival. But I refused this course of action. I've been on a spiritual journey since I was twenty-one years old, and I believe in holistic, alternative healing. Chemotherapy wipes out your healthy cells. It can lead to your body's demise in a more rapid time frame than the cancer it is attempting to treat… the cure can be worse than the disease."

"Wow," I interjected, somewhat speechless. My mind was racing in response to what I was hearing. I was captivated by his story, especially because of his belief in alternative healing. Western medicine had not healed my skin condition, and I wondered if an alternative approach might be more effective. "What did your family think?"

"Oh, my family was quite fearful and uneasy at my decision. Friends and other doctors told me I would die after a few months without chemotherapy, and that my decision was a death sentence. They said I was crazy, but I knew I wasn't. My belief that the body can heal itself has exposed me to numerous forms of alternative healing. I had heard of an alternative cancer treatment called Biological Resonance Therapy years before."

Peter described how the therapy worked. He explained that all the tissues in the human body have an ideal electrical frequency. These frequencies coordinate to various forms of physiological activity. When there is a disruption in this frequency because of inflammation or another inhibitor, the ideal frequency is subject to change. Alterations in frequency can cause major problems to physiological activity in the body, including the formation of cancerous cells. This form of therapy, Peter noted, is not widely accepted by Western medicine. Most people have never even heard of this type of treatment—including me, until I met Peter.

"The price of a biological resonance device is not cheap, but I bought one. I set the device to emit the ideal frequency level that matched my brain. For the next year, I placed the device under my bed with the antenna correctly aligned and slept over it every night. A few months after my diagnosis, my tumor grew to three centimeters, and my doctor was really worried. He had been very supportive and wanted to help in any way he could despite his thoughts on my decision to abstain from chemotherapy. But after a year of sleeping with the antenna under my sheets, the tests showed no sign of the tumor. It disappeared entirely."

My mouth was hanging half-open. I had never heard such a story in my entire life. I felt my heart pump rapidly, and my legs bobbed up and down as my mind flooded with wonder.

"Did your story make national news?" I asked eagerly. I pictured him being interviewed on a major television show. I imagined millions of people tuning in to his interview, and that his story would revolutionize cancer treatment.

He chuckled again. "No, no, nothing even remotely close. Of course, my family and friends were astonished at the outcome. And so was my doctor. But the form of healing I went through goes against the common method of modern cancer treatment. Other doctors called it luck and other sorts of names. There is also a lot of money involved in chemotherapy. At the expense of individuals fighting for their lives, there are pharmaceutical companies and physicians who reap enormous sums of money from the price and administration of chemotherapy. My story would never gain any press because it would threaten that industry."

"And so how did that bring you to a small town in Guatemala?"

"After my ordeal with cancer, I wanted to leave Germany. When I was diagnosed with cancer, I was no longer allowed to fly planes. I wanted to move to a quiet place where I could practice farming, maintain a small, earth-friendly, ecological footprint, and connect with nature. Germany has many rules and regulations, and I wanted to move to a place where I could live more freely, a place of peace and tranquility. I came to Guatemala based on a friend's recommendation and fell in love with the town of San Juan."

I assimilated Peter's story, in particular his desire for a peaceful, productive life. In the Western world, our everyday lives can become so stressful and chaotic. We often become so consumed with work, school, social status, keeping up with social media, and the acquisition of material goods that we fail to recognize the truly important things in our lives…the things that bring us gratification and a sense of fulfillment and that reflect our true passions.

We talked for a while, and I noticed that the town was beginning to stir. More and more people were out walking around. I remembered Mike telling me that there was an Internet café in town, and I figured that my best chance of finding him was there. I asked Peter if he would help me find it, and he happily agreed. We rose from the table, and Peter asked the woman who sold us the coffee where the Internet café was. She pointed to a shop about twenty yards away. I laughed, finding it funny that what I was looking for was right before my eyes. Often, what we are seeking is right in front of us. We just have to open our eyes fully.

We walked up to the shop, which was painted a glowing royal blue. As I entered, I heard a voice inquire, "Hey, Jake is that you?" I turned my head and saw Mike sitting with his back up against the wall. This was the man I'd seen in the Workaway pictures. He had a dark beard and mustache tinged with some subtle gray hairs. His hair wasn't tousled, yet had a sort of freedom to it. His jaw, although covered by a bush of facial hair, receded toward his neck as if it were cut at an angle. He had a sort of kick to his voice—not quite a lisp—yet it didn't sound completely natural. He was wearing army cargo shorts and a black tank top. I noticed a few tattoos, some were military insignia and others were tribal art. He was dark, as if years in the sun had leathered his skin. His appearance revealed that he had a story to tell, a complex one at that.

"Hey, yeah, it's me. You must be Mike!" I exclaimed enthusiastically. A wave of relief swept over me.

"Yeah, it's me. I was out looking for you last night. I drove to the bus station and waited a few hours but saw no sign of you. I figured you would eventually make it here. Everyone has some sort of trouble finding me, but they all succeed one way or another."

I nodded my head. I turned to Peter and thanked him for helping me. We exchanged contact information, and he assured me that we would see each other again. "Our meeting was no accident," Peter guaranteed me. "The energy that you radiated out to the world brought us together. Stay positive and continue on your spiritual journey. Good-bye, for now."

I said good-bye to Peter and he took off. I let his words sink in.

"Well, let's take you to the house and meet the others," Mike suggested. And off we went.

"The Universe corresponds to the nature of your song."
—Michael Bernard Beckwith

CHAPTER 8

A Shift in Perspective, A Shift in Reality

March 21, 2015

"It's not necessarily reality that shapes us, but the lens through which your brain views the world that shapes your reality."
—Shawn Achor

I followed Mike through town, and he told me about the schools and the people of San Andres. We walked past a huge, green soccer field, and positive memories of my soccer days flooded my mind. Although it was a beautiful field, its natural beauty was marred by the profuse amount of trash that covered it. Mike explained to me that he was working on a project with the town mayor to get trash cans placed around the field.

"People here do not understand the concept of trash," Mike stated. "They think that if they just throw their trash on the ground, it will magically disappear. It's unfortunate, but most of the people in San Andres were never taught about the environment. It's a shame, because it is such a beautiful town, yet it's always covered in trash. Environmental awareness is one of the biggest things we try and teach the kids in school."

I listened intently as I stared at all the trash lining the soccer field. I always took for granted the clean conditions of the area I grew up in as well as my knowledge about science and environmental sustainability. It had never occurred to me that millions of people around the world were never educated about the importance of recycling and the proper disposal of trash. It caught me off guard to see all of this waste strewn about so casually.

I followed Mike down a trail surrounded by green grass, bushes, and trees. The trail sloped downward, and we were walking closer and closer toward the enormous lake, which gleamed in the background. Little shacks and huts lined the trail on both sides. The roofs were comprised of thin, metal sheets spotted with rust and dirt. Three chickens crossed the trail right in front of us, a sight that would become common to me.

Finally, Mike hooked a left off the trail and announced that we had arrived. The house in front of us had a yard lined with rocks, which formed a path leading to the main trail. A little wooden table was built around a palm tree that sprouted in the middle of the small yard. Clothes hung from a laundry line that spread across the twenty-foot yard. Magnificent trees bordered the yard, creating an incredible silhouette, a natural fence through which you could see the lake in the background.

And the house—oh, was it beautiful. The concrete walls were painted a mix of beige and white. Hand marks and indentations sprinkled its surface. I soon learned that the house was built by one of the locals in town with just his hands and basic materials. A small wooden hut was attached to the main part of the house. Mike later explained that was where he slept.

It suddenly struck me how the world is not what we see, but how we see it. On one hand, someone could look at this "house" and claim it was a tiny, dirty shack with a filthy, tin roof. But to me, it was beautiful. The imperfections of the construction only made it that much more marvelous. The home was a piece of art, a handcrafted creation. A rustic, blue wooden door was embedded in the center of the house, and two square holes on either side served as windows.

The house had an aura of humility and ingenuity. It was down to earth, physically and metaphorically.

I was happy to be in a home just like the others in town. I wanted to experience life here to the fullest extent possible, and that included sleeping and living like the locals. That was the only way I figured I could truly understand how these people lived.

Mike escorted me in, and I happily slumped my bag down. The floor was painted a sky-blue color with swirls of gray and silt intermixed. A wooden, triple-decker bunk bed in the corner grabbed my attention. Mike explained that the volunteers who were here just a month before— two carpenters from Germany—built it with just hand tools and wood from trees out front. I loved its rustic, natural appearance and I was impressed with the volunteers' inventiveness. A mattress lay in the corner opposite from the bunk bed, with a large, white mosquito net hovering over it.

"The shower is right in there," Mike stated, pointing to a wooden, makeshift door in the corner that rested upon three dingy steps. "Feel free to rinse off. There's only cold water by the way. Lunch is usually around noon, so probably in about twenty minutes or so. After you're washed up, we can head over and you can meet the family and the other volunteers. They're still up in town."

"Great, thanks! I think I will hop in now," I replied. Mike walked out, and I stripped off my clothes, grabbed my towel, and proceeded toward the steps leading to the shower. The wooden door creaked as I slowly edged it open. It was a five-foot by five-foot gray, concrete room, with a small toilet, a sink, and a single pipe that hung overhead that was the shower faucet. There were six, red, aluminum beer cans tied together by a piece of string hanging from a small window slit. Toothbrushes and toothpaste rested in each one. I marveled at the creativity and resourcefulness of the display. I turned on the shower, although it was more of a hose than anything else.

The cool water sent a refreshing chill down my spine, and I felt the sweat and dirt on my face being washed away. The water temperature was quite soothing, and I had no desire for warmer water even if I could've gotten it. I reflected on the past two days of travel and how, despite the obstacles I had faced, I made it here. I smiled at this realization, thinking of Arthur C. Clarke's words: "The limits of the possible can only be defined by going beyond them into the *impossible*." The previous forty-eight hours seemed daunting, but nonetheless, things had worked out. The possibilities seemed scary because they were unknown to me—that is, traveling alone in a third-world country not knowing the language. But having done it now, I laughed. Maybe the best way to persevere through fear is simply to take action, courageously stepping toward your goal despite the voice in your head telling you it's too frightening.

I dried off and put on a fresh pair of clothes. I stepped out of the house into the yard where Mike and six other unfamiliar people were sitting around the wooden table that circled the palm tree.

"Hey, there he is!" Mike exclaimed. I smiled and introduced myself to the others who were also volunteering. Emma was from the Netherlands. She had thick, carrot-orange hair that was arranged in dreadlocks. I sensed an aura of glee around her—all from the simple words of greeting she offered me. It's amazing how we make judgments and assessments of people within seconds of meeting them. Anna was from Germany, although her parents were from Sri Lanka. She had the dark skin color that matched the local Guatemalans. She was Mike's wife, although they were not legally married. Matteus was from Switzerland and had dark, sloppy curls that matched his five-o'clock shadow. He spoke in a peculiar accent, sounding almost like Dracula, as English was one of the six languages in his repertoire. He had a tattoo of a bull on his right shoulder that reflected his headstrong, self-determined demeanor. Suzy and Jonathon were a couple traveling from San Francisco who blended in with the locals. Suzy had short, black hair and an inviting smile. Her parents were from Mexico, and she spoke fluent Spanish. Jonathon was Filipino and had polished, inky hair and piercing eyes that spoke of kindness and understanding.

They had packed and sold all of their belongings in the United States and were now nomads, living out of their backpacks. After talking for a while and getting to know them, I heard someone call out a phrase in Spanish from a house just twenty yards away.

"Lunch is ready!" Mike announced. I followed the others, eager to meet the Guatemalan family. I walked in and was captivated by the clayish, salmon-colored walls. A wooden table was in the center of the room with a plastic, flower-patterned cover. A large, open square in the wall served as a window to the outside world, and the sunlight coming through lit the house. The house lived openly to nature, the wind always breezing through to say hello, with the sounds of birds ringing like mellow chimes.

"*Hola! Hola! Hola!*" a woman exclaimed cheerfully, approaching me with welcoming arms. She had a smile wider than the horizon as she reached up to hug me. I bent my knees and leaned over slightly so I could accept her warm embrace. She stood a little over five feet tall yet contained the energy of a thousand suns. She had a dark complexion like most of the Guatemalans I had met so far. Her frizzled, black hair was raised behind her shoulders and held together in a hair tie.

She unleashed a barrage of rapid-fire Spanish, and I barely understood a single word she said. Not totally sure how to respond, I gave her a huge smile, reciprocating the one she gave me. I simply responded, "*Gracias!*" which was at least one word I knew. Her presence fueled me with a comfort and joy that made me feel like the happiest kid in the world. Her name was Juanita. She was the mother of the family that I was to live with, and she would prepare all my meals. Although I had known her for just minutes, I already felt as if she were my mother away from home.

I was then introduced to her three kids. Alejandra, twenty-five years old, was the oldest of the three and the only girl. She also stood around five feet tall and had a lighter complexion than her mother. She had a certain spunk and zest about her. Juan Carlos, twenty-three years old, had a mop of dark, curly hair that stuck out prominently. He had a sly, yet humorous aura about him and stood closer to my height, around five feet seven inches. Winder, the youngest child, was twenty years old and built like a tank. His dark hair was short, almost like a crew cut, and slicked smoothly atop his well-built frame. He was also around my height but had the body of a linebacker. At first, he looked quite intimidating, but when he smiled, he could light up a room. I later learned that their father, Juanita's husband, had left the family a few years ago, and they hadn't seen him since.

We all sat down at the table and enjoyed a tasty meal of beans, rice, chicken, tomatoes, and, of course, tortillas. Not only is the tortilla a staple of Guatemalan cuisine, it also functions as an edible utensil.

The conversations were essentially in Spanglish, changing from Spanish to English and then back to Spanish. I listened intently to the Spanish, trying my absolute best to interpret what I could. Luckily, Mike and all of the volunteers spoke English, so they translated for me.

"Hey, Jake," Mike addressed me, "would you be interested in going on a six-day jungle trek the day after tomorrow? It's a trek of over seventy-five miles through the ancient Mayan civilization. It's deep within the jungle. La Danta, a pyramid in the jungle, is the largest in the world by volume."

"Yes!" I replied instantly, not even hearing the full description as I was so enthralled by the idea of adventure.

"I was recently granted a certified document so I can now take people on official tours. I no longer need to do it secretly," Mike informed us. "That's how I make money here in Guatemala. Yesterday, I went to Flores, a touristy town nearby, and found a couple of people who are interested in going. They're going to sleep over at the house tomorrow night so we can set out early Monday morning. Tomorrow, we will gather all the food and supplies we need for the trip. This is definitely not your average hike. This trek is deep in the jungle, and less than 10 percent of the ruins have been excavated. That's why it's so special. It's a hidden gem."

"Awesome, I'm definitely up for going!" I exclaimed. I had never been camping before in my life, so why not just jump straight in? Six days and over seventy-five miles sounded like an adventure that was calling my name. The thought of being immersed in a remote jungle, something I had never experienced before, ignited a fire in my stomach.

This excitement was partially blinding...I had no idea what I was in for.

"Everything you want is on the other side of fear."

—Jack Canfield

CHAPTER 9

Welcome to the Jungle

March 23, 2015

"If at some point you don't ask yourself, 'What have I gotten myself into?' then you're not doing it right."
—Roland Gau

Mike woke us up at 5:00 a.m. to begin our jungle trek. We had all packed our bags the night before, so we were ready to catch the 5:30 a.m. bus to Carmelita, a remote town with no electricity or running water that was the last trace of civilization before the jungle completely took over. The sun was slowly awakening on the horizon, feeding the new day with light.

Our group of twelve lugged our bags up to a dirt road where we waited for the bus. A grumbling rumble could be heard in the distance, and the bus arrived soon after, spewing small clouds of exhaust and dirt into the air. It was a "chicken bus," or at least that's what foreigners commonly call it, because chickens are common passengers. Essentially, it looked like a typical yellow school bus in the United States; however, it was painted with other colors and decorated with Christian ideology. The locals in Guatemala use these buses for everyday transportation.

We piled into the bus and arrived three hours later at our destination, Carmelita. We went to pick up the mules, which would transport our food and bags. The people who were renting the mules to us lived in a small wooden house with a roof of palm leaves. Their yard was filled with skinny dogs, bobbing chickens, and multicolored pigs of all sizes. Small children were running around completely naked, shoeless, and covered in dirt. They naturally played alongside the animals. A man in the family who looked to be in his thirties, Alfonso, was going to be in charge of the mules on the journey. He wore an unbuttoned, red-flannel shirt that revealed his chiseled abs. I watched with interest as he easily loaded the bags onto the mules, communicating with them in a sort of unspoken "mule language."

Everything was finally packed up, and we began our journey into the jungle from their yard. Luckily, it was the dry season, so we didn't have to worry about trudging through mud and puddles. I looked down at Emma's feet and noticed that she was not wearing shoes.

"Where are your boots?" I asked, as we were about to begin our hike.

"They're in my bag. I always walk barefoot. I prefer to feel the texture of the ground on my feet. I feel more connected to the earth."

Amazed, I asked, "But aren't you worried about stepping on something sharp or slicing your foot?"

"Not really," she replied, a smile forming across her face as she was clearly entertained by my curiosity. "I walk barefoot all the time. Plus, I have my shoes in my bag. If my feet are sore, I can always throw them on."

I was astounded by Emma's decision but found her answer admirable. She definitely fit my definition of a free spirit. She was one of those people who constantly smile and find the joy in every situation. She had been traveling the world for the last five years and was full of interesting stories. I enjoyed talking with her—she had many experiences that were different than mine, and I enjoyed hearing her perspective.

We finally set off, and after about one hour hiking through the outskirts of the jungle, we entered the shade that the giant trees provided, protecting us from the scorching sun.

"Rahhhh!" In the distance, I heard the most terrifying howls echoing through the jungle. It sounded like a noise from Jurassic Park, and I half-seriously wondered to myself if somehow there was a possibility that dinosaurs lived in this jungle. These roars were unlike anything I'd ever heard—deep, chest-born, grunting growls.

"Howler monkeys," Mike informed us. And before long, I shot my head up to see four of them effortlessly swinging in the trees above us. The monkeys were cracking the tree branches, and various-sized branches rained down upon us. I didn't know if I should be laughing or concerned. "Be careful," Mike warned. "They often throw down sticks and branches. If you're not paying attention, one could knock you out."

We kept a quick pace as we traversed through this part of the jungle, all of us aware of the monkeys barking behind us with smirks on their faces. I imagined what story the news would conjure up if I were hit by one of the monkey's thrown branches. *An eighteen-year-old male from California was trekking through the Guatemalan jungle when suddenly a monkey launched a branch downward, knocking the young man unconscious. And now, here's Cindy with the traffic update.*

We were moving at a swift pace, and I enjoyed talking with everyone about his or her culture and experiences. Mike stopped up ahead and bent down, picking up a kiwi-looking ball. "*Chicozapote*," Mike informed us. "The monkeys love these fruits. They're delicious." Mike whipped out his knife and sliced the fruit in half, handing me a chunk. I sunk my teeth into the fruity flesh, my taste buds dancing at the new flavor. It tasted cinnamony and had the composition of a kiwi. I marveled at the fact that we were eating fruit fallen straight from the trees. It was a cool feeling, eating food directly from its original source. I felt like Tarzan.

Every few minutes, Mike stopped to point something out. He was so knowledgeable about the jungle, and I found his insights fascinating. He engaged us all with his tales about ancient Mayan shamans and blood sacrifices, sacred rituals, and ghost stories.

After five hours of hiking in the dry heat, we finally reached the first campsite. I pulled off my shoes and sweaty socks, the wind now giving my feet space to breathe openly. I already had burning blisters on both of my feet. Emma's feet were fine, although she said they were sore. The sun was descending toward the horizon, so we set up camp. I assembled my luxurious bed—a thin blanket on the hard jungle floor with a mosquito net hanging over it.

Once we set up our sleeping arrangements, Mike announced that we were heading to a pyramid to watch the sunset. I slipped on my flip-flops, and we all followed Mike down a trail. After about ten minutes, we arrived at El Tintal, an enormous ancient Mayan pyramid. At first, it was hard to fully decipher that it was actually a pyramid—it looked like a huge, pointy mountain immersed in trees. Yet as we approached the structure and began our ascent, I could more clearly see the rocky steps and shape of the pyramid. After trudging step after step, developing a hearty sweat, I finally reached the peak.

Atop the pyramid, I gazed at the shining sun, now just a few feet from the horizon. In every direction there was lush jungle as far as my eyes could see. There was nothing but miles and miles of different shades of green trees. No people, no cars, no buildings, no electricity. Nothing.

I felt like I was on top of the world peering down at earth and marveling at the incredible creation before my eyes. The vastness made me realize how small I was in comparison to this boundless Universe. I suddenly grasped how vulnerable and inferior humans are to the world we live in. We are minute specks of energy among this enormous ball of matter spinning through space in a solar system so large that we cannot even fathom its true dimensions.

Paradoxically, this gave me a surge of confidence. Thinking of how inconsequential I was invigorated me with a sense of freedom. My own personal failures, mistakes, and rejections now seemed insignificant compared to the world before my eyes. My individual actions were of little importance in the scheme of the cosmos, yet they were hugely important in the scheme of my own life. Powerful and meaningful change starts with the efforts of one single individual. *Your fear of failure will only hold you back. But your successes—your potential to make a positive impact— have the ability to transform you, and, perhaps, the world.*

The bright pink sun was now halfway under the horizon. All of us sat in silence, lost in thought. The sky was painted with bright violets and oranges and yellows, contrasting beautifully with the dark and light greens of the trees underneath.

Once darkness started to drift in, we headed back down the pyramid toward camp. Alfonso began preparing the corn tortillas, placing circles of dough on an iron skillet. We boiled eggs and rice and took out packs of prepackaged beans. Ravenous, I devoured my food, inhaling it as if it were the best meal I'd ever eaten. After trekking over eleven miles in thick heat, along with climbing the pyramid, I was exhausted.

I could feel the dry dirt and sweat that had seeped into my skin but ignored my desire to jump into a cool shower since that was not an option in the middle of the jungle. I brushed my teeth and washed my face with some of the drinking water at the campsite. I then slid under my pop-up mosquito net onto my blanket, which was to be my nightly resting place for the next week. The hard, bumpy ground lumped against my back. The mosquito net was missing a rod by my feet, so it drooped along my body from my torso to my toes. I didn't care. I was drained and we had a big day ahead of us. The sounds of the jungle lessened as I finally drifted into sleep. Yet, no amount of rest could prepare me for what the next night had in store.

"We are part of this Universe; we are in this Universe,
but perhaps more important than both of those facts,
is that the Universe is in us."
—Neil de Grasse Tyson

CHAPTER 10

Praying to the Shit Gods

March 24, 2015

"Everything can be taken from a man but one thing: the last of the human freedoms—to choose one's attitude in any given set of circumstances, to choose one's own way."

—Viktor Frankl

"RAHHH!" I awoke to the thundering roar of howler monkeys. Chirping birds sang their tunes as I flipped onto my back. My whole body was sore; my legs ached and my back was stiff as a pole from sleeping on the hard ground. I pushed away my body's discomfort, focusing on the wonder of waking up in such an incredible atmosphere. I absorbed as much of the cool morning breeze as I could, knowing that shortly the day's heat would replace the soothing dawn temperature.

Sunlight crept in, and I got up from my blanket, making my way toward the wooden table where the campsite "kitchen" was located. The others joined me soon, and we spoke haltingly, still waking up. We began boiling water for instant coffee and eggs, preparing for the new day at hand.

"Today's a big day," Mike announced. "We're heading to the Mirador campsite, where we will stay for two nights. We have a fifteen-mile journey ahead of us, so drink lots of water this morning."

I took Mike's advice and guzzled down as much water as I could. The thought of another fifteen-mile jaunt through the hot jungle didn't exactly seem like a walk in the park. But at the same time, I was excited for the day ahead.

We packed up all of our sleeping mats, food, and backpacks and headed on our way. Mike again led the way and set a rapid pace. Being a fast walker myself, I enjoyed the long, swift strides. Some of us walked faster than others, and every now and then those at the front waited for the others at the back to catch up. We drank water at these breaks and sucked on lollipops, savoring the sugar as we marched through the dry jungle.

Conversations among us ebbed and flowed, and after awhile, I found myself alone with Mike at the front of the pack. We were both trekking at a swift pace, and as a result, had distanced ourselves from the others. I wanted to get to know Mike better. He had a unique, distinctive aura about him—a singular energy seemed to emanate from him—I couldn't help but feel that here was someone who had lived his life in a dramatically different fashion than anyone I had ever known. By now, it was also apparent that Mike was fearless and an incredible leader. He took care of people's needs and knew how to deal with just about any problem that surfaced. He was one of those people who never complained and seemed to have a solution for everything.

"Hey, Mike, what was life like in the military?" I asked. Mike turned his head and directed his attention toward me. He grinned, yet his eyes told a different tale, as if the simple question I had asked him might actually be the most complicated question in the world.

"Well, it was a lot different from life back in the States. A lot different from life here as well." He spoke firmly; I sniffed out a small piece of anguish in his tone.

"What branch were you in? And how did you end up in the military?" I inquired. Because Mike was so open, I didn't feel as if I were crossing boundaries by asking him any question that surfaced in my mind. Yet, I could sense there was something about my questions that were causing Mike to recall a tragic past.

"In a way, I was destined to serve in the military. My dad, grandfather, uncles, cousins—they all served. My family ran a SERE training camp, which stands for Survival, Evasion, Resistance and Escape. In Delaware, where I grew up, woods surrounded us. My grandfather, who directed the training, used me in drills, so I learned everything there is to know about survival. When I acted out, my grandfather sent me to the woods for a few days to collect myself."

My mind began to piece together the information I was receiving. No wonder Mike knew so much about the outdoors, resourcefulness, and survival. Those were the foundations he grew up on.

Mike continued, now as deeply engaged in telling his story as I was listening to it. "After graduating college early and working a few jobs, I entered the Special Forces working for a private contractor. I served eight years, my unit's focus mostly in hostage recovery and raids. During that time, I accumulated over eight and a half months of combat time."

My eyes practically burst out of their sockets. From my standpoint, that job was something I had only seen in the movies, like *Saving Private Ryan* and *American Sniper*. And here was someone who had actually lived that life. And over eight months of combat time! I could not even begin to imagine the ordeal of over eight months of my life being filled, every second, with the physical, mental, and emotional strains of being in constant battle and turmoil and having to make spur-of-the-moment, life-and-death decisions.

He resumed, "I was mostly in Iraq and Afghanistan. We engaged enemy forces who were blowing up schools, guys who threw acid in girls' faces. Death became a part of life. It was like the sun coming up in the morning or the moon at night. It happened regularly, every day." Mike's face remained stoic.

"Did you ever have any close calls?" I probed, trying to be sensitive and careful with my words. As prepared as I thought I could be, the story that Mike was revealing had my jaw dropping to the floor.

He began, "One day, my partner and I were assigned to drive an armored vehicle through a danger zone. We did rock-paper-scissors to see who would drive. I won, and because I like being in control, I took the wheel. As I was driving, I glanced up and noticed a man on a building with his phone in the air. Suddenly, there was a huge blast. The next thing I knew, I was on the ground, dazed, crawling for my gun. We had guys behind us, and they were firing ahead, providing cover. I didn't realize it in the moment, but I had a huge piece of metal stuck in my jaw, among other wounds. I was dragged to cover where the medic performed emergency tracheotomy surgery on the spot." He grimaced, as if he were reliving the events he was detailing. "It was awful; I couldn't breathe, and they were pumping air through a hole in my throat. I lost consciousness, and when I awoke, I was in a hospital bed."

I peered at Mike with eyes full of shock and awe. The hairs on the back of my neck shot up, and goose bumps formed on my arms despite the day's roasting heat. Deeply engrossed in his story but not knowing exactly what to say, I asked, "What happened next? What happened to your partner and the guy who detonated the bomb?"

"Our guys shot down the guy who set off the IED." Mike paused, glancing upward toward the beams of sunlight that were escaping the barrier of the trees. It was as if he were searching for an answer in the sky, one that could not be found. He was silent for a few seconds, and then continued, "My partner was killed in the explosion."

The sounds of the jungle suddenly became silent. No birds chirping, no leaves rustling, no monkeys howling. The boiling air weighed down heavily on my shoulders. My tongue searched for saliva yet came up empty; my mouth felt like a dry wasteland. My arms and legs and toes and feet no longer ached with pain.

Mike resumed. "After surgery, where they removed the metal from my jaw and other shrapnel from my body, I was flown back to the States where I was hospitalized for six months. I lost sixty pounds. It took me almost two years to recover, and I had to learn to speak with part of my jaw gone. Those years recovering were some of the darkest in my life. The military asked me to return to duty even after everything that had happened."

"What?!?" I exclaimed, having a hard time believing that someone who went through such a traumatic experience would be called back to duty. "Did you go back?"

Mike smirked, acknowledging my response as if my reaction conveyed common sense. "I didn't go back. After everything that had happened, I was done. Done with war. I had a lot of time to reflect on my life. War is a never-ending hell. Violence does not solve violence. I've had friends die in my arms. I've seen people's limbs disappear in a flash. I've seen sacrifice that goes beyond the deepest roots of what it means to be selfless. I've taken the lives of people I didn't even know. And for what?" He stopped momentarily, gathering his thoughts.

He resumed with an emotional passion that pulsated through the protruding veins in his forehead. "I had friends who killed themselves just days after returning home, unable to cope with the contrast of the cruel world they knew during their time on active duty to the reality of life in America. A medic in my platoon killed himself two weeks after coming home. All he wanted was to be an elementary school nurse. But his training and certifications didn't transfer over. He could stitch on a blown-off leg but wasn't "qualified" to put a Band-Aid on a ten-year-old's cut. Many soldiers I knew often returned to war because it was the only thing they knew. The ignorance, the mass consumption, the materialism; these unfortunate truths pierced the deepest depths of my own justification for fighting a war... a war that I had now forgotten why I was fighting. Every single place that I went to over my eight years of service, conflict broke out when we left, resulting in more death and more violence."

Mike rested his voice for a minute and then raised his eyes to my level, looking directly at me. "Hate and violence are easy. Anyone can be hateful and cause harm. Love and compassion are hard. It takes effort to have self-control. It takes effort to step back from a situation and take a deep breath—to look at the bigger picture. It takes effort to hold in your ego, to understand a situation from someone else's perspective you disagree with. That is true power. That is the first step toward love and compassion. Love and compassion are the only way toward peace."

I let Mike's words sink in, repeating them in my mind again and again. Here was a man who spent years living a realistic hell, witnessing atrocities on a daily basis, and who, himself, lost parts of his body. Yet, despite the violence that had been his everyday life, he knew that it wasn't right. He knew that love and compassion are the only way to conquer hate and violence. He knew that darkness, does not combat darkness but that light does.

"We are all connected," Mike explained. "When you take a step back, you realize that people from every culture, every religion, every country all want the same thing: to be loved. When we realize that at some point in time we have all sat at the same table—that we are all family, connected in some indescribable way—then we will be one step closer to peace."

I was locked in concentration, listening to Mike as if he were revealing the world's greatest secrets. I smiled, acknowledging him. I had a deep belief as well that we—all humans and other life forms—are all connected in some inexplicable way. Hearing Mike's perspective only reinforced my own thoughts. His story invigorated me with passion. I wanted to scream Mike's message into the jungle, a roar of inspiration that I hoped would echo to every civilization on earth.

We stopped and waited for the others to catch up since we had walked far ahead of them. I didn't even realize we had been hiking for seven hours until Mike signaled that we were within one hour of camp! The others finally approached, and we all marched the last haul together.

As the campsite came into view, we all cheered. The sight of huts filled with palm leaves always meant that we'd made it. There was a large, green field right next to the campsite with about twenty wild turkeys hanging out in the center. Fifteen miles of hiking had taken its toll on our aching legs, and we all happily plopped down at the campsite's wooden table. We sat for a while, not moving, chugging water. I was too exhausted to get up. I barely gathered enough energy to pull my shoes and socks off, yet the relief was unlike any other feeling in the world. The air met my feet, and the refreshing sensation of the breeze flowing between my toes was pleasurable beyond what words can convey. I wiggled my toes, glad to give them space to breathe. I now had stinging, raw blisters in between my toes as well as on my heels. I tried not to think about it or the fact that we still had over fifty miles to go.

*   *   *   *   *

As the sun's heat subsided and dusk approached, we all gathered around Alfonso to collect our sleeping gear from the mules. Worn out, I mustered up the minimal amount of energy needed to set up my blanket and mosquito net. I figured that since I was so spent from the day's hike, I would pass out like a rock despite the hard jungle ground beneath my blanket.

We all gathered around the communal "kitchen" and began preparing dinner: rice, beans, eggs, tomato sauce, and tortillas. My stomach growled, reminding me how hungry I was. I wolfed down my dinner, refueling my exhausted body. I knew I probably looked like a mad man shoveling heaps of tomatocy rice and beans and eggs into my mouth, but I couldn't have cared less. Out of the corner of my eye, I noticed many of the others inhaling their food in a similar fashion. The food seemed to restore us all, recharging our batteries.

The moon was shining, a piercing, white crescent that brightened the black, night sky. All twelve of us convened on the grass field to watch the stars. I lay down, too tired to care about the bugs crawling on me. We all talked for a while and listened to Mike tell exciting stories and legends about the ancient Mayans. He shared myths and fables as well as the history of the jaguar, which roamed around this part of the jungle. This was no ghost story; he had actually spotted a jaguar on his last journey in the jungle.

I gazed up at the stars that rested in the clearest sky I'd ever seen. I pondered how extraordinary the world is, the wonders of space filling my brain. I pictured Neil Armstrong landing on the moon, and how he had achieved what had been considered impossible. So many failures had preceded that monumental accomplishment that I couldn't help but dwell on the concept that experiencing failure is part of achieving success. *What if everyone's view of failure is actually distorted? What if success is only possible with failure, at least most of the time? What if people realized that failure—along with hardships and obstacles—are essential steps in the process of achieving success?* A shooting star soared across the sky, and everyone acknowledged the blessing before our eyes. I began to drift off to sleep.

After a while, I felt an uneasiness stir in my stomach. I had been feeling lightheaded earlier probably because of dehydration after the strenuous amount of energy I had exerted. Even the beauty of the night sky couldn't distract me from the pain that I was now feeling. I slowly lifted myself off the ground, feeling my head rush in the process. I said good night to everyone and made my way to bed, my flashlight providing a meager trail of light among the pitch-black air. I settled under my mosquito net, anxious to get some sleep, the net draping against my feet. My stomach stirred and my head pounded. I closed my eyelids, praying to fall asleep.

Some time later, I awoke with my body dripping in sweat; cold chills were simultaneously shaking my weary body. My head throbbed as my stomach turned and twisted in painful knots. It was the middle of the night, and everyone was asleep. I felt sick as a dog, and I was huddled up in the fetal position on my blanket unsure if I was hot or cold. *What if I've contracted a disease or a parasite? What if I'm going to need a helicopter to somehow fly in and rescue me? Should I wake up Mike?*

My stomach rumbled, and I knew I had to go to the bathroom quickly. The campsite bathroom—a wooden box with a hole in it where hundreds of bugs roamed—was too far away. Plus, I was fearful of going there in the middle of the night. According to Mike, there had been a snake in it on one prior occasion. I stumbled out of my mosquito net toward the direction of the grass field. I was so disoriented that I was unsure of exactly what I was doing or where I was going. I felt a surge in my stomach and knew I couldn't hold my dinner in any longer. I squatted by a tree, clenching my abdomen, and looked up to the sky as if it would heal me instantly and answer my prayers. I stood there for a while in a half squat, flailing my flashlight around me in case the jaguar decided it was hungry. After what felt like an eternity in this uncomfortable position, my stomach cramps subsided. With nothing to wipe with—and frankly, I was too discombobulated to care—I pulled up my pants and made my way back to bed. Matteus was sleeping in a hammock just a few feet away from me. He heard my moans as I approached and got up to help me.

"You need water," he commanded. "Here, let's go to the water tank." I began stumbling in the direction where I thought the water was, and Matteus quickly grabbed my shoulders and turned me around. "Where are you going? You're walking toward the field; the water is in the opposite direction. Come with me." He put an arm on my shoulder and directed me toward the water jug, which was by the wooden dinner table. I could barely focus on my steps, feeling lighter and weaker by the second. Matteus put a bottle of water in my hand and helped me lift it to my mouth. I took a small sip, unable to absorb much as my stomach rumbled in disagreement. "You need to drink more," Matteus directed me. I obeyed his command as best I could, sipping small mouthfuls of water at a time.

After Matteus forced me to drink more water, he escorted me back to my blanket. He assured me that he was there if I needed anything and to wake him up if necessary. I mumbled a thank you to him, unable to fully express my appreciation for his help. I crawled back to bed, praying for my burning fever and stomach pains to go away. The hard ground was now the least of my worries. I got up five more times during the night to poop, squatting painfully as I let nature take its course. I finally made it back to bed with no more interruptions and managed to rest my eyes for a little while before daylight slowly dawned.

With the onset of morning, I got up gingerly and made my way toward the wooden table in the communal kitchen. My shorts were covered in poop, pee, sweat, and dirt. My previously white shirt looked tie-dyed—and not with warm, bright colors. My feet stung from blisters, and my legs had red bumps on them, which I assumed were bug bites. I staggered over slowly, feeling like a zombie. Luckily, my fever was mostly gone as well as my stomach pains, although my belly felt empty and fragile. Delicately, I eased my butt onto the wooden table and grabbed my water bottle, taking a few sips.

Thankfully, today was an easy day. We didn't have to pack up our stuff; we were spending the night again at the same campsite. The only walking we had to do was to La Danta, the biggest pyramid in the Northern Hemisphere. Knowing that my day was going to involve summiting one of the largest pyramids in the entire world filled half of me with elation. The other half of me couldn't imagine doing anything in the state I was in. I closed my eyes, exhausted, trying to let my body ease into the new day.

As daylight approached, the others awoke and soon joined me at the table. I filled them in on the ordeal I endured over the course of the night. Emma went in her backpack and handed me some Imodium pills and a dehydration packet, which I graciously accepted and swallowed instantly.

"Man oh man, you looked funny last night," Mike chuckled. "I looked over at you during one point. You were butt naked, squatting over, and looking up toward the sky. It looked like you were praying to the shit gods." He was bent over in hysterical laughter, wheezing, unable to control himself. I was glad that someone found the experience funny, because I definitely didn't.

We cooked breakfast and relaxed for a while; today, we were in no rush. We could spend the day hanging out at the pyramid, which wasn't far off from the campsite. The food and water immensely lifted my spirits. My stomach was now filled with some food, and the water helped replenish my weak limbs. Slowly, I felt my energy restoring itself. *Maybe this was the jungle's natural way of welcoming me?*

After hanging out at camp for a few hours, I was beginning to feel as good as new. My head no longer throbbed, and my stomach had finally calmed down. Mike announced that we were going to head out to La Danta, the enormous ancient Mayan pyramid. We followed Mike on the trail that lead to La Danta. Leaves covered the ground, providing a carpet for each step. Tall trees stood like giants all around, shading and sheltering us from the beating sun.

My head was angled down, entranced in the art of each step I took. I could feel the leaves crunch as my shoes met the jungle floor. The uneven surface of the ground, which was hidden with branches, logs, and roots, demanded my full attention. Focusing so intently on each and every step I made was tiring but oddly soothing. It was the only thing I was aware of; my thoughts about the intense night before—my fear of contracting a parasite, my stinging blisters and achy feet—all ceased to exist because I was now solely conscious of my body's movements.

Suddenly, everyone stopped to look up. As I lifted my head, I was mesmerized by the sight before my eyes. In the middle of the jungle, far away from even the fringes of civilization, lay one of the most spectacular structures I have ever seen. It was like looking at the Empire State Building as if every other building in New York ceased to exist. It was extraordinary, rising far above the trees that encompassed it. A pyramid so enormous, in both volume and height, that just viewing it sent chills down my spine. It was one of those moments in life in which something is so remarkable that you can't help but question the wonders of the world and what humans are truly capable of. The thought that over two thousand years ago this masterpiece was built without any modern technology stunned me. I looked around and noticed that everyone else was also awestruck, their mouths hanging open and eyes glistening at the reality that lay in front of them.

We followed Mike as he guided us toward the steps that led to the top of the pyramid. We began the march up. Slowly but steadily, we advanced toward the top. It felt like an eternity ascending the steps. I was breathing heavily, my legs ached from exhaustion, and my shirt dripped with perspiration. Finally, I could see the top. The excitement of reaching the peak filled me with adrenaline and enabled me to ignore my body's pain and exhaustion. I surged up the last few steps and found myself standing on the summit.

I stood there for a moment, feeling accomplished, as if I had climbed Mount Everest. All around me, an endless warp of green stretched out toward the horizon. Fluffy, white clouds were scattered across the light-blue sky floating along effortlessly. The thoughts in my mind drifted just like the clouds. I couldn't believe that I was standing at the peak of what was once home to one of the world's foundational civilizations of over two hundred thousand people. Standing where ancient kings and shamans stood, I tried to imagine what life was like when this ancient society was at its height. We listened to Mike as he explained the history of the Mayan civilization. He pointed his finger in different directions, showing us how close we were to Mexico and Belize. We all talked for a while, marveling at the vastness before our eyes. We were in awe of being in the presence of something greater than man.

I laughed at how peaceful I felt compared with the previous night's horror. It reminded me that sometimes in life, things get worse before they get better. We wouldn't appreciate the joys in life if we didn't experience pain. Our emotions are relative; they are only understood in comparison to our previous feelings and emotions. Therefore, happiness cannot be understood without suffering because if all we knew was happiness, then we wouldn't know any other feeling. We only appreciate light because we know what darkness is like. Without joy and pain, our lives would be boring and monotonous. We would flat line, which speaks of death, not life.

After sitting for a while, we all agreed that we were ready to go back to camp. We leisurely walked back because we didn't need to set anything up. We sat around the wooden table and talked for hours until the sun set. No one was distracted by their phones or itching to check into social media. There was no electricity, no Wi-Fi, and no cell phone service. And it was amazing. We were stimulated by each other and the energy that we radiated. We were connecting face-to-face, eye-to-eye, not through a screen. I felt this indescribable wholeness, immersed in the wonders of nature, immersed in a shared experience with friends, without any artificial distractions.

We prepared and ate dinner, all of us feeling so happy to be exactly where we were. When darkness settled in, I slid into my blanket and under my mosquito net, closing my eyes. Oddly, the hard ground didn't seem to bother me this time. The sounds of the jungle comforted me as I drifted away.

> *"The present moment is filled with joy and happiness.*
> *If you are attentive, you will see it."*
> —Thich Nhat Hahn

CHAPTER 11

Breaking Past Limits

March 25, 2015

"Human beings, by changing the inner attitudes of their minds, can change the outer aspects of their lives."

—William James

The next day was intense. We faced our longest part of the trek, over twenty miles. We set out soon after daybreak. After trekking for hours in the scorching sun and stiff, dry air, I felt my inner thighs and legs stinging ferociously. Mike announced that we were halfway there, so we took a break, sitting on a few fallen trees and drinking as much water as we could.

I pulled up my shorts to see that my thighs were covered in an aggravating heat rash. It consisted of red, burning hives that were irritated by even the slightest grazing of my shorts. I grew quiet and fearful. Although attempting to hide my emotions, I became upset. Until this point, the skin problems that had plagued me before my trip had almost disappeared, but now I felt like I could never escape them. I found myself becoming mad at Mike as if he were somehow responsible for making us go through this ridiculously long hike in scorching heat. I felt anxiety creeping in the same way it always had.

As Alfonso approached with the mules, he noticed my shorts pulled up unusually high and he pointed to my thighs. I watched him tie the mules to a tree and disappear into the brush. He returned shortly, carrying a bunch of greenish-purple leaves. I watched him rip them up and grind them between his hands. He then added a few drops of water into the green mush in his hands. He motioned for me to extend my legs, one at a time, which I did. "*Plantas medicinales,*" he explained. Alfonso squeezed the mush in his hand and a brownish liquid seeped out and onto my thighs. He poured the juice over my entire rash, getting every ounce of liquid he could from the plant mix.

In that moment, I had an epiphany. My grumpy, self-pitying mood vanished instantaneously. I realized that regardless of my skin problems, I had a choice. I could enjoy this incredible journey despite my skin rash, or I could drown in my own misery. Whether the plant that Alfonso used on my skin actually lessened its pain was irrelevant. The action that Alfonso took in attempting to heal me changed my entire perspective. His act of kindness, showing me that he cared about my situation, lifted my spirits. I no longer felt my skin's inflammation; I chose to focus on how lucky I was to be in the jungle in the first place.

It was in this moment that I truly realized the power of the human mind. My response and perspective toward this situation was more important than the reality of it. Bob Marley's words of wisdom rang in my ears: "Emancipate yourself from mental slavery; none but ourselves can free our minds." *Only I can free my mind.* We still had a few days and many miles ahead of us. Yes, it was hot. Yes, I had a rash. And yes, I was physically uncomfortable. I couldn't control those things, but I could control my attitude. I decided that from there on out, I would enjoy every remaining minute of the trip.

* * * * *

The next three days were just as amazing as the first three. We explored ancient pyramids and temples, hiked for miles, and then set up camp each night. Over the course of six days, we trekked over seventy miles in the jungle through stifling heat. At the end of it, I was covered in dirt, dried sweat, pee, poop, insect bites, and an itchy rash. I had not showered and had eaten only packets of beans, boiled eggs, rice, and tortillas. I slept on the rocky ground with just a blanket underneath me. And I loved every minute of it.

It's a funny thing, looking back. I had never been camping before and didn't know what to expect. Six days and seventy-five miles in the wild jungle was no easy feat. I had no doubts that I could do it beforehand. It sounded exciting to me, and I wasn't paying particular attention to the strenuous challenges the trip demanded. Of course, certain obstacles arose. But I did it. Those hurdles didn't stop me. I realized that things are never as bad as they might seem if you can manage to put them into perspective. Humans are naturally adaptable. We have to be in order to survive. The thought of change or living without certain comforts that we've come to rely on can sound frightening. It's this idea of the unknown, something we can't wrap our heads around, which strikes fear within. But just doing it is empowering. This feeling of empowerment was starting to blossom within me, though I wasn't yet fully aware of it.

"The only thing that stands between you and your dream is the will to try and the belief that it is actually possible."

—Joel Brown

CHAPTER 12

The Universal Language

March 29, 2015

*"The man who says he can, and the man
who says he cannot are both correct."*
—Confucius

I awoke Sunday morning as if I had been asleep for weeks. Sleeping on rough ground the past six days made my bunk bed feel like a five star hotel bed. I strolled over to the wooden table and plopped down on a seat next to Mike and the other volunteers. They were talking about the week ahead, and Mike was about to fill me in on school.

Suddenly, Mike realized, "Wait! There is no school this week because of *Semana Santa.*"

"What's *Semana Santa*?" I inquired.

"It's the holy week that's celebrated before Easter Sunday. There are usually festivities throughout the week and up until Sunday. It's one of the biggest holidays in Guatemala."

"Awesome!" I exclaimed. Along with being excited because I would get to experience a religious holiday, I was relieved to have a full week to practice my Spanish before school started.

I walked inside and perused the books that Mike kept in the house. A protruding, yellow *Spanish for Dummies* textbook caught my eye.

I grabbed it and strolled toward the wooden table. I made a promise to myself right there that I would spend time every day practicing my Spanish. Mike gave me a notebook where I could write down what I learned and use it as a reference. I spent the next few hours engulfed in learning Spanish verbs and phrases, trying to etch new grammar rules into my brain.

Anna, Mike's wife, announced that she was going to swim to San Juan, the next town over, and invited everyone to join. Not having any idea how far of a swim that was, I accepted along with Emma and Suzy. I figured that if the three girls could do the swim, I could, too.

As we went down the steep hill to the lakeshore, I noticed a sunken house in the lake about twenty feet from the shore. The roof was flat and rose six feet above the water. Anna explained that the lake level had risen throughout the last few years, and the house had become almost entirely submerged. There were stairs leading up to the house, and the roof was a perfectly square platform. I soon learned that everyone called this house "*la Casana.*" Anna pointed out a red, triangular speck in the distance.

"That's the pier we are swimming to, the one with the red tent over it. We did the swim for the first time right before we left for the jungle. It's definitely a challenge."

I couldn't believe how far away the pier was. It was literally a small red dot in the horizon. I brushed aside any concerns that were trying to enter my mind. *If they can do it, I can, too*, I reassured myself. We climbed up the steps from *la Casana* and dove in. I started to swim in a freestyle stroke but soon realized that it exhausted me much too quickly. I couldn't believe that I was struggling just minutes into the swim. I glanced around only to notice that we had barely moved from *la Casana.* Our destination still appeared as a remote speck. The others were preoccupied in a smooth breaststroke using a frog-style kick. They glided through the water in a slow yet fluent motion. I tried replicating their technique and found it to be much more effective.

I found myself in a rhythm focusing intently on each stroke I made. I soon realized that turning around to see how far I had come didn't help me at all. I decided to focus all of my attention on maintaining a continuous, steady stroke. Just like I had felt when trekking through the jungle, I found myself in a trance. Before I knew it, we were halfway there, and the red tent was now taking form. Every couple of minutes, I turned onto my back to rest. After floating on my back, I flipped back over, feeling renewed with energy. Ralph Waldo Emerson's words came to mind: "Once you make a decision, the Universe conspires to make it happen." I smiled at this thought, knowing that a force deep within me was guiding me down my destined path. Just like the Universe, I realized I had to work *with* the motion of the lake, not against it.

I swam now with confidence, my tired limbs and lungs no longer bothering me. *Mind over matter, mind over matter,* I kept repeating to myself. I knew that the biggest obstacles in life were not physical, but mental. The mind has the ability to inspire the physical body to transcend limitations and achieve what has been deemed impossible.

The red tent was now just a few hundred feet away, and I could read the small letters printed on its canvas shell. I drove myself forward and finally grasped onto the ladder of the pier and hoisted myself up. I turned and looked at *la Casana* from my new vantage point. It was just a speck of gray in the distance, rising squarely above the water.

We sat on a bench in a little park overlooking the lake while regaining our breath. Anna asked someone walking nearby what time it was. We found out that we had been swimming for over an hour! I couldn't believe how long and far the swim was. After talking and relaxing for a while, we walked back to San Andres.

Back at the house, everyone was hanging out and enjoying a day of relaxation. I got out my book and began to read as well. Other than the wooden table, there weren't many places to sit in the yard or even in the house. I sat on the steps of the house consciously pushing my shoulders back trying to maintain good posture. A few clouds rolled in, and a slight breeze glided by. Juanita, who was standing two feet in front of me, interrupted my thoughts. I was so absorbed in my book I hadn't even noticed she was there. Smiling, she handed me a cup of hot cocoa and signaled for me to follow her. I graciously accepted the cocoa and walked behind her.

She escorted me to a little area tucked away in the front of her yard. A denim-blue hammock was perched in the middle of a hidden little outdoor loft with an incredible view of the lake. "*Aquí*," or "here," she indicated, pointing toward the hammock. My face lit up as I thanked her. I couldn't imagine a more picturesque setting to read in. I eagerly plopped down in the hammock, grateful for this new dwelling spot. I was in a cocoon, the snug denim fabric wrapped tightly around my body.

After reading for a while, I got up and made my way through Juanita's kitchen, which was the best way back to our house. Her home was a mere fifteen yards away from the shack that housed the volunteers. Juan Carlos, Juanita's son, was sitting at the table and asked me if I wanted to go for a ride with him on his motorbike. "*Sí!*" I gladly replied. I followed him out to the street where his elegant blue motorbike was parked. Motorbikes were used everywhere in San Andres, and cars were less prevalent.

Juan Carlos revved the engine, and I hopped onto the seat behind him. We took off into the center of town. Famished dogs wandered the streets and alleyways, their skeletons protruding from their skimpy bodies. We passed the main food markets and tortilla stands, waving at the locals with whom Juan Carlos was acquainted. They studied me with curiosity, and I smiled and waved, feeling comforted by Juan Carlos's presence. He took me all around and into the next town, telling me about different sights and buildings. We eventually headed back and I thanked Juan Carlos for the tour.

During dinner, Mike suggested that I could take a few Spanish lessons if I wanted. "The man who helped build our house has a son named Miguel. He's twenty years old and wants to be a teacher but can't find a job. I talked with him earlier today, and he said he would love to teach Spanish to any volunteers. He's asking a very reasonable price."

"Yeah, I would love that!" I exclaimed. I couldn't think of a better way to learn Spanish than with one of the locals.

"Great. I will talk with him tomorrow and set you guys up," Mike replied.

I washed up and got ready for bed. Because there wasn't much electricity in the house—or all over town for that matter—it became pitch black by about eight o' clock after the sun had dipped under the horizon. My internal clock adjusted to the rise of light and the fall of darkness. When the sun rose, I awoke, usually around five thirty; when the sun set, I went to bed, usually around eight thirty. Neither time seemed abnormally early to me. Rather, I was just abiding with the flow of nature.

*　*　*　*　*

The next day, Mike strolled into the yard midmorning. A teenager who looked to be around my age was standing next to him. He had a mop of maple-brown curls that stuck out at all angles, icy-blue eyes, and freckles that dotted his tawny-colored skin. He stood slim and composed.

"Jake, come over here and meet Miguel. He will be your Spanish tutor," Mike said.

I hopped off of the wooden table and approached Miguel who had a broad smile on his face. I introduced myself in Spanish and shook his hand, trying to give off an aura of welcoming positivity. He reciprocated my intention, his smile widening even further and dimples forming on his face. After talking for a few minutes about town, soccer, and other things through both spoken and unspoken words, he directed me toward the trail. He knew of a cool spot to study and wanted to take me there.

I followed him up the grassy trail that veered away from both the house and the lake. We meandered through town, which was now alive and filled with local merchants going about their business. Miguel led me through the town center and up a hill. Finally, after cutting through a few streets and making a swift right, Miguel looked at me and smiled, curious to see my reaction. In front of us lay a browning grass field with a wooden table and an umbrella made of palm leaves. And the icing on the cake was the magnificent view of the lake in the background. The spot was tucked away, and I could tell that Miguel took pride in taking me here.

We both sat down, and Miguel began going over the basics of the Spanish language. He had me write down key words and pronounce them aloud. Every now and then, he would cackle in laughter at the way I pronounced something, his curls bobbing up and down as he tried to control himself. I couldn't help but laugh myself whenever he did. The two-hour session seemed to pass at warp speed, and when we finished, we made our way back to the house. We set up our next meeting time, and he highlighted the words I should practice. I thanked him for his help. We said good-bye, and just as he was about to head up the trail, he turned back and called my name. He told me that he and his friends were playing soccer up at the local field later and wanted me to join. I gladly accepted his invitation and told him I would meet him at the field at five, the time he suggested.

At lunchtime, I practiced my new vocabulary on Juanita and her kids. I still struggled to understand all of Juanita's words. Whenever I couldn't comprehend her words and didn't feel like admitting my confusion, I would just give her a warm smile and nod my head. It was going to be a challenge to fully understand the fast-paced Spanish that Juanita and the other locals spoke, but I was up for that challenge.

Five o' clock rolled around, and I jogged up the hill to the field. Miguel and his friends were sitting in a circle putting on their soccer cleats. He got up to greet me and bumped my fist with his, welcoming me to the group. I stretched my legs, waiting for the others to get ready to play. We started kicking a ball around, warming up and getting familiar with the touch of the ball and the bumpiness of the uneven ground. The group split in two, forming teams. Miguel directed me toward his team. We set up rocks, which were to be our goal posts, and let the game begin.

My legs worked tirelessly as they propelled me back and forth across the uneven field. I zigged and zagged, wanting the ball to be at my feet. I called for the ball in Spanish and then passed it on to my teammates, creating space to move toward the goal. Miguel threaded me a perfect pass in-between two players on the opposing team. I launched myself forward like a gazelle, all the while controlling and maneuvering the ball as I sped toward the goal. I slowed down the speed of the ball with my outstretched right foot and took a shot at the open goal, which was angled just a few feet to my left. The ball skipped wide past the stone posts out of bounds. Annoyed with myself, I uttered a cuss word in Spanish, which I had picked up from playing soccer in my youth. To my surprise, everyone dropped to the ground howling in laughter, clearly shocked at my use of a slang word. I guess it was pretty funny and out of the blue, and I laughed with them or maybe at myself. I didn't really know and didn't care. I was enjoying myself and my newfound teammates. The game resumed, and we played for a while until everyone was too drained to exert any more energy.

We all made our way toward a little shop and bought Gatorades. I guzzled down the sugary, refreshing drink along with Miguel and the rest of the locals. We sat on the steps talking and laughing for a little while. Feeling my stomach rumble with hunger, I said good-bye to the guys and set off toward the house. I practically swallowed my food whole, eating more than my fair share of warm, fluffy tortillas. Exhausted from the game, I showered and settled into bed.

"Sport has the power to change the world. It has the power to inspire and unite people in a way that little else does. It speaks to youth in a language they understand."
—Nelson Mandela

CHAPTER 13

The Happiness of Pursuit

April 3, 2015

"Dance is the hidden language of the soul."
—Martha Graham

Alejandra and Winder had been telling me about a party to be held on Friday night. It was going to be one of the most special and fun nights of the year with a DJ and dancing. Winder talked about the different types of dances that he liked and that a style called *Punta* was his favorite. I warned him that he better be able to bring the heat Friday night, because I was ready to dance.

For most of Friday, we had seen people setting up the DJ equipment on the shore near *la Casana*. It seemed as if everyone in town was counting down the minutes for the dance to begin. When Friday evening finally rolled around, a festive atmosphere filled the air and almost all of us—Mike, Anna, Emma, Suzy, Jonathon, Winder, Alejandra, and I—headed down for the party. We were quite a diverse group.

The music was blaring, and I could feel the vibration of the bass from the shore. In the distance, a crimson moon was ascending above the horizon. I was shocked at the color of the fiery moon and almost thought the sun had risen too early. Suddenly, everyone cheered as an Enrique Iglesias song began to blast into the night. Alejandra clutched my hand and pulled me toward the dance floor. I felt the rhythm of the music taking over my body as my shoulders loosened up, my legs tapped against the floor, and my arms swayed in whatever way the music pulled them. I grabbed Alejandra's hand and spun her in a circle, grooving as spontaneously as the flow of the wind. I turned to my right to see Mike and Anna jamming out and dancing like there was no tomorrow. Emma was in awe as Winder swayed his hips in a way that I didn't know was possible for a man. Suzy and Jonathan were also lost in the musical tempo, busting out moves left and right.

As a crisp breeze brushed against my cheeks, I pondered how I ended up in this exact spot at this exact moment. There was not one place on earth I would have rather been. The calmness and simplicity of life in San Andres gave me a new zest for life. Time seemed to stand still as we danced to the music, totally absorbed in the moment. The moon transitioned from a burning scarlet to a piercing white that lit up the night sky.

It struck me later that this was the first time I had truly danced without a care in the world—while sober. In high school and during college, I had always felt that I needed alcohol in order to dance. Yet that night, I realized that dancing is an expression of feeling and emotion. Everyone knows how to dance; it's instinctual. Dancing is the unspoken language of the soul that syncs up the internal rhythms of our minds and bodies with the resonance and frequency of sound. Melody and beat have the power to inspire movement of the body that is beyond our conscious control if only we release our body to the rhythm of the music.

I went to bed that night with a warm buzz radiating in my chest. I was having trouble falling asleep, not because of discomfort, but because I realized that my reality was better than my dreams. The natural high I was feeling fueled my body with adrenaline. I lay awake now knowing what it meant to be living life to its fullest.

"It is not in the pursuit of happiness that we find fulfillment,
it is in the happiness of pursuit."
—Denis Waitley

CHAPTER 14

From Student to Teacher

April 5, 2015

"If it scares you, it might be a good thing to try."
—Seth Godin

S unday rolled around, and I suddenly remembered that tomorrow was Monday. I hadn't been paying attention to the days of the week.

"Are you excited about teaching tomorrow?" Mike asked me.

"Yeah. I'm kind of nervous but excited. Do you know how old my kids will be?"

"Right now, there is a class of fourth-graders who have never had any English teachers. Kids will range in age from about nine to twelve years old, and most of them won't know a word of English. I thought that could be a great class for you to teach, so you could start from scratch with them."

I nodded in acknowledgement. "Yeah, sure, that sounds great!" I replied, trying to mask my feelings of uncertainty.

"You'll do great, trust me. There's no pressure. We're just trying to give them a basic foundation of English so they can build upon it as they get older. English can be the opportunity that will enable these kids to get better jobs and have a better life. If we weren't here, they would have no one to teach them English. This is the poorest school in San Andres. Most of them will do what their parents do, if their parents even work. So just know that even if it's just a few things they learn, it's better than nothing."

"Okay, thanks. I guess that makes me feel better."

I had no idea what teaching was going to be like. I was about to teach a class full of fourth-graders who didn't speak my language, and I could barely speak a word of theirs! I didn't know if it was going to be highly structured or laid back. I didn't know how it was going to all play out. *What if the kids don't like me? What if I totally freeze and don't know what to do or say?* I found myself beginning to worry about tomorrow and steered away from those negative thoughts. I reminded myself that as long as I was myself and smiled, things would work out. I just needed to stay positive.

I had been brainstorming ideas since I found out that I was going to be teaching. Mike gave me a notebook that I could use to plan my lessons. I had tentative ideas for the week but decided to take it day by day, as I had no idea how much progress the kids would make after each lesson. I wrote down my lesson plan for day one. *What would I want to learn if I were in their shoes? Or more importantly, **how** would I want to learn?* I designed my lesson for the day based on these questions. *Everyone has to start somewhere,* I reminded myself.

* * * * *

The sound of roosters crowing filled my ears at the crack of dawn. I climbed down and made my way toward the wooden table outside. When everyone awoke, we all gathered for breakfast at Juanita's. She prepared us a warm plate of eggs, beans, cheese, and tortillas. Juanita was dressed in a white T-shirt that had a collar with a red badge sewn on the front. This was her teaching uniform. She also taught at the school where I was going to be teaching; however, she taught subjects in Spanish.

Mike announced that it was almost 8 a.m. and time to start walking to school. I followed him, eagerly playing out over and over in my head how my first class would go. We approached a large, faded, lime-green building, and I could hear the chatter and voices of school children growing louder and louder. We entered through a wooden door and were greeted by other teachers in the school. We were the only ones there who spoke English, as well as the only non-native Guatemalans. The center of the school was an open, gray basketball court with soccer posts at each end. The lines of the court were barely visible, and the concrete was cracked in many places. Classrooms surrounded the court, and chain-link fences served as windows. The roofs were lined with tin sheets that were browning with rust.

Mike escorted me to my classroom. We passed by other classes, and kids ran to the chain-link windows. They waved and shouted "*Hola*" at me as I walked by, their eyes fixed on me inquisitively. I waved back, smiling, taken aback by the excitement and fascination that my presence seemed to generate.

We approached a door with the word "*Cuarto*," or "fourth," hand-painted in black above it. I followed Mike into the classroom and turned my head to the left where the students were sitting. Thirty glistening sets of eyes gazed at me with wonder. Mike introduced me to their teacher, Omar. He gave me a firm handshake and welcomed me. He told the class that I was going to be their English teacher. The class roared with enthusiasm. Kids ran up from their desks and hugged me, and I felt an instant affection for them. I could not have dreamed of a better introduction. I greeted each child, unable to stop myself from smiling and laughing at each new student who came up and hugged me.

Mike let me know that he was teaching in the class next door if I needed anything, and then he was gone—I was the lone English speaker in the room. Omar gave me the floor and left the classroom. He would return when I had finished giving my English lesson. I stood alone now, watching as thirty expectant kids looked up at me. In the best Spanish I could muster, coupled with body movements and hand motions, I signaled for the class to join me in a circle on the floor. I plopped down on the floor. I wanted the class to know that as well as being a teacher, I was their friend, their equal. I thought a great way to make that clear was to sit with them at the same level.

A raucous screeching could be heard as kids enthusiastically jumped out of their seats and pushed their desks to the edge of the classroom. They gathered around me without the slightest hesitation, all smiling and giggling. I pulled a hacky sack out of my backpack and introduced myself in Spanish, then in English. I passed the ball to my right. An adorable little girl with silky, chocolate eyes and hair in pigtails eagerly grabbed it. She introduced herself in Spanish and then paused. She froze, her eyes searching for an answer. She glanced up at me with innocent, bewildered eyes, conveying to me and all of her classmates that she had absolutely no idea how to introduce herself in English. The circle burst out in laughter. I slowly repeated the instructions in English and tried to enunciate as clearly as possible.

She began. "Hi, my name Silvia."

"*Buen trabajo!*" or "Good Job!" I exclaimed. It was a start. The hacky sack was passed around the circle, and every child got the chance to introduce him or herself. Most of the kids forgot how to say it in English, and I would repeat, "Hi, my name is…" each time they froze and giggled. After we all introduced ourselves, I stood up and asked everyone to please move his or her desk back and have a seat. Obediently, they all raced to their desks and moved them as close to me as possible at the front of the room.

I started writing out the alphabet and writing the phonetics of each letter so the students had the proper pronunciation. Each kid wrote down the alphabet and the phonetics in his or her notebook. I noticed that it was taking the students much longer to write the translations than I had expected. I reminded myself that these were young kids and what might have seemed easy and quick to me could be seen as challenging and time-consuming to them. I went around the class to check on how they were doing and to help them with anything they were finding difficult.

Once everyone had finished copying the alphabet down, I walked back to the front of the room. I started singing the alphabet, pointing to each letter as I sang it. "*A, B, C, D, E…*" my voice cracked as I was hitting the high note of "*E.*" My face must have broadcasted my embarrassment, and the class erupted in hysterical laughter. I gathered myself together and quieted everyone down, trying to contain my own laughter in the process. I managed to finish singing the rest of the song without any other awkward surprises. I then asked the class to sing along with me. Although out of tune and not necessarily in harmony, we sang from A to Z. After practicing this together multiple times, I then asked the students to do it alone. "*Uno, dos, tres...*" I counted out loud. They began and did well until about the middle of the alphabet, where they started to mumble and steer off the correct pronunciation.

I noticed the class's attention shifting toward the door. I turned my head and saw Mike standing in the doorway. He signaled that class was over, and I could wrap up my lesson when I was ready. The children were starting to lose their focus and talking among themselves. I pulled some stickers out of my bag and gave a few to each kid. I explained that this was a thank you to them for accepting me into their classroom. Their faces lit up with joy and curiosity as I passed out the stickers. I announced that class was over and thanked them for an incredible first day. Just like when I entered the classroom, they all rushed toward me like a stampede, lining up to hug me. I happily returned their hugs, with intense appreciation and gratitude filling my body. I thanked the class and waved good-bye to them. Walking past the class window, thirty hands were swinging in the air waving back at me. I smiled and made my way toward the school's exit to meet up with Mike.

We got back to the house and plopped onto the wooden table. I couldn't believe how exhausted I was after just one hour of teaching. I felt like my brain had just worked out; my mental energy was drained. It takes unbelievable effort to try to teach kids in a manner that is both fun and effective. I had a new, profound appreciation for teachers. To be able to teach for six hours every day while staying focused, calm, and composed is remarkable. As much fun as I had with the kids, I had the impression that the actual *learning* part was going to be challenging. My connection with the kids formed almost instantaneously, and I was no longer worried about that aspect of teaching.

I told Mike my thoughts about how my first day had gone. Even after one day, I could relate to all of the things he had been saying about being patient and calm, making it fun but also maintaining a learning atmosphere.

"The hard part is that their parents don't speak English. When the children go home, they don't have any guidance on practicing and reinforcing what they learned. I called a parent meeting a few weeks back. A lot of the parents actually showed up, which surprised me. I explained to them that the volunteers and I are teaching to give their children an opportunity for a better life. The parents seemed to be so appreciative and excited about it. I told them that they could help reinforce their child's English by checking on their kid's homework every day and asking them to share just one thing that they had learned in school that day. But the parents don't do that even though they say they will. The school culture here is so different."

"Yeah, I could sense that," I responded to Mike. I really let his words sink in. I was here to make a difference and was determined to teach the kids something that they would not just remember, but that would also help. I knew that I was going to need to get creative. We then talked for a while about our views on the world and our philosophies on life. I listened intently to Mike; I valued his opinion and perspective.

"Have you finished *Unbroken* yet?" Mike asked me.

"Yeah, I actually finished it yesterday. It was an amazing story," I answered.

"I have a book you might be interested in. It's called *My Big TOE*, which stands for 'My Big Theory of Everything.' The author is a quantum physicist who has worked in nuclear defense for the United States and spent much of his career exploring parapsychology. The book changed the way I view reality. He talks about the power of focused intentions. But he never once forces his beliefs upon the reader. He clearly states that the reader must test his theory out for himself."

"I'd love to read it!" I exclaimed. This sounded exactly like the type of book that I would find interesting. There were already some crazy "coincidences" that seemed to be happening in—and shaping—my own life. After arriving in San Andres, Mike explained to me just how lucky I had been to find Peter. He said that in all of the time he had spent in San Andres, he had never met someone who spoke English. I had never thought about much of my interaction with Peter until Mike mentioned it. Maybe the Universe was conspiring to make it happen. Maybe my intentions were picked up through some indescribable force of energy that modern science can't yet explain or detect. Peter did say it was destiny that we met each other.

Winder strolled into the yard with that highly infectious smile painted across his face. He suggested that we could do a Spanish/English learning exchange. He could teach me some Spanish, and I could teach him some English. It would be a win-win situation. I gladly accepted his proposal, and we both sat down at the wooden table. We alternated from Spanish to English and then from English to Spanish. We taught each other slang words and other funny expressions. We focused on aspects of the two languages that were used on a day-to-day basis. Just like that, we formed a bond that would continue throughout my time in San Andres. Multiple times a week, Winder and I sat together and taught each other about our own native languages. I cherished the time we spent together.

My next few days at school were great yet challenging. Each morning, I received the same incredible greeting that never ceased to impress and delight me. Yet I felt as if the children weren't actually learning anything. They all claimed that they wanted to learn English but wouldn't actually focus and spend time learning the material. I had introduced a few basic words, and by the end of the week, they were still having trouble remembering them. I found my patience being tested and gladly looked forward to the weekend. What I thought would be a relaxing Friday night turned out to be quite the opposite.

"Have patience. All things are difficult before they become easy."
—Saadi

CHAPTER 15

Danger in the Night

April 10, 2015

"The years teach much which the days never know."
—Ralph Waldo Emerson

Friday meant physical education, or more specifically, "*Futbol* Friday." That morning, I pumped up the soccer ball that I had brought with me from home. I tied my sneakers extra tight and made my way to the school. As I entered the building, an extra ounce of anticipation seemed to be stirring in the air, which I assumed was from the soccer ball that I carried in my hands.

When I turned the corner and walked through the door of my own classroom, I was met with an enormous burst of enthusiasm. All eyes were locked on the soccer ball. Julian, one of the smaller boys who sat in the front, dropped to his knees, raised both of his fists in the air, and tilted his face up to the sky, screaming with delight as if he had just won the lottery. The class charged forward and circled around me, belting out cheers.

After a few minutes of chaos, I settled the class down as best as I could. By this point, Omar and a few other teachers approached the classroom to witness the craziness that apparently was the talk of every classroom. Omar helped me organize teams, and we split up the class evenly, boys and girls intermixed. I was chosen to join one of the teams. We stepped out of the class and onto the courtyard. The cracked, gray court was the field of dreams for these kids. The white goal posts, which had no nets, were the entrances to the golden treasure—and getting the ball past the posts was the Holy Grail. The teams took their respective sides, and I whistled as loudly as I could, signaling the start of the game. I punted the ball into the air. Game on!

Both teams swarmed toward the ball like bees chasing honey. Footsteps stomped in every direction. Bodies juked, pivoted, and accelerated like cheetahs, lunging toward the ball. Everyone called for the ball in Spanish, words flying out of every kid's mouth. I kept my distance from the stampede, waiting for the ball to pop out. When it did, one of my teammates passed me the ball. I glanced up and saw Julian, who was on my team, waiting by the opposing goal. I booted the ball up the court, and it bobbled up against his body. He had only seconds to spare before he would be engulfed by the opposing players charging toward him. As the ball dropped to the ground, Julian's leg retracted as he prepared to swing. With all of the might his little body could muster, Julian blasted the ball between the goal posts; the goalkeeper had absolutely no chance to stop the ball's destined course. Half of the arms on the field shot up in pride, and my team flocked toward Julian, our arms stretched out wide as if we were flying toward him. Julian's face beamed with a mixture of fierce intensity and overwhelming ecstasy. We all embraced him, and I hoisted him in the air. Our team was chanting "Goooooooooal!" and "*olé, olé, olé, olé!*" as we celebrated like world champions. Julian wore a permanent smile.

We finally settled down, and the game continued. The ball bounced off the classroom walls and steps surrounding the court like a pinball, followed by a herd of children as if they were magnetized to the ball. They kicked and fought and ran, ignoring scrapes on their knees and stains on their pants, which were badges of honor to their competitive spirit. The smallest kids were fearless as they competed with the hearts of lions. Although the boys were predominantly controlling the game, many of the girls were just as much in the mix of things.

The sun shone down strongly, and perspiration dripped from my forehead, stinging my eyes. I was exhausted and announced I was taking myself out of the game. I sat down on a wooden bench, now just a spectator. Seeing the young boys play brought back memories of my childhood. I remembered when I played soccer tirelessly for hours on end with my friends. Julian reminded me of my own self, smaller than the others but still playing fiercely and putting forth every ounce of effort he possessed. The thought brought to mind what Mark Twain once said: "It's not the size of the dog in the fight, it's the size of the fight in the dog." The joy these kids experienced from the game was a delight to behold.

When I was younger, I never fully understood how my parents got so much pleasure from watching me play. I always thought that it would be boring to just watch my games without physically participating. But watching the schoolchildren play, I finally understood. There is something mysteriously beautiful about watching people you care about enjoying themselves. I could absorb the happiness and love for the game that radiated from the children. It was as if nothing else mattered except the game at hand. And witnessing it was a treasure.

After a while, Omar announced that the children had to return to class. The kids sighed, accepting the decision that the game was over. They headed toward the lone drinking fountain, swallowing mouthfuls of water as if they had just come across a desert oasis. I said good-bye to my students and went back to the house where Mike and the other volunteers were. I hadn't realized how long I had been at the school. Yearning to cool off, I took a dip in the lake. The soothing lake waters soon had me feeling refreshed, and I made my way over to Juanita's hammock with *My Big TOE*. A soft breeze cooled my warm body as I swayed slowly in my cocoon.

Although the book was extremely dense and hard to read at times, I was fascinated by it. I read the author's advice on focused intentions and meditation. He explained that someone meditating twice a day over a three-month period for just twenty minutes could reap significant benefits that included clearer thoughts, improved energy levels, a boosted immune system, and decreased anxiety and stress levels, just to name a few. I was fascinated by the proclaimed benefits of meditation and decided to give it a try. After all, the author kept stating, "Taste the pudding," or in other words, try it out for yourself.

I sat in the hammock, my back perched up, and closed my eyes. I tried focusing on my breath but found it extremely difficult. After a minute or so of attempting to mediate, I found myself thinking about a million other things. Finally, after multiple attempts, I gave up. I realized, as the book had clearly stated, that meditation takes effort and practice. Like any other skill, it takes time and diligence to master. I told myself I would try again tomorrow.

Mike was sitting at the wooden table back at the house. Three little chickens meandered through the yard, a sight that was no longer unusual to me.

"Hey Mike, I'm kind of struggling to meditate. How long did it take you to get good at it?" I asked curiously.

"Honestly, it takes some time. I think that meditation is different for everyone. Each individual has a unique way of meditating. For me, I meditate using 'focused intentions,' like what *My Big TOE* talks about."

"Yeah, I was reading about that. What exactly does that mean?" I questioned.

"Basically, it involves concentrating all of your energy on something you desire to happen. Ideally, you should be focusing on positive intentions that not only help yourself but others as well. Through repeatedly focusing on what you desire, you program your subconscious thoughts to align with your conscious thoughts. This reaffirms your belief that this intention *will happen*. This helps increase your inner coherence and resonance. The author describes all this in terms that can be really confusing. I mean, he's a quantum physicist explaining this complicated process to the average Joe. But that's the way I see it, and it's worked for me countless times in my life. It takes time; just remember that. Time and deep focus."

I sat there trying to fully grasp what Mike was saying. I was open-minded to the idea of focused intentions, but I knew that I had to experience it for myself. Little did I know that something would happen in the near future that would help me understand the concept and power of focused intentions. I had a question that I needed to ask.

"But to me, it seems weird how just thinking and hoping for something to happen will make it happen. Wouldn't people just sit around all day if they could just pray for things to magically happen?"

Mike acknowledged my question. "I had the same thoughts when I first read the book. You have to understand that almost every action you take in your life is related to a prior thought that you had. Your thoughts control your decisions, and decisions control your actions. You always have to act in life. But what you need to understand is that your thoughts help manifest your reality. They play a huge role in helping you act in the way you do."

Mike's explanation made sense to me. I had never viewed my thoughts in this way before. It sounded so compelling. I promised myself that I would work on focusing my thoughts and practicing meditation.

That night, I settled into bed early. Playing soccer with my students had tired me out. I slept on the middle bunk because Matteus had left San Andres the day before. He was heading south toward Costa Rica. I could actually sit up when I was in the middle bunk without having to be wary of crashing my head against the ceiling. Plus, the bugs on the ceiling were now even farther away. Emma slept under me on the first bunk, Jonathon and Suzy slept on a mattress in the corner, and Mike and Anna slept in a single room attached to our house.

In the middle of the night, I awoke from a deep sleep. The air had an eerie feeling to it, and I found my senses to be strangely alert. I turned my head toward the door and saw an unfamiliar man with a flashlight in his hand. I heard Jonathon yell at him, and the man uttered something in Spanish. I didn't understand what was going on. I was dazed from sleep and apparently the last one to notice that a strange man, unknown to any of us, had snuck into our house. Jonathon's tone warned me of the possible danger of the situation. It was pitch dark except for the flashlight the man was holding. I couldn't make out his facial features, but his presence sent a chill down my spine. Luckily, the man turned and left the house. Jonathon, Suzy, Emma, and I talked for a minute, all trying to understand what had just happened. We always slept with the doors open and never had any problems. The man had approached so secretly and quietly that none of us noticed him at first. We were all confused and a bit shaken up. Jonathan went into the other room to wake Mike. Seconds later, Mike charged into the room. He stormed outside, only to return a few minutes later.

"I am so pissed off right now," Mike grunted in a low, deep voice, smoke practically coming out of his ears. "The fact that someone thinks he has the right to come in here…" he couldn't complete his sentence. He voiced his frustration that none of us woke him up sooner. We explained that it shocked us all, and we weren't even sure what was going on.

"The man claimed that he was here to protect us from danger," Jonathon told Mike. "I screamed for him to get out."

"I ran up the hill but couldn't find anyone…Damn it!" Mike fumed. "We come into this community to help make a difference, and someone decides to invade our house at three in the morning. Emma's here sleeping in just a shirt and short shorts, and some creep is just standing there looking over at her." Even in the darkness, Mike's enraged face was impossible to ignore. "I'm going to the police station tomorrow."

We talked for a while and let our nerves settle down. I felt safe being around Mike, but the idea that some random guy just snuck up on us spooked me.

Mike shut the doors, angrily stating, "Now we can't even keep the doors of our damn house open because some guy…" he trailed off again. It was pleasant with the doors open and the cool breeze that flowed through. But we all agreed that we would feel much safer with the doors closed. We eventually fell back to sleep, but I felt myself waking every few minutes as if every sound—or what my brain thought was a sound—was potential danger.

This encounter reminded me how the nature of traveling isn't always smooth and jolly. There are real dangers that can arise. This is part of the package and the only thing you can do is be aware of your surroundings and act accordingly. This experience didn't deter my desire to continue living here and explore other parts of Central America. It was just a reminder to be alert and keep my eyes fully open.

> *"Experience is not what happens to you;*
> *it's what you do with what happens to you."*
> —Aldous Huxley

CHAPTER 16

Escaping Time

April 11, 2015

"Life can only be understood backwards
but it must be lived forwards."

—Soren Kierkegaard

The chirping of birds and the glimmer of sunlight notified me that morning had finally arrived. I climbed out of bed like a mouse, trying not to make any noise since the others were still sleeping. I sat on the wooden table, and the hard, square surface supported my tailbone. The lake glistened with the sun's reflection; a beaming trail glittered on the surface. The earth stood still, or at least it seemed to. A rustling from the trail caused me to turn around.

Mike stumbled into sight with an energy that hinted he had been up for hours. "I just got back from the police station," Mike stated. "I talked for a while with the chief mayor. He says he might have a couple of ideas about who it could be. I laid into him that we are here helping the community, and that this stuff cannot happen. He knows that we are the only gringos in town. He promised that he would send some guys to patrol the trail at night from now on." Still clearly aggravated about last night, Mike shook his head. "In all my time here, I've never had any problems." He turned toward the trees and gazed reflectively into the heart of the lake in the distance.

The others woke up, and we chatted for a while about the night before. Luckily, no one seemed too frightened. We took it as a warning sign, a reminder to keep our awareness levels up and look out for each other.

*　*　*　*　*

The weekend whizzed by, luckily with no more scares. Juanita and Mike alerted everyone about the incident, and it felt as if all the locals were looking out for us. I was now becoming a familiar face in San Andres. I waved to the regulars I saw walking through town. I struck up a conversation with the store clerk from whom I always bought a Gatorade after playing soccer. I hung out with my students whenever I saw them wandering about. Between relaxing in the lake, lying in the hammock and reading *My Big TOE*, practicing Spanish with Winder, and playing soccer with Miguel, I was enjoying myself.

It suddenly struck me that I had lost all concept of time. I had now been in Guatemala for almost a month and rarely knew what time it was. I rose with the sun and slept when darkness settled in. I had no need to check the time. I had always been punctual in my life before arriving in Guatemala. Not once had I ever completely lost track of what day or time it was. Here, I was truly living in the present moment, not worrying about the past or the future. I wasn't concerned about what my friends or family were up to back home while I was away. I had even forgotten to think about how my dad was doing. My focus was on the world in front of me.

The simplicity of life in San Andres provided me with a sense of freedom from stress and worry that I had not previously known. With just basic electricity, small huts, and a peaceful atmosphere, the people of San Andres lived happily—and it was contagious. The town lacked complex technology, big houses, and lots of money. Some people didn't even know where their next meal was coming from. And still, people were generally calm and happy and not worrying about things outside of their control. They took things day by day, a stark contrast to the hustle and bustle of where I grew up. I also realized that other than bug bites, my skin was clearing up! I couldn't help but wonder if my medical problems had been aggravated by—or even caused by—the anxiety and stress I felt at school.

I was living with significantly less in terms of material goods in San Andres yet felt significantly more whole inside. I felt a new sense of control over my own life. A confidence was building inside me, pushing me to continue living a life conducive to my own happiness. This different way of life had shown me just that—that there are different ways to live. It struck me that the hardest part of my journey thus far was not getting to San Andres, or trekking seventy-five miles in the jungle, or the bugs, or adjusting to simple living conditions. The hardest part had been leaving school and booking my flight. The hardest part had been taking action despite my fears. *Maybe true courage is the act of persevering toward one's dream despite the presence of fear?* I felt my eyes opening wider and wider with this realization.

> *"The most difficult thing is the decision to act.*
> *The rest is merely tenacity."*
> —Albert Einstein

CHAPTER 17

When You Hit a Wall, Cha-Cha Real Smooth

April 20, 2015

"Creativity involves breaking out of established patterns
in order to look at things in a different way."
—Edward de Bono

The kids in my class were beginning to slack off a bit. Despite my efforts at hangman and other games, I knew I needed to try something different. Keeping the attention of thirty kids for an hour was no easy task. Luckily, my Spanish was improving at a rapid pace. Not only had I finished the *Spanish for Dummies* textbook, but practicing with Miguel and Winder, along with teaching and speaking to everyone in town, was paying off. Being able to communicate more effectively with the students in my class made things much easier. I just needed them to put in a similar effort to learn English.

There was one girl, Lucia, who was leaps and bounds ahead of the other kids in the class. At ten years old, she was one of the younger kids, yet her English was substantially better than the others. When I asked Lucia how she knew so much, she simply replied that she loved watching movies in English and listening to music from the United States. When she told me that, a light bulb went off in my head. *Music.*

When I arrived in class the next day, I didn't pull out my usual notebook and pens. Instead, I pulled out a speaker and Mike's phone. Curious eyes scanned the devices in my hand. With his head tilted sideways and his forehead scrunched up, Julian questioned why I had brought the speaker and phone. I smiled at him, hinting that he would find out soon enough. I signaled for everyone to move their desks to the borders of the room. In unison, sixty scampering feet pushed their desks along the outlines of the classroom, producing a symphony of screeches as the desks were dragged across the floor.

The afternoon before, I had gone to the Internet café and downloaded the "Cha-Cha Slide" onto Mike's phone. I directed the class to line up in rows, and I drew arrows on the front whiteboard indicating, "left," "right," "back," and "forward," along with the Spanish translations. I turned up the volume on the speakers as loud as I could and pressed the play button. The music blared and rang out in a groovy tune, "This time we're gonna get funky." I joined the kids on the floor, standing in front of them, facing the board just as they were. Above the sound of the pumping music, I could hear giggles of anticipation and excitement. The tunes thumped, and I waited for my cue. It was go time!

I shuffled to the left as the upbeat words, "Slide to the left," chimed out. The class followed my lead, slightly delayed, and I felt a wave of feet sway to the left with me, the ground now vibrating. "Slide to the right," sounded, and I abided, pointing and singing along. "Take it back now, y'all," I stepped backward, feeling like I was in a dance club. I turned to see my students laughing and copying my moves. The line, "Cha-cha real smooth," chimed aloud, and I let myself flow in a spontaneous movement of twists and turns, dancing like there was no tomorrow. I felt like Mick Jagger but probably didn't move like him. I shouted out, "*Todos a bailar!*" or "everyone dance!" Half the class joined in, boogying to the right and to the left. The other half stood shyly, their faces bright red, giggling with their hands covering their faces.

The song continued, and after a while, the students' movements were corresponding to the words of the song without me dancing. I paused the music and decided to test them. I shouted out different directions, and they had to move in the appropriate direction. I was surprised and delighted to see that they were getting it now. I signaled that a dance competition was about to begin. I would be the judge and watch as the kids had to move appropriately in the direction that the song demanded. When I announced that the prize would be a batch of stickers, the kids uttered a loud "Ooooo" and jumped up and down.

I hit the play button on the speakers and focused my attention toward the little bouncing bodies of energy in front of me. During the first verse, almost half the class moved right instead of left. A gust of laughter broke out as half the class knew they had made a mistake. I signaled for the ones who moved in the wrong direction to take a seat. Cheers exploded from the students who were still alive in the game. It was like a language version of "musical chairs."

The song continued, and eventually only three kids were left dancing. The song rolled out to the finish, and all three managed to make it to the end. I rewarded each of them with a handful of assorted stickers. They hoisted the stickers in the air as if they had won Olympic gold medals. The excitement finally settled down, and everyone took their seats. I instructed the whole class to write down the directions that we had practiced along with the visual arrows. For the first time, *everyone* in the class seemed to be following my instructions and I felt a tremendous sense of satisfaction. In the past, I never took offense that the class didn't always follow my directions. Now, however, every student was either focused on copying the information into his or her notebook or glancing up toward the whiteboard at the directions.

When class finished that day, I walked back to the house, contemplating how successful the day had been. Before today, I felt as if the class were plateauing. I sincerely wanted my class to learn at least some important concepts of English by the time I left. I realized that the process of teaching the class paralleled my own life's "growing pains" in many ways. *If you do the same thing over and over again, you are going to get the same results. If nothing seems to be going right, try going left.*

It struck me again that every individual on earth is unique. There isn't just one way to learn, just like there isn't just one way to live. By trying an alternative teaching style that involved singing and dancing, I noticed a dramatic improvement in both the attention span of the class as well as their ability to retain the information. For the remainder of my time in San Andres, I was determined to continue with creative and fun teaching methods.

"Creativity is not the finding of a thing,
but the making something out of it after it is found."
—James Russel Lowell

CHAPTER 18

Money Stolen, Blessings Gained

April 25, 2015

"The only thing you sometimes have control over is perspective. You don't have control over your situation. But you have a choice about how you view it."

—Chris Pine

The next week at school went smoothly. My class became nearly obsessed with the "cha-cha slide," and I almost forgot whether I was teaching English or dance. I built on the enthusiasm of using music to teach by integrating new songs and vocabulary into my lesson plans.

As the weeks passed, the composition of the volunteer group evolved. Suzy and Jonathan were preparing to leave for Mexico; like modern nomads, they were ready to move on and continue their quest for exploration and adventure. I hugged them both good-bye. I was sad to see them leave but thankful to have met them.

Mike announced that a Japanese volunteer named Takeshi was supposed to arrive later that afternoon. I helped Mike tidy up our house and then made my way over to the hammock, intent on reading my book. But after lying down in the hammock, I had no desire to read. I just swayed slowly and peacefully back and forth, my thoughts wandering with the wind. For what felt like an eternity, I did just that—nothing. I found it oddly blissful and invigorating.

Mike and Anna were soon heading for Germany so that Anna could finish her teaching degree. I started making my own plans, trying to figure out where I would go next. Part of me feared being back on my own. I had grown comfortable in San Andres and developed relationships with Mike, the volunteers, and Juanita's family. It felt like ages since I had been totally on my own, journeying from Los Angeles to San Andres. The reality that I would soon be by myself again was now sinking in. I wouldn't have Mike or the others to watch my back. But I was deeply curious to see what the Universe had in store for me. I knew I had to rid myself of my need for always knowing what was going to come next and just take the world in stride. After all, it's the unknown that makes life interesting.

I had read about Lake Atitlan, the deepest lake in Central America, and heard from others that it was breathtaking. It is a region encircled by two enormous volcanoes and mountain ranges. I was informed that this region held a mix of indigenous cultures, rich traditions, and astonishing scenery. In addition, San Marcos, a town on the shores of Lake Atitlan, was supposedly a world-renowned spiritual mecca where shamans, teachers, and other healers resided. I was excited and intrigued by the possibility of meeting new people with drastically different lifestyles and world views. I decided that in a week's time, right before Mike and Anna were set to depart, I would set out for Lake Atitlan.

I climbed out of the hammock and cruised up to the Internet café. I ran into Mike, Anna, and Emma. They introduced me to Takeshi, the volunteer who had just arrived.

We talked for a while and Takeshi told me about his travels through Mexico. He had sold all of his belongings in the United States and was backpacking through Latin America. Once his money got low, he planned on buying a ticket to Japan to live with his family who he hadn't seen in years.

I was craving a *Choco* banana—a frozen banana covered with chocolate and peanuts that many locals sold from their homes—and invited the others to join me. They declined and said they would meet me back at the house later.

I made my way back to the house alone and went inside to retrieve my wallet. I pulled out my wallet from my backpack and froze. It was empty. There was no cash. I knew there should have been about *600 quetzals* in there, roughly $80. I did a double take, checking again and meticulously searching every crease and fold in my wallet and backpack. No cash. Luckily, my bank cards were untouched. But I felt uneasy because my wallet had been tucked away in a safe, concealed pocket in my backpack. For someone to snag my money, they must have searched my bag very carefully. My thoughts were interrupted by some noise coming from the trail.

Mike and the others turned into the yard. "Have you guys been gone for a while?" I asked them. "I just checked my wallet, and all of my cash is gone, about $80." They looked shocked, their scrunched foreheads revealing worry.

"We've been up in town the last few hours," Mike replied. He reached down and squeezed his pants pocket, letting us know he had his wallet. Mike asked everyone to check their belongings.

When everyone returned, Takeshi looked very pale. "My money is gone," he muttered. "All of it."

Takeshi's tone caused an edgy pit to form in my stomach. I asked, "When you say 'all of it,' what exactly do you mean?"

We all stared intently at Takeshi. He continued, "I mean all of my money is gone. I had $1,000 with me. That was the money I was going to use to purchase a flight to Japan. It was everything I had."

I felt terrible for Takeshi but couldn't help wondering *why in the world anyone would be carrying $1,000 in cash on them?* Especially as a backpacker traveling though Central America, I was stupefied by his choice to leave himself so vulnerable. But this was no time to judge. I felt sick as I tried to put myself in his shoes. His family, whom he hadn't seen in years, was halfway around the world. And he was stuck in the middle of rural Guatemala.

Anna's soft cries broke the awkward silence. She managed to stutter, "I-I, I'm so-so sorry."

"Please, you do not need to cry," Takeshi answered. "Look, here," he declared, pointing to his hands. "I still have my fingers, my arms, and my legs. I am healthy and my family is safe. So many people have it much worse than I do. Yeah, I'm upset, too, but I have everything I need. I'm alive, and I will survive. Life will go on."

Takeshi's stoicism and positivity had an uplifting effect on all of us, and Anna's whimpers died down. I was astounded by Takeshi's outlook on his situation. After a moment of pity, Takeshi picked himself up and showed me that there are two ways to view hardships in life. You can either be grateful for everything you do have or feel self-pity about things you don't have. His amazing spirit of optimism and appreciation made me realize how lucky I was for everything in my own life. Instead of counting the money that was taken from me, I began to count my blessings.

"Be thankful for what you have; you'll end up having more.
If you concentrate on what you don't have, you will never,
ever have enough."
—Oprah Winfrey

CHAPTER 19

On My Own Again

May 1, 2015

"The oneness of human beings is the basic ethical thread that holds us together."

—Muhammad Yunus

My final days in San Andres were a blur. The sun rose as it always did, majestically ascending above the placid lake. The roosters, pigs, and other animals woke from their night's rest, crowing, snorting, and whistling at the dawn of a new day.

My last day of teaching began just like all the other Fridays. We marched out to the courtyard and divided into teams, kids jumping up and down, unable to contain their buzzing energy. The game kicked off, and nothing else in the world seemed to matter for the next hour. When the game wrapped up, I took a rest on the wooden bench alongside my class. We sat and talked as the sun beamed down overhead. The kids were summoned to return to their next lesson, and I stood up to say good-bye to them. They looked different that day, a little older. It was strange to think that I wouldn't be kicking the ball around with them next Friday. I wouldn't see their big smiles walking around town; I wouldn't be swarmed by cheerful greetings every morning.

The class lined up, and I hugged each student good-bye and gave each one a bundle of stickers. A couple of students had drawn cards for me, which I graciously accepted. After a stretched-out good-bye, I waved to my students one last time and made my way toward the school exit. Walking back to the house, I felt mixed emotions. My nose scrunched up and my eyebrows knitted together as I stared out at the lake, confused. I had come here to make a positive impact in the children's lives, and it struck me that the positive effect went both ways. The students inspired *me* to be creative and showed *me* unconditional support. They reminded me with their daily hugs that every day is a new day, a fresh start. I was filled with a bittersweet nostalgia. It had been an incredible experience, one that was both frustrating at times and also rewarding. I cherished my time spent with my fourth-grade class, but I knew I was ready to move on. I came to give and ended up receiving more than I could have ever imagined.

*　*　*　*　*

The weekend flew by, and Sunday, the day I was departing, was fast approaching. I found myself intently focusing on everything in sight as if I could store it in my backpack and carry it with me on the rest of my journey. I wanted to take with me the scintillating lake and the denim hammock and the bumpy soccer field and my new chicken friends. I tried capturing the smell of the morning dew and the brisk, barky smell of the trees and the shrubs and the other plants. I wanted to remember the sweet taste of a *Choco* banana and the pizzazz of Juanita's cooking that was infused with a dash of love as the main ingredient in all my meals. I strived to relive and memorize the feelings of the stiff board on the wooden table out front and swaying in the hammock, feeling light as the wind yet full as the sun. I wanted so badly to take San Andres with me, to imprint it in my senses so I could unravel and experience it on demand.

There is something profoundly strange and sad about having to say good-bye to people with whom you've formed a tight-knit bond. The surrealism of leaving blinded my understanding that I wouldn't see them tomorrow, or the next day, or the day after that. I felt my senses heighten immensely, as if my awareness of everything going on around me was enhanced as never before. No words could express our relationships, and this reality both frustrated and fulfilled me. But I knew that they appreciated what I was feeling. We all felt it. The most heartfelt moments in life contain elements of mysticism, a warm fondness that can only be illuminated through an impalpable energy.

The bond that I had formed with Juanita's family illustrated the power of human connection despite differences in culture, language, and customs. I found a family that I never knew I had. Juanita cared for me as if I were her son, making sure I was never hungry, talking with me cheerfully, and hugging me good night. My relationships with Alejandra, Winder, and Juan Carlos had grown extraordinarily close. I was going to miss joking around with Alejandra and her spunky attitude; riding around with Juan Carlos, enjoying his dry sense of humor; and practicing Spanish with Winder, with that permanent smile etched across his face and that infectious laugh that expressed his lighthearted nature.

I hugged Anna and Emma and Takeshi, wishing them well on their own journeys. I turned to Mike and gave him a hug as well. It was one of those manly hugs that only last a second or two. Mike wasn't one for all the lovey-dovey, touchy-feely stuff, and neither was I, yet I struggled to find the words to express my gratitude. I thanked him for everything and tried my best to show how much I appreciated him. I looked up to him as a teacher, a leader, and a role model. His outlook on life, despite what he had been through, deeply impacted me. His stories fueled me with powerful lessons that I planned to carry with me.

Winder escorted me up to the stop in town where the *colectivo*, a van that picks up people en route to other destinations, stopped on the way to the Santa Elena bus station. He sat with me on a bench. Other than a few words uttered between us, the whizzing of motorbikes and locals' conversations filled our ears. A mutual silence—an underlying understanding—spread between us.

The *colectivo* rumbled forward, and the man standing inside the car but hanging outside barked out, "Santa Elena! Santa Elena! Santa Elena!" I lugged my bag onto my back and turned to face Winder. I hugged him, and he cautioned me to "be safe." I thanked him and stepped into the *colectivo*, which was already packed with people. I squeezed into the middle window seat and dropped my backpack between my legs. The driver slammed the door shut, and I glanced out toward Winder. He waved at me, smiling one of his irresistible smiles. I laughed and waved back. The engine revved, and I felt my feet vibrate as the van grumbled away.

I peered out the window as we departed San Andres, the outstretched trees and gray streets now a blurry whirl as we bumped along. The memories of six weeks filled with events so far removed from anything I had ever experienced were condensed into the blink of an eye. Every day had been an adventure, a new thrill. It dawned on me that in the past six weeks, I had grown accustomed to sleeping without a pillow and taking cold showers. I had never once found it strange after the first few days that I had no pillow or warm water for a shower. The prospect of change is often scary, not because of what will be, but because of what we *think* it might be. Humans were made to adapt and evolve. The change in routine and commodities became normal after just a few days. It became my current reality, and I didn't think of it any other way. The scarce number of words in my Spanish repertoire when I arrived had increased to a point where I was now capable of having in-depth conversations with the locals. I discovered a new tranquility, a composure that was manifesting in my clearing skin. The stress that had plagued me just two months before felt like ancient history.

But being on my own again did bring about fear. My path was wide open, and I didn't know for certain where I would end up next. Yet, reflecting on my time in San Andres awakened an inner confidence. I realized that people are never actually ready for anything in life. Paradoxically, this also signifies that people are always ready. We wouldn't be breathing if we weren't ready. We are never fully ready for anything, and that is what makes us ready for everything.

I inhaled a gust of air. My hesitations and worries filled my raised stomach and chest for a moment as I kept the oxygen inside of me. *Breathe.* I exhaled, releasing a gust of warm air, my shoulders dropping and my muscles relaxing. My hesitations and worries were now unleashed from my body into the atmosphere. I embraced the unknown trail ahead, ready to accept the flow of the Universe.

"If we wait until we're ready, we'll be waiting for the rest of our lives."
—Lemony Snicket

CHAPTER 20

Say Yes

May 3, 2015

"Life is a series of natural and spontaneous changes. Don't resist them—
that only creates sorrow. Let reality be reality.
Let things flow naturally forward in whatever way they like."

—Lao Tzu

When I arrived at the bus station in Santa Elena, I stood there baffled amid the throngs of people in the chaotic terminal, watching everyone scramble to their desired destination. As nice as it would have been to stand in the middle of a hectic bus terminal all day, I shook myself out of my reverie and focused on finding where I could purchase a bus ticket to Lake Atitlan. I approached a clerk working at one of the desks, and he pointed across the room, signaling it was in the other direction. Still having no idea which line he was pointing to, I thanked him and walked aimlessly in that general direction.

As I wandered over, I saw two guys with backpacks. They stood out among the dozens of Guatemalans scrambling about. There was something about them that drew me toward them. I walked over and asked them in Spanish if they knew where the line for Lake Atitlan was.

"Uh, do you speak English? I barely know any Spanish," one of them replied, chuckling. He seemed surprised at the fact that I questioned him in Spanish, not English.

"Yeah, I do. I had no idea if you guys spoke English or not," I responded, smiling.

"Where are you from?" the other one asked me. There was something about the way the two of them looked that seemed familiar to me. I couldn't decipher exactly where they were from, but I felt a connection to them.

"I'm from the United States. What about you guys?" I countered.

"We're from Israel. We are with two of our other friends as well. We just got out of the army and have been traveling down from Mexico."

"No way! My sister was in Israel this past summer and loved it," I exclaimed. I knew I had heard the accent before, but I hadn't quite been able to identify it until he said so.

"Yes, it's a beautiful country. I'm glad your sister had a good time. You have to come and visit one day as well. Are you Jewish?" he questioned.

"Yeah, I am!" I replied, laughing a little. Never in a million years did I expect to find other Jewish people in the middle of rural Guatemala.

We discussed life in Israel and the United States and acknowledged how funny it was that we found each other.

"You should come with us," one of them encouraged, his eyes lighting up.

"Yes, come with us!" the other one added. "We're going to Semuc Champey, an incredibly beautiful place. It has turquoise pools and beautiful rivers. It's in the jungle!"

While I had planned on going to Lake Atitlan, Semuc Champey sounded mystical. I felt a little funny going to a place I'd never heard of before, but it hit me that spontaneous adventure is about accepting opportunities as they arise. I was here to flow with the wind, and it had taken me here, to the Israelis. I trusted them—it was a gut feeling. Listening to my intuition hadn't failed me before, and I found no reason not to follow it this time.

"Yeah, I would love to! My name is Jake," I replied enthusiastically.

"Great!" one of them exclaimed. "I'm Leo, by the way." He stuck out his hand and I shook it, feeling his firm squeeze, which I took as a good sign. He was thickly built, and his tank top revealed his burly arms. He had a faux hawk haircut that emphasized the dark curls resting on top of his head, which matched the color of his protruding chest hair.

"And I'm Dor," the other guy announced. He stood short, yet compact. He had olive-tan skin and a stylish haircut and outfit that made him look European as if he were straight out of GQ magazine.

"Hey guys, this is Jake," Leo announced as the other two members of their group approached. "He's going to come with us to Semuc Champey." I shook their hands, and we talked for a while, connecting over our Jewish bond and exchanging information about our own lives.

Idan was the tallest of the crew and lean but not skinny. He had brown hair, thick brown eyebrows, and maple-colored eyes. Igor had golden-brown skin, a result of some Brazilian flair mixed into his demographic. He was also wearing a tank top, which revealed his sculpted biceps. The four of them definitely fit the physical description of what I imagined soldiers to look like.

The five of us gathered in line for Semuc Champey and bought our tickets. An hour later, we piled into a van that would take us to our destination. Upon entering the van, I was stunned—not by the overly packed van full of people, because I was used to that by now. Rather, the type of people surprised me. Non-Guatemalan people. English speakers. Travelers. They seemed almost foreign to me, and English had never sounded so amazing. I felt a wave of comfort as I relaxed both physically and mentally. Up until this point, it had never struck me how exhausting it was to constantly try and speak and understand a foreign language that I didn't know very well.

I squeezed onto the tiny, removable box of a seat that was added so twenty of us could squish into a fifteen-person van. I was the unlucky one, being the last to board. My knees touched, and I tucked my elbows inward to prevent pressing up against the others in the van. It didn't help much as Dor drifted into a deep sleep soon after we took off, and my shoulder ended up being his pillow. I had no window or headrest to lay my head against, so I stayed awake for the eight-hour journey, trying to balance my head from tipping over as sleep overcame me. I was a miniature human statue scrunched together like a hedgehog in a ball.

I let my thoughts roam free, reflecting on my time in San Andres. Occasionally, I talked with Dor and the others in the van as they awoke from their sleep and took a break from their iPods. Dor told me about a fascinating opportunity in Nicaragua that he had heard of from another backpacker. "There's a guy who is building an eco-lodge on a deserted beach near Leon. Volunteers can camp on the beach and eat for free in return for a few hours of work on the project. I've met a few people who've been there and loved it."

"That sounds awesome!" I exclaimed.

"Yeah, I'll give you his e-mail. All you have to do is shoot him a message and ask if you can volunteer."

"Thanks," I said as Dor handed me a piece of paper with the contact's e-mail on it. I figured that could be a perfect place to go after Guatemala. I had heard great things about Nicaragua.

I was happy to peer outside and see the countryside and wilderness that we were crossing through. We approached giant green mountains that soared out of the ground like divine creatures. The van zoomed down the winding roads, and we traveled to the base of the forested valley. A misty haze of clouds loomed over and under the mountain peaks, creating a mystical feeling as if we were in a fairytale. Locals were trudging along the mountain paths and lugging ridiculously large amounts of firewood, which they pulled with a rope attached to their foreheads. A few women walked along the edges of the road with large baskets of fruit on their heads, the cliff's edge just a few feet away. They diligently executed each step as if they were walking on a high wire. I wondered if I had somehow ended up in the Hobbit and would soon see dragons and other magical creatures.

Finally, we arrived at our destination. It was drizzling outside, and dusk was approaching. Gray, twirling clouds blanketed the atmosphere. We were in a small town, and people surrounded our vehicle as we pulled to a stop. I climbed out of the van and extended my arms up toward the sky, letting my limbs stretch out as long and as far as they could. I grabbed my backpack and joined the Israelis. They had already made a reservation at a hostel, and the advocate for that hostel said they had room for me. I exhaled with relief, and we followed the worker to the vehicle that would take us there.

The hostel was an eco-lodge. It had only four hours of electricity a day and no Internet service. It was tucked away from town along the river of Semuc Champey. To get there, we had to ride in a truck that could handle rough roads. The worker escorted us into the back of a pickup truck, which had metal bars about five feet high on the sides. The five of us, along with four other travelers, hopped into the back of the truck. The vehicle started up and took off, and the nine of us gripped the bars tightly. I felt like Indiana Jones as I clutched the cool metal rail, struggling for balance as we bounced through a muddy, unpaved road surrounded by the most magnificent mountains. The wind breezed against my face as I gazed at the wondrous vistas before me.

After about thirty minutes, we approached a wooden bridge that looked like it hadn't been repaired in years. The uneven wooden planks that would bear the weight of our truck were shades and tints of faded brown. The splinters and cracks were evidence that it had endured years of nature's forces. The suspension cords that held the bridge erect looked like rusty, dented pipes. Many of the planks were loose, which I discovered as we gradually teetered onto the bridge. The truck creaked and rasped as the wheels rolled over the wobbly planks. I rocked back and forth in the back of the truck, holding on tightly. A river of greenish, cerulean water flowed underneath the bridge, producing a lulling whisper.

I let out a breath as we finally got to the other side. A number of beautiful, oak-red huts were scattered among the hostel's property overlooking the river. Alluring greenery filled every empty space, and the vibrant jungle landscape teemed with life. The truck rolled to a stop, and we all hopped out and grabbed our backpacks. We followed the driver to the hostel's check-in desk and purchased a tour for the next day, which included a full day of exploring the park's limestone pools and pitch-black caves. The Israelis and I were escorted to one of the huts. We had it to ourselves, and we plopped down our stuff, making ourselves at home.

After settling in, we washed up and grabbed a quick bite to eat. We were informed that the adventure tour started bright and early the next day. Exhausted from the day's journey, I was more than happy to go to sleep early. I slid into bed and closed my eyes. The room was still lit as the Israelis were not in their beds yet. A few minutes later, Idan switched the lights off, and I turned over, relieved to finally get some rest. The Israelis continued to chat for a little while in Hebrew, and I couldn't understand a word. The chatting turned to debating and arguing, their voices rising louder and louder. I so badly wanted to pass out into a deep sleep yet could not drift away as the loud rambling filled the room. I let out a sigh and rolled over onto my side, turning toward the wall.

"Hey Jake, are we keeping you up?" Dor asked in a thoughtful manner, clearly having heard my sigh.

"You really think I can sleep with four Israelis jabbering in Hebrew?" I responded in a joking tone.

They all burst out laughing, and I ended up joining in. We talked for a little while, in English, and then finally silence ensued. I was glad the Israelis had such good senses of humor, and I found them highly entertaining. But I was more than relieved to only hear the sound of crickets outside as I drifted into a deep sleep.

"Say yes and you'll figure it out afterwards."
—Tina Fey

CHAPTER 21

Spontaneous Adventures

May 4, 2015

"The adrenaline and stress of an adventure are
better than a thousand peaceful days."

–Paulo Coelho

We awoke early the next day and quickly got dressed. We gathered for breakfast, eating at a table overlooking a magnificent valley of green jungle. The sun was shining, and the sky was a clear blue, uninterrupted by even a single cloud—a stark contrast from the gray clouds and drizzling rain of the night before.

The tour guide from the hostel signaled for all of us to join him for the day's adventure. Along with the five of us, an Australian couple, a Brazilian couple, and a trio of girls from France were in our group. The twelve of us followed our guide as he led us through the park entrance. Upon entering, we followed a trail that ascended up toward the lookout point where we would be able to see the natural pools from above. We climbed higher and higher, surrounded by green vines and a variety of trees.

After about thirty minutes, we arrived at a wooden platform. I walked eagerly toward the edge of the platform and couldn't believe the sight that lay before me. In the middle of the rich jungle valley beneath us, a series of aquamarine pools sat atop a natural limestone bridge carved out by the river beneath it. The turquoise water in the pools was so crystal clear that you could see the texture of the pools' bottoms from our vantage point, which was hundreds of feet above. The description "crystal clear" now had a whole different meaning for me. This was nothing like I had ever seen before. The water's mesmerizing color seemed straight out of a fairytale. Our guide signaled for us to follow him down to the pools.

Our entire group practically sprinted down the trail, all of us wanting to quench our thirst in the pools that teased us below. Upon reaching them, I noticed the water trickled calmly, each pool spilling its fresh water into the next, abiding with the natural flow of the river. I took my shirt off and eagerly strode toward the first pool. I tiptoed along the uneven limestone surface, each step bringing me closer to the sanctuary of the water. I finally reached the first pool, the Israelis following closely behind. I entered, breaking through the surface, and felt the water's fresh welcome, which cooled my heated body. I opened my eyes underwater, seeing my hands so clearly I checked to see if I was actually under water. I was. I lifted my head above the surface and stared down at my feet. My toes and veins and hair were displayed as if observed through glass. I flipped over onto my back, staring at the light-blue sky. I floated happily, still shocked to be swimming in what felt like a dream. I swam with the current of the water and hopped out from the pool I was in to the next one. Each pool had its own treasure, its own unique beauty that I had to discover for myself. I momentarily looked around only to realize that all of the others in my group were behind me. I didn't mind. All I wanted to do was immerse myself in each body of water. It was a rare occurrence to be in such a magical place. I was happy to hear only the sounds of the river peacefully flowing downstream.

I cruised from pool to pool, floating untroubled, constantly reassuring myself that *yes, this is real, I am actually here.* I felt like a kid wandering onto a playground, each new attraction as alluring as the one before it.

I approached a waterfall that dropped off about thirty feet, which signaled the farthest point that you could go. The Israelis soon caught up with me and we eventually made our way back to the starting point, swimming upstream. The tour guide said we were only supposed to be there an hour, yet it was clear to everyone we had been there much longer. I would have been more than happy to spend the entire day wading in the limestone pools, but the guide assured us that there were other exciting parts of the day ahead.

We went back to the hostel and ate lunch. Everyone seemed to be in an upbeat mood as if the pools had stirred up a sense of ecstasy in us. The guide signaled it was time to explore the Kanba caves. I expected some short, easy excursion into a cave where people could snap some photos and then be on their merry way. I was wrong.

Our guide spoke no English, yet everything seemed straightforward up until this point. I left my shoes back at the hostel and soon realized that I was the only one barefoot. The mouth of the cave loomed in complete blackness. The trickling of water sounded from inside the cave. The guide handed each of us a ten-inch candlestick, our only source of light.

Upon lighting each of our candlesticks, the guide gestured for us to enter the cave. I snorted, surprised by my own reaction. I thought he was joking. Surely he would go first. None of us had any idea what was inside or how to navigate. I felt a slight push from behind. Dor indicated for me to enter. I turned around and saw the guide in the back, behind the group, helping the girls.

Without really thinking, I turned and made my way into the cave. The brisk water washed up on my ankles and sent a shiver up my spine as I slowly edged my way into complete darkness. The roof of the cave was populated with stalactite formations that looked like melted candle wax seeping downward in an array of spikes. I heard a bat flap its wings and whistle through the chilling air. I moved my feet ever so slowly; the jagged rocks warned me not to step too quickly. I immediately regretted not wearing shoes. I could not see more than one foot in front of me since the entrance of the cave was now well behind us. Other than my candle, which provided me with a meager few inches of light, blackness enveloped me. The rough ground began to drop, and I felt the water snaking its way up from my legs to my chest as we proceeded through the eerie cave. The cave floor dropped off, and I was now swimming with one arm, my other hoisted in the air holding my candle, struggling to keep the water from splashing out my light.

So here I found myself leading a pack of thirteen people in a pitch-black cave with only a candle, barefoot, doggy paddling frantically with one arm, having absolutely no idea where the hell I was going. I had not the slightest clue as to how deep or far the cave was, when I would be able to stand again, or what lay ahead. I struggled to keep my head above water and my candle dry. My feet finally touched rocky ground, and I let out a sigh of relief, grateful to be standing again. I turned around to see a flickering trail of light. A line of candlesticks were lighting the way behind me. The guide shouted for us to wait for him. *Oh, so now you want to lead us.* I was still in shock about what we were doing and where we were. I put my candle behind my back and held out my other hand in front of my face. I couldn't see it. Not even a speck of my hand.

I was relieved that the guide was now taking the lead. He directed me toward a skimpy black ladder, which he gestured for me to climb. The next thing I knew, I was ascending the ladder with one hand, my other clutching the burning, diminishing candle. The steps of the ladder must have been less than an inch thick, and I fiercely gripped each ring with my free hand. I made it to the top of the platform and waited for the guide and the others. Once we were all there, the guide took the lead again, and we followed. The rugged floor scraped my feet as I blindly took each step, the sense of touch my only real guide. Idan was now in front of me, and the guide in front of him. The others were closely behind. I felt better not being in front. I could actually see more of what I was doing and observe the cave that entrapped us.

We came to a drop-off where I watched, in bewilderment, as the guide ushered Idan down a compact black hole. I heard a splash and saw the guide checking to see if Idan was okay. Idan smiled and held up his thumb through the hole that he had just dropped down through, so I figured he was fine. It was my turn now, and the guide directed me over to him. He guided me to sit down and placed my feet and hands in specific positions against the cool, rough ground. He directed me to let my hands and legs go so I could fall down into the ridiculously tight hole that Idan had just dropped through.

I tucked my head inward and released my grip. My stomach dropped as I stretched my arm over my head, hoisting the candle up to prevent the fire from being put out. I splashed into the dark abyss and quickly lifted my head up, surprised to find that not only was I fine and unscathed, but what remained of my candle was still burning. Relieved, I paddled toward the platform where Idan rested, and we waited for the others to take the plunge.

We followed our guide up another ladder, this time onto a platform about two feet wide. A horizontal rope hung overhead for us to hold onto. If you let go of it or slipped, you plunged ten feet down onto the sharp rocks jutting out beneath us. *This setup would definitely not fly in the United States.* It suddenly struck me how none of us had signed a waiver. We were adventuring at our own risk in a country with almost no limitations or regulations compared to those of the Western world. I gripped the rope for dear life, carefully edging my way across the rocky bridge to safe ground.

When we were finally escorted out of the cave, I jumped with delight at the sight of daylight. I could literally "see the light at the end of the tunnel." My candle was just the length of a cigarette butt hanging between my fingers. I had taken it as a challenge to keep my candle burning until the end and was proud of my accomplishment. I was so relieved to have made it out unharmed, with only sore feet and tense muscles from the perilous adventure. My eyes squinted shut as I adjusted to the brightness of the midday sun. From pitch black one moment to beaming light the next, the day had been full of new experiences, relaxing and adrenaline pumping, soothing and intense.

After leaving the cave, we each grabbed inner tubes that the guide provided for us and bounced into the river. I laid back in my inner tube, the Israelis and the others floating alongside me, unwinding from the intensity of the cave adventure.

I was truly grateful to have met the Israelis. Not only were they great guys, but they also showed me the rewards of spontaneously accepting an invitation. I would probably never have known about the gem of Semuc Champey and the unbelievable Kanba cave expedition. I *definitely* wouldn't have experienced it. But that's the beauty of exploring the unknown. Boundless opportunities are possible when we can overcome our self-imposed limitations and accept the potential of the unknown. Spontaneity is a vine with a sweet fruit at the end. When we expand our horizons, only then we see how far we can go.

> *"The Universe will reward you for taking risks on its behalf."*
> —Shakti Gawain

CHAPTER 22

Forcing Chemistry, Ignoring Signs

May 5, 2015

"You can ask the Universe for all the signs you want but ultimately we only see what we want to see when we're ready to see it."

—Ted Mosby

I said good-bye to the Israelis and promised that I would visit them one day in Israel. They were heading to the colonial city of Antigua, and I was heading to Lake Atitlan, the majestic Guatemalan Highlands of the Sierra Madre mountain range. Upon entering the van that would transport me to Lake Atitlan, I was relieved to see multiple open seats. I took a comfy spot where I could rest my head against the window.

I had heard of a so-called *sabio*, or "wise man," in Lake Atitlan named Arnulfo. I didn't know much about him other than what I'd heard: that he had incredible knowledge and insight into the human condition. Also, I heard he worked with orphans in the region, and I wanted to help out in any way I could. His mother apparently owned a small Mayan restaurant called "*Los Abrazos*" in the town of San Marcos, so I knew I could find him by asking around.

The seven-hour drive was by no means quick, yet felt light-years faster than the drive to Semuc Champey. I fell in and out of sleep, the glass window serving as my pillow. I opened my eyes as the van slowly wound its way down the mountain range. Two enormous volcanoes shot out from over the glimmering lake like divine creatures in the distance. Numerous little huts and houses were scattered along the lakeshore. They looked like specks in the distance as we descended from the top of the mountain range.

The van decelerated at each turn in the road, as each twist was narrow, sharp, and steep. Huge chunks of asphalt were missing from parts of the worn-down road, and the van kicked up dust, rocks, and dirt. At every turn, the driver let out a honk to warn any possible drivers climbing upward. The sun shone down on the vast lake and gentle waves shot off shards of reflected light.

The driver pulled to a halt. "San Marcos!" he announced loudly. Everyone else in the van was headed to San Pedro, a town on the other side of the lake. I hopped outside, and the driver climbed onto the roof and handed down my backpack. He said this was as far as he could go and that I needed to catch a *tuk-tuk* to town. I thanked him and seconds later, the van rumbled off.

I stood there, turning 360 degrees, observing my surroundings. With the van gone, I was blanketed by the surrounding silence. This absence of man-made sounds felt both strange and serene; the temperature was toasty, yet pleasant. I quickly grew accustomed to the pervading stillness.

The silence was broken as a bright-red *tuk-tuk* mounted up the road before me. I waved at the driver, and he pulled to a stop next to me. I greeted him and asked if I could catch a ride to town. I wasn't quite sure if I was even in San Marcos yet or if the town was at the bottom of this seemingly endless road. The driver smiled and said he would take me, so I climbed in. The seat cushion I sat on was imbedded with an FC Barcelona design, which is a professional soccer team. I struck up a conversation, and we talked about soccer for the entire ride, my driver enthusiastically spilling out his knowledge and passion for FC Barcelona.

Again, soccer served as a positive form of connection. I smiled inwardly, amazed at the power of this universal language, which had helped me time and time again.

As we traveled toward the lake, more people began to appear. Other *tuk-tuks* whizzed by, and little stores and shops started to pop up. Finally, the driver pulled to a stop alongside the lake, where a red stone path led toward the shore. He signaled for me to follow the path to find a few hostels. I thanked and paid him, and then he sped off.

Almost the instant I stepped off the *tuk-tuk*, a Guatemalan-looking man greeted me warmly with a wide smile, standing there as if he had been expecting me. He wore round sunglasses, a purple-collared shirt, and crisp, denim jeans.

"Hi, friend," he exclaimed in Spanish. "I'm Sergio. Are you looking for something?"

"Hey, I'm Jake," I replied, wondering what this spontaneous meet-and-greet would lead to. "I'm looking for a hostel; do you know where one is?" I questioned.

"Yes!" he exclaimed, "This way," he directed with his hand.

I followed him down the stone path that led toward the lake. I told him about my journey, explaining that I had come to San Marcos to discover for myself the spiritual energy that San Marcos was known for and to meet interesting people from all over the world.

"Then you must meet my father," he announced. "He's a shaman who lives in San Pedro."

I stopped dead in my tracks, trying to contain my excitement. I had heard fascinating stories about shamans and was curious to meet one myself. I voiced my amazement to Sergio, and he replied that it was "*destino*," or destiny, that we met. I chuckled, not so much at what he said but the idea of it. I wasn't a firm believer in destiny but laughed at the possibility of it. I was feeling open to whatever lay ahead—"destiny," if you want to call it that.

"If you want, we can have a Mayan meditation ceremony," Sergio offered. "My father leads them often, and many members of the community gather, and we send our intentions to the elements."

"Yes, I would love to experience one!" I exclaimed. I pictured myself huddling around holy symbols in a ceremony with Sergio and a bunch of his Mayan relatives.

I checked into the hostel and was surprised at how empty it was. I dropped my bag off in an empty room and headed back outside. I suddenly remembered my plan to search for Arnulfo. I decided that I would wait to find him and follow Sergio for now. It seemed almost supernatural how I had met him and how he had a connection to exactly what I was looking for—a shaman. I started playing with the idea that maybe it was destiny that we had met.

I met up with Sergio, and we stopped at a small store in town. Sergio asked if I could purchase the candles for the ceremony, and I agreed. I didn't think anything of it as my mind was in a daze, pondering the upcoming ceremony. I followed him up the road and then off into a trail leading up toward the mountains. Bushes and trees surrounded us as we ambled up the narrow dirt path. I was feeling slightly confused as to where we were going and how the others would join us for the ceremony. I decided to stay silent for the time being, following Sergio up the trail.

After about fifteen minutes, we came upon a towering cliff that rose strikingly in the middle of the shrubs and greenery. The cliff slanted toward the ground at an angle, creating a shallow cave. Beneath the cave, a circular platform that looked like a fire pit rose from the ground. It was surrounded with little rocks, creating a border. Luscious trees surrounded the cliff, and the melody of chirping birds rang peacefully in the air.

"When are the others coming?" I asked, feeling somewhat anxious.

"What do you mean?" Sergio responded. "It's just us."

Sergio had given me the impression that there would be others joining this ceremony. At least, that's what I thought he had conveyed. Sergio spoke no English, and although my Spanish was proficient, I felt as if my lack of fluency had caused a misunderstanding. For whatever reason, I was feeling somewhat cautious. Sergio didn't strike me as dangerous or ill hearted, yet there was something about him that was strange. It felt as if his overly wide smile was hiding something. When he had mentioned his father was a shaman, I disregarded my other feelings and became solely fixed on meeting his father and experiencing a part of the Mayan culture.

"Oh," I mumbled, shaking my head in an effort to help myself understand. "I thought you said others would be here with us when you mentioned the ceremony?"

"No, no," he replied, smiling. "It's just us. I know how to lead the ceremony."

"Hmm, okay," I said. Feeling that Sergio seemed harmless, I switched my focus to a more optimistic state.

We stood in the natural cave immersed in shade. Sergio gathered a handful of the colorful candles and placed them in distinct places. Red, black, green, and white candles now stood on the platform. Sergio handed me four candles to hold and proceeded to light the other candles in the fire pit. Once all of the candles were lit, Sergio took a seat on the ground. His demeanor appeared to be one of relaxation yet deep concentration.

"The red candles represent blood," Sergio explained. "All humans, despite skin color and race and religion, share the same color of blood. We are all one. The black candles represent respect for the dead. It is important to honor our ancestors. The green candles represent the earth and the power of nature. We must flow with the elements, not against them. The white candles represent purity and bliss."

I was now deeply focused, giving my full attention to the experience at hand. I knew that in order to fully appreciate the significance of the ceremony, I needed to go with the flow and have an optimistic, open-minded attitude. He directed me to close my eyes and focus on the important people and things in my life and express appreciation through my thoughts. I watched him close his eyes, his face locked in concentration, softly and rapidly uttering phrases to himself in Spanish. I closed my eyes and fixed my attention on what I was thankful for. I thought of my parents and sisters, my friends and family. I thought of my health and the opportunity to become what my heart desired. My shoulders loosened, dropping as I exhaled. I could feel the tension leaving me like the smoke from the candles.

Once the candles burned through after about fifteen minutes, Sergio concluded the ceremony. He bent down and kissed the earthy floor and then looked upward, his eyes conveying gratitude. He signaled that the ceremony was over and smiled to me, asking what I thought of it.

"It was an interesting experience," I honestly revealed. I found it fascinating what the colors represented in the Mayan culture.

I watched as Sergio dug through his backpack and pulled out a joint. "Do you smoke weed?" he asked, smirking.

"No, I'm good. Thanks, though," I responded firmly. A wave of uneasiness settled into my stomach. It wasn't the weed itself that made me feel apprehensive. I had smoked countless times in my life. But now I wanted to experience life completely sober so I could see the world unfiltered through my own thoughts. I wanted to be fully alert and tuned into my authentic senses. There was something about Sergio that struck me as shady, though I couldn't quite put my finger on it; this feeling of something being awry started to gnaw at my gut. While Sergio finished smoking his joint, we hung out by the cave and talked. When we walked back into town, he stopped at a street vendor.

"Jake, can you give me some cash? I have no money, and I'm so hungry," Sergio voiced in a tone spoken to get my sympathy.

"Yeah, sure," I replied simply and handed him the money he asked for. Although it wasn't much money, I had reservations about giving it to Sergio. It wasn't the money that bothered me, but rather Sergio's appeal for it. The documentary I had seen, which was filmed in Lake Atitlan, featured countless children and families living on less than a dollar a day. I knew that it was wrong for me to make judgments based on looks, but Sergio was well dressed and definitely didn't come across as starving. Yet he appealed to me as if he hadn't eaten all day. Confused, I pondered how he could afford to buy marijuana but not food. He seemed so sincere in the ceremony. I was stuck in an internal battle. *Is Sergio as sincere as he says he is? Or is there something else lurking behind his wide smile? I would feel awful if he truly was starving. Does he actually have no money to eat?*

After Sergio munched on a few chicken tostadas and stuffed a few bags of chips into his backpack, he said that he needed to get back home. "You can meet my father tomorrow if you want. I can talk to him and see if he can drop the price down for you."

"Uh, okay," I uttered, hesitating. "I'm not sure what my plan is for tomorrow," I continued, deepening my voice in an attempt to convey confidence. I didn't realize that it would cost money for me to meet his father. The concept of paying to meet a shaman who would tell me about myself seemed wrong. The notion sat uneasily in my stomach. It felt unnatural and inauthentic, the opposite of what I desired and expected based on what I had read and heard.

"I will be back in San Marcos tomorrow morning around nine. I can take you to him then if you would like," Sergio announced. "Also, can I have a few more *quetzals* so I can get a ride back to San Pedro?" he pleaded in a way that I could only say yes.

I handed him the money he asked for, and he thanked me, that wide grin again forming on his face. We said good-bye to each other, and I watched him hop into a *tuk-tuk* and speed off. *Why do I feel so discontented right now? Why is this nagging feeling in my gut not going away?*

It struck me that my desire to meet a shaman had resulted in my ignoring my own gut feelings. If the Universe desired for me to meet a shaman, it would happen. The world would pick up my intention and act accordingly. I needed to stop pushing so hard. The world operates in mysterious ways, and things have a way of working out if they're meant to be.

The sun was settling on the horizon, and I made my way back to the hostel. I was the only one in my room; the other beds were vacant. I grabbed a towel from my backpack and stepped into the shower. I turned the knob, but nothing happened except the creaking sound of the dial turning. I kept turning, but no water poured out. I threw my clothes back on and approached the hostel front desk, explaining the situation.

"There hasn't been any water all day," the receptionist explained. "This happens sometimes, but we have no control over the water system."

I nodded and then trudged back to my empty dorm. I really craved a shower now, not so much because I was dirty, but because of the fact that I wanted to shower and couldn't. The absence of water seemed to add to my feeling of loneliness. After a peculiar afternoon, I was looking forward to meeting people at the hostel. Being alone in this new place, along with the day's events, took me some time to fully process.

Luckily, the Wi-Fi was working in the hostel. I decided to e-mail the guy constructing the eco-lodge volunteer project in Nicaragua. I sent him a message asking if I could come and volunteer in a few days. I longed to be in a place with many volunteers.

I was exhausted and climbed into bed. I reminded myself that tomorrow was a new day, a new opportunity waiting. I would go in search of Arnulfo in the morning, accepting whatever the day offered.

"You can't force chemistry to exist where it doesn't in the same way you can't deny it when it does."
—Unknown

CHAPTER 23

Trust Your Hunches

May 6, 2015

"Synchronicity is choreographed by a great, pervasive intelligence that lies at the heart of nature and is manifest in each of us through intuitive knowledge."

—Deepak Chopra

I awoke with the rising sun ready to embrace a new day. I felt refreshed despite the fact I hadn't showered in a couple days. The water was still not working. The peculiar events of the day before were behind me now. I checked my e-mail and was happily surprised to see an e-mail from Gabe, the man in charge of the volunteer, eco-lodge project called "Carpe Diem." He said I was welcome to come and volunteer! He said to shoot him an e-mail when I knew what day I was arriving so he could plan to have enough food for me. I immediately began researching flights. The best deal for a flight to Nicaragua left in a week. I booked it and sent him an e-mail, feeling ecstatic and hopeful about the upcoming experience.

After breakfast, I made my way over to *Los Abrazos* in search of Arnulfo. It was another beautiful day with clear skies and endless opportunities. As I approached the entrance to the restaurant, I doubted myself for a second. It looked more like a small hut than a restaurant. There was a wooden door at the entrance that rose to my chest height.

The small building was crafted in white concrete with various stones strategically placed to fill in the gaps. A beautiful, rainbow-colored *quetzal*, the national bird of Guatemala, was painted above the entrance. The windows were just empty space to the left of the door, and a few plants and pots rested on the floor. Tin sheets covered the roof, a now-familiar sight to me. I stood beneath the steps leading to the door, peering inside. No people. A clayish color coated most of the restaurant, and intricate designs and words were inscribed on the walls. They were symbols of the Mayan calendar and glyphs, which I was soon to learn. Each picture was unique and represented symbols of the indigenous Mayan language.

"*Hola?*" I questioned in a voice as genuine as I could compose. I waited a few seconds but heard nothing. I tried again, this time a little louder. A few seconds later, an old woman approached the door. I could sense her tenderness from her delicate, gentle movements. Her wrinkles and deliberate steps spoke of her fragile age. She couldn't have been more than five feet tall, if that. Her dress radiated with color, an artwork of sophisticated patterns.

"*Hola,*" she replied softly, almost whispering. Her dark, fibrous hair was sprinkled with gray and rested smoothly on her shoulders in a ponytail. Her smile formed slowly, revealing a genuine kindness.

"*Hola,*" I voiced cheerfully in Spanish, trying to convey my complete sincerity. "My name is Jake. I was looking for Arnulfo. Is he around by any chance?" She glanced up momentarily as if in search for the answer.

"He is out right now but should be here in about an hour," she replied softly.

"Oh, okay, thank you," I responded, unsure of what else to say.

"Would you like to sit inside and wait for him?" she kindly offered.

"Yes, that would be great," I happily replied.

She opened the wooden door, and I stepped inside. The room must have been less than twenty feet in length. It was compact but cozy. The stone floor matched the surrounding walls and created an earthy feel. Two handcrafted, clay fire ovens were built into the far corner. One oven was sculpted into a condor, the other an eagle. It looked as if they were hugging each other.

I sat down on the stone bench that rested beneath the wooden table. We talked for a while, and I asked her about Arnulfo who, she informed me, was indeed her son. Her name was Antonia. Deeply curious, I asked her about her restaurant and her culture. She was separating beans that were nested inside their shells. Her frail arms moved gradually but precisely. I offered to help her, and she gladly accepted. I sat next to her at the wooden table, and we continued to talk and learn more about each other while we plucked beans from their shells and put them into a steel bowl.

Soon after, the wooden door creaked open, and a man walked in. He had short, dark hair and thick, chocolate eyes that looked impenetrable. His white shirt emphasized his amber skin. He had a calm and composed demeanor.

I smiled at him as Antonia introduced me to him—Arnulfo, her son. I stood up and shook his hand. When I looked into his piercing, dark eyes, they seemed to convey a sense of deep understanding. I was relieved to hear that he spoke English pretty well. He asked me where I had previously been, and I told him about my time in San Andres and Semuc Champey. It seemed as if he knew and understood me from the second we locked eyes. He was one of those rare people who carefully listen to every word you say with utmost attention. His openness and empathetic demeanor were inviting. I immediately felt I could trust him with my darkest secrets and fears. And I did; they all came tumbling out of me. I told him about my anxiety and unhappiness at school and my father's depression and my worry of ending up in a similar situation. I expressed to him my overall confusion with life.

"Breathe deeply," he advised. "Now and always. Breathe. Calm down and breathe." It struck me that I had just poured out my deepest insecurities and feelings so rapidly that I was not aware my body was shaking. Never in my life had I revealed such personal information to someone so soon after meeting. But Arnulfo had a special aura about him, a supernatural empathy. (I had no idea that his book, which I was about to read soon, *Light of the Soul: A Secret Blueprint for Revolutionary*

Happiness and Realizing Your Dreams, would have a profound impact on my life and give me insight into how Arnulfo had developed such wisdom about human nature.)

I took his advice and inhaled deeply. I held my breath for a few seconds, feeling my chest and lungs expand. I exhaled, releasing along with my breath the jittery nerves that were apparently stacked inside of me. I instantly felt lighter.

"It is important that you keep calm. Don't go flying off; come back down to earth and connect with all your Five Elements –mind, body, heart, spirit, and soul and the Source of Life. The Center of Nature is the bond through which all of life is connected. It's where your most natural self is, where your soul stems from."

I intently listened to every word he spoke as if each one contained valuable wisdom.

"You must unconditionally love your father. He needs your support. Learn from him. Emulate his positive qualities and separate yourself from the ones that result in his suffering. Be the light through which he can find his way out of the darkness."

I was fixated on his mysteriously deep eyes, feeling as if he were reaching into the depths of my soul with his gaze. I absorbed his words, which pulsed powerfully through my mind and heart. Arnulfo was right. My father was struggling, and that was a fact. Part of me felt that I shouldn't be around him—that his sadness and depression were dragging me down, and I would sink into an abyss of isolation from the world, devoid of happiness. But I knew that this part of me was wrong. I had to be there for him, now more than ever. By shining my own light, I would give him permission to shine his. By offering my support and expressing my love and gratitude for having him in my life, I could give him hope. My dad had given me the greatest gift of all: the opportunity to live a life of my dreams. His unrelenting support and care for me growing up provided me with the foundation to find my own beat, my own trail.

I asked Arnulfo about the orphanage that he worked with and expressed my desire to assist him there.

"There is no orphanage here in San Marcos," he explained. "There is a small village near San Marcos where many orphans live, but there is no orphanage. There are many poor people. If you would like, you can come with me tomorrow when I go over there. It is too far to walk, but you can ride on the back of my motorbike."

"Yes, I would like to come!" I responded, enthralled.

We talked for a while more, and I felt myself gaining more self-insight through Arnulfo's stories and advice. I felt a bond to him that needed no words to explain. His eyes spoke the language of the Universe, and each word he uttered was carefully crafted, illuminating with remarkable clarity the confusing things that were tangled in my mind. He told me about the book he wrote, *The Light of the Soul*, and I promised him that I would read it. It was more a promise to myself than to him—I knew that the message in his story would add to my understanding of the world. In the same way I had felt about Mike, I knew there was something special about Arnulfo—a powerful story inside of him that was ready to be heard by the world.

When he pulled out his phone and announced it was almost three in the afternoon, my mouth dropped open. I had been there for nearly four hours! Yet again, time seemed to stand still. Arnulfo announced he was going back to his home, which was close by in town. I joined him walking out, saying good-bye to Antonia. I thanked her for her warm hospitality and told her I would see her tomorrow.

"Why don't you meet me here tomorrow morning at nine?" Arnulfo suggested.

"Yes, that sounds great. Thank you for taking the time to talk with me," I gratefully responded.

We parted ways, and I walked back to my hostel, the sun beaming as bright as ever. I was glowing with enthusiasm and clarity, which was a stark contrast to my feelings the day before. It suddenly hit me that the beautiful things in life cannot be forced. Chemistry cannot exist where there is no possibility of connection. Powerful relationships and spectacular events happen naturally like the bonds in a chemical reaction. Things that are meant to happen *will* happen as long as you put forth an open mind and have the courage to be proactive and live in accordance with the principles you value. Like attracts like, so when things don't work out, then they're simply not meant to be.

I realized that my desire to find a shaman was too forced. While meeting Sergio may have seemed like destiny or a magical coincidence, it was only because I had chosen to convince myself of that. I was so caught up in believing that Sergio was some magical omen that had fallen upon me that I failed to acknowledge the warning signs my gut was signaling. It takes incredible awareness and practice to effectively tap into your intuition. I noted to myself that I would try my best not to lose track of my inner voice again.

But maybe meeting Sergio was still destiny at work. Maybe the Universe conspired for me to meet him so I could distinguish true from false, sincere from counterfeit, right from wrong. Sergio's nature only made me feel much more confident that Arnulfo was as genuine as he seemed.

I walked back into the hostel dorm feeling lighter than the wind. When I entered, a man with gray curls was standing beside one of the beds in the room with his backpack plopped on the floor. He turned to me as I walked in, giving me a warm greeting.

"Hi! I'm John," he introduced himself in a delighted manner, waving his hand hello from a few feet over.

"Hey, I'm Jake! Nice to meet you," I reciprocated. John was older than most of the travelers I had seen—or at least, the backpackers who stayed in the cheap youth hostels with multiple beds in a shared room. He had dark-gray curls that rested freely on his head. His sparkling eyes revealed remarkable energy and a youthful spirit that seemed to contrast with his gray hair.

"Did you just arrive?" I asked.

"Yeah, a few hours ago. I came from El Salvador. I was there for a month or so helping out in an orphanage. I'm a teacher by training, actually," he laughed to himself, his easygoing nature percolating through the air. "It's beautiful there on the beach. I've thought about buying some property in El Salvador."

"Wow, that sounds awesome!" I exclaimed, intrigued by his story and tranquil demeanor.

"Yeah, it was a great experience," he responded. He looked around for a moment, examining the empty beds. "It's awfully quiet around here. I was surprised to see only one backpack in the room when I arrived. I was sort of hoping for a communal atmosphere."

"Me, too!" I acknowledged in agreement. "It would be nice if more people were around."

"When I was walking over here, I met a nice gal who told me of a great hostel where she is staying called *Hostel del Lago*. She said it has a cool vibe, and a lot of people are staying there. I already paid for the night here, but maybe tomorrow we can go check it out."

"Yeah, that sounds like a great idea," I replied. "Hey, I'm getting kind of hungry. Do you want to get dinner?" I asked.

"Yeah, sure!" he replied. "I would love to take a shower first, but the water's not working."

We walked to a little restaurant in town and sat down at a table. After ordering our food, we talked for a while. I learned that John was sixty-three years old and lived in Canada with his wife and that his kids were already grown up. He spoke English, French, and Spanish. He told me about his love for traveling and discovering new places. He'd been to Togo in Africa on multiple occasions where he taught in schools and lived in a local community. We connected on the idea that age doesn't define what you can or can't do. I didn't feel I was too young to be out exploring the world on my own, and John obviously didn't feel he was too old. We laughed about the various stereotypes in the world and how we both felt like free spirits defying our society's expectations of what travel is or how old you have to be.

John's outlook on life struck a chord in me, forcing me to see the everyday aspects of my own society through a different lens. It's a funny thing about appearances, status, rankings, numbers and titles. Our lives seem to be governed by these external differences, yet true connection stems from within. Your spirit and character define who you are, not your job title or age or race or religion.

I thought about how whenever I met someone back in the United States, I almost always asked the same few questions. "What do you do? How old are you? What school do you go to?" I had never thought much of this. It seemed to me that was just the way people met other people—plain and simple. I realized that as I was growing older, I was comparing myself to people based on their answers. I wasn't even aware that I was doing this, but I was making assumptions about their intelligence or character based on what careers they were pursuing, what school they went to, and how many organizations they were members of. I had been sizing myself up and deriving my own self-worth based on the numbers and titles of my peers. This only exacerbated my ever-present anxiety. Life was blown up in my mind as this rat-race competition to the "top."

John reminded me that I always have a choice of how I can view the world. Nothing was stopping me from asking different questions like: "What do you *love* to do?" and "What do you value in life?" I had the power to become *aware* of my preconceived judgments of other people. I could change this. I could judge people based on their integrity and personality—on what lived inside of them, not outside.

John and I were so wrapped up in talking that I hadn't even noticed it was now nighttime. We finished our meals and headed back to the hostel. On our way back, we ran into the girl from the hostel John had mentioned. He introduced me to her—Lauren, from Australia. She told us that tomorrow at four in the afternoon she was going to check out this special ceremony she had heard about.

"There's this guy named Scott who lives in San Marcos and is a so-called *cacao shaman*," she informed us. I tried to focus on what she was saying but found myself distracted by her amazing accent. "It sounds strange to me, but I've heard from the others in my hostel that his ceremony is incredible. You guys should come along tomorrow!" she offered.

John and I both looked at each other. I turned back to Lauren and replied, "Yeah, why not! It sounds like a cool experience." John chimed in, saying he was up for going as well. We both agreed that traveling was all about trying new things. This definitely sounded like something neither of us had ever experienced, and I was excited to see what awaited us.

> *"Trust your hunches. They're usually based on facts filed away just below the conscious level."*
> —Dr. Joyce Brothers

CHAPTER 24

One Action Can Change Someone's World

May 7, 2015

"How lovely to think that no one need wait a moment, we can start now, start slowly changing the world! How lovely that everyone, great and small, can make their contribution toward introducing justice straightaway....And you can always, always give something, even if it is only kindness!"

—Anne Frank

I met Arnulfo in front of *Los Abrazos* at 9:00 a.m. I had a small backpack containing stickers and a water bottle. Arnulfo pulled up in his sleek, black motorbike wearing a matching helmet that made him look like a secret agent. He was the only person I had seen during my travels to wear a helmet while riding a motorcycle. He took off his helmet, climbed off his bike and greeted me with a warm smile.

"Thanks for coming with me today. The village we are going to, Tsununá, is very poor. Many of the children don't have parents, and food is scarce. They don't receive any care for their health. They have no doctors. I want you to see how these people live."

He directed me to sit on the back of his motorbike and to hold on tight to his shoulders. I hopped onto the seat behind him, and he revved the engine. We took off, riding through the paved roads in town. It wasn't long before buildings and huts became scarce as we wound our way around the untouched, green mountain. The paved roads became rocky trails, and my grip on Arnulfo's shoulders tightened as I bobbed up and down on the backseat, praying that I wouldn't fly off.

As we continued to travel, the most remarkable view of Lake Atitlan appeared. An opening in the green trees to my right showcased the two vast volcanoes that rested majestically above the cerulean, shimmering lake. White, fluffy clouds drifted slowly behind the enormous peaks. To my left, extensive arrays of trees filled the mountain, a wash of jade and grassy greens. The raw beauty of the landscape contrasted starkly with the environment we were about to enter.

We pulled up to an opening on the rocky road. Huts were scattered throughout. Arnulfo decelerated his bike to the side of the dirt road, and we hopped off. This was Tsununá. Silence permeated the dry, toasty air. No birds were chirping, no motorbikes were whizzing by, no travelers were wandering about. The stillness in the air wasn't eerie or peaceful—it was loud. It spoke to me of the magnitude of the situation I was entering. It weighed heavily on my shoulders. The only sound I heard was my own footsteps on the dirt.

"These people speak almost no Spanish," Arnulfo informed me as we walked across the gravel toward the huts. "They speak *Kakchiquel*, a native Mayan language. I'm from *el Quiché* where we speak *K'iche'*, but when I came here, I had to learn to speak Kakchiquel. I am going to pass out some money to the families here so they can buy food. Usually, I bring them standard food parcels, but today I'd like them to buy whatever food they need."

"Can I give out stickers to the children?" I tentatively asked, not knowing if that would be allowed or not.

"Yes, of course," he replied instantly, supporting the idea.

The hut we were about to enter was constructed of cylinder blocks. It looked to be about fifteen feet wide and fifteen feet long. A thin metal sheet served as the roof, a mix of browns from rust and blacks from smoke. A couple of kids lingered nearby, running around and playing with each other.

Arnulfo voiced a greeting before we entered to give notice of our arrival. He spoke in *Kakchiquel,* a variety of ticks and clacks clicking from his mouth. Walking through the open door of the hut, I saw a woman sitting on a small mat in the corner holding a small child in her arms. The room was shadowy, a sharp contrast from the bright sun outside. The woman had dark-black hair that matched the darkness in her eyes and her suntanned skin. Wrinkles scrunched together on her forehead and saggy cheeks as she peered up at Arnulfo and me. Her eyelids were half-open, and her eyebrows rose yet slanted downward. The corners of her mouth drooped after we greeted her. These facial movements made it look as if it took copious amounts of energy for her to stay awake, and fatigue seeped out of her skin. Her stoic face looked cemented and told of hopelessness and exhaustion and years of hardship and dismal living. The child she held looked to be around two years old. His head was buried in the woman's chest, and I could only see the dirty bottoms of his dusty feet.

Arnulfo spoke with her and handed her some money. They spoke in *Kakchiquel,* and I listened intently as if I could somehow understand a few words of this intricate, ancient language. I gazed around at the desolate room. The ground inside the hut was the same dirt and gravel that we walked on outside. The mat the woman sat on was raggedy yet beamed with the same beautiful colors that matched her dress. After speaking with her, Arnulfo said good-bye, and we left the hut.

Upon walking outside into the bright light, three young boys approached us. All were barefoot, and their tattered clothes were covered in dirt and stains. Two of them looked about seven years old, the other one a few years younger. They each stared up at me with wide, searching eyes as if I were an extraterrestrial creature, someone whose skin and appearance didn't exist in their world. Still, their gazes didn't hint of judgment—only curiosity and wonder. Their small faces had open cuts, scabs, and dirt on them. Their expressions weren't happy or sad, angry or calm; they just were. They were impassive and accepting of their situation, which was normal to them and depressing to me.

Arnulfo talked with them in *Kakchiquel,* and it was evident that he knew them well. He handed each of them some money as they conversed. I turned to Arnulfo and asked him if I could give them stickers, and he nodded yes. I pulled my backpack off and took out my bag of stickers. I pulled out about a dozen strips and handed them to the kids, not knowing what to expect. I will remember their reactions for the rest of my life.

Their faces lit up instantly, a wave of joy practically surging through them like a volt of electricity. Their glistening eyes and dimply smiles emitted radiant delight that I didn't know they were capable of producing. They were silent at first, holding their stickers up in the air, studying them fastidiously as if I had handed them a million dollars. They hunched together, their heads touching one another as they gazed at the different stickers each was holding and uttered a few words. They held up their prized possessions in the sunlight, turning them in different directions and watching in amazement at the various colors reflecting off the stickers.

I stood there silently, watching them smile as they giggled and talked about their new gifts. Arnulfo exchanged a few words with them before we said good-bye, and they waved at us with smiles as wide as the ocean.

"I found those three children sleeping in the coffee plants," Arnulfo revealed to me matter-of-factly. "Their parents had died, and no one was taking care of them. I approached the grandmother and told her she had a responsibility to take care of the kids." Arnulfo was silent for a few moments and then continued, "This is common here. It's unfortunate, but true. They have no money and no one to take care of them. I've been providing them with food and sending them to school, but it's difficult for me to control them because society has an influence on them."

Arnulfo's words stung. All of my complaints and problems paled in comparison to those of these children. Many of them had no parents, no food, no place to sleep, and no doctors. They wore ragged clothes that were blanketed in dust and dirt and had untreated cuts all over their bodies. Arnulfo explained the complexity of the situation in Guatemala and how it dated back to the intense discrimination that provoked the dark times of genocide when countless indigenous Mayan tribes, including his, were oppressed, murdered, raped, and tortured. Yet this dismal reality was, and still is, relatively unknown to the modern world. I knew that almost half of the world's population—over three billion people—were living on less than $2.50 a day, but it was another thing for me to see it with my own eyes.

We spent the next hour or so passing through various huts where Arnulfo passed out money and I passed out stickers. Everyone knew Arnulfo. It seemed as if he were everything to them—their father, watchman, protector, doctor, and caregiver. I was continuously blown away by the reaction of the children as I handed them stickers. I asked Arnulfo how to say good morning in Kakchiquel. "*Saqarik*," he told me, putting an emphasis on the "rik" while making a clicking sound.

Each hut we went to was more or less the same: a grim, small enclosing with minimal objects in a somber room. The faces of the adults all revealed withering spirits and a history of destitution and hardship, and the children all gaped at me with wonder, unsure of what to make of me. "*Saqarik*," I greeted them, which immediately broke the silence as the children giggled at my awkward pronunciation. After giving them the stickers, pure ecstasy emanated from their small bodies as if I had given them the whole world. It seemed as if the stickers symbolized hope for them, something that appeared lacking in the adults.

I had an epiphany walking back to the motorcycle with Arnulfo after we finished passing through each of the huts. The drastic change on the kids' faces from sheer, unemotional stillness to total euphoria replayed over and over in my mind. I realized how truly powerful humans are, not in the sense of building technology or giant skyscrapers, but in the sense of making a difference in someone else's life. Every individual on this earth has the ability to show someone else they matter, that someone cares about them. Rich or poor, having one arm or leg, black or white, religious or atheist—any person can make a difference in someone else's life. The fact that a few stickers created such bliss in these children's lives sent a powerful message to the heart of my soul. That something so small and seemingly insignificant on the surface could bring about such rapture to someone else struck a chord in me. This experience was a gift and one I thanked Arnulfo for. The Universe reminded me what I had inside me: *limitless potential to make a positive impact on the lives of others.*

As we rode back to the town of San Marcos, I was surprised by the irony. Right next to this touristy town where travelers flock exist some of the world's poorest people. If it weren't for Arnulfo, I would never have known they were there. This stark reality infuriated me—yet it exists all over the world and even in my own country. For those lucky enough like me who have the resources to live a healthy life and one with opportunity, we get so caught up in our own lives that we aren't even aware of the brutal suffering of so many people around us. The wind brushed my face, reminding me that awareness is power if knowledge can be translated into action.

We arrived back at Los Abrazos and walked inside. Antonia greeted us warmly, and we both sat down at the wooden table. I sat silently, trying to fully process the last few hours.

I never believed that there could be a "saint on earth" until I met Arnulfo. Every night, Arnulfo told me, he goes into the remote mountains alone and feeds and heals the sick and poor people where there are no doctors. These people don't speak Spanish, only their indigenous Mayan languages.

"During the night?" I asked, confused. "When do you sleep?"

"I don't, really," he replied in the most straightforward, casual manner. I felt my eyes practically bulging out of their sockets. "I usually sleep for two or three hours when I return. It's enough for me." He looked over at me, and it was apparent that I was shocked by his words. He continued, "When people have an intention that is pure, they can bear any task in order to fulfill their mission. These people have no one. I have to help them. It is my soul's duty."

Suddenly, I remembered excerpts from a book I recently read in San Andres, *Autobiography of a Yogi*. It details the life of one of the world's greatest spiritual leaders, Paramahansa Yogananda, and his life journeys; it explains life's lessons and describes the lives of various "saints," many who defy the limits of what Western medicine believes is possible. Many of the "saints" had the ability to prosper with minimal food, sleep, and other "necessities" through their complete dedication to the practice of meditation and helping others. It seemed as if the Universe had conspired for me to read this book.

Arnulfo's way of life no longer seemed so crazy to me—that he literally sacrificed his sleep to help heal and provide for these sick people—as I had the context to understand that this was, in fact, possible. What seemed crazy, however, was that I was staring at him with my own eyes, seeing this person whose mission of helping people was so important that he didn't need sleep to flourish. He was nourished by a spiritual power, a fuel that cannot be described, but which nonetheless gave him the ability to fulfill his mission. I was staring at a human anomaly.

"Wait, so you do this every night? And how do you help them?" I asked curiously, still somewhat amazed.

"Yes," Arnulfo responded, "I treat the sick using natural medicine, and I bring food and clothes to those in need. I also help the women, who are abandoned in the mountains, through complicated births. I do this with my own funds, earned through the sales of my art, my international talks and therapies, and my construction work. What I earn during the day, I share with people at night." I listened intently, deeply fascinated by Arnulfo's words.

"The path of light is the path of the Center of Nature. It requires discipline and seeing through the eyes of the soul. This is the path of truth. We come in this world with a unique light to fulfill our mission and serve humanity."

He informed me that during weekday mornings, he welcomes the poor children from surrounding villages to his house to eat because they are almost all malnourished. He also teaches classes in the local school about consciousness and physics, directing the children to live honestly and with respect for others and the world around them. Moreover, he has built homes for orphans in Tsununá. He does this in addition to going into the mountains alone each night, which is not safe.

As the afternoon approached, I said good-bye to Arnulfo and Antonia and planned to meet up with them the next morning. I thanked Arnulfo for taking me to the village and for reminding me of the power I have inside of me—the power to help others.

"There are two ways of spreading light: to be the candle or the mirror that reflects it."
—Edith Wharton

CHAPTER 25

Why Were You Born?

May 7, 2015

"If you wish to understand the Universe, think of energy, frequency, and vibration."

—Nikola Tesla

When I arrived back at the hostel, John was gathering his stuff together on his bed. "Hey!" he greeted me. "I was just about to head over to the other hostel. I went earlier today, and they said they had room for us."

"Awesome!" I replied. In less than a minute, I packed my backpack, and we left the hostel. Hostel del Lago was only a five-minute walk away. We entered the hostel and walked toward the front desk, which was attached to the kitchen and less than twenty yards from the lakeshore. There were fifteen or so people hanging out in the lounge area, the breathtaking lake and volcanoes lurking elegantly in the background. I spotted Lauren and waved to her. She cheerfully waved back and greeted John and me.

"The cacao ceremony starts in an hour!" she shouted over at us. "Let's meet at this table in half an hour so we can walk over early and grab a good seat. I've heard these ceremonies are packed!"

The kind lady at the front desk checked me in and led me to a six-person dorm. I thanked her and plopped my backpack on an open bed, eager to hop in the shower. The cool water sent a shocking yet refreshing wave through my body, and I felt a layer of sweat and grime fall away as I scrubbed my body. Feeling rejuvenated, I got dressed and strolled to the lounge area where Lauren and John were waiting. Above the lounge area and resting above the lakeshore lay a beautiful, raised wooden platform that was used for yoga in the mornings.

The minutes flew by, and the three of us proceeded to the cacao ceremony. I was feeling slightly skeptical about the ceremony. For one thing, I didn't know much about it. I was told it could last anywhere from two to eight hours, and that it all depended on the "energy in the room." I decided to approach the ceremony with open-minded skepticism; I would "taste the pudding" for myself.

We approached the cacao shaman's cottage, which lay on the outskirts of the village. A wooden gate with the words "Cacao Ceremonies" emblazoned on it signified we were at the right place. I opened the gate and stepped into a beautiful courtyard filled with vibrant flowers and plants. A young man with a Bob Marley shirt and long, maple-brown hair that reached down to his shoulders escorted us past the garden and onto a porch. He was the shaman's helper, we were told, and he handed us a jar, announcing that the suggested donation for the ceremony was roughly $10. We all put money into the jar. We took our shoes off as he instructed and then began to look for a seat in the small room where six other people were sitting.

The room was draped with colorful blankets and mystical patterns, lush vines and tribal insignia. A small, rectangular table lay in the middle of the room covered in a shiny, purple cloth. One reclining chair sat beyond the table, which is where I assumed Scott, the shaman, would be sitting, although he wasn't present yet. A wooden bench bordered the snug porch, and flowery pillows and cushions lay casually scattered in the middle. I took a seat on the bench with John while Lauren sat on the ground with one of the cushions. Before long, the small room was packed with people: men and women of different generations wearing diverse outfits and hairstyles including jeans and simple blouses, dreadlocks, extravagant tie-dyed shirts, and crystal, beaded necklaces. I wondered if I had somehow time-traveled back to the 1960s and ended up at Woodstock. The room had a mystical aura about it that seemed appropriate for the events to come.

A man resembling Dumbledore approached; he had a long, gray, scraggly beard and long, wispy, white hair that reached all the way down his back. He looked like an ancient wizard with soft, steel blue eyes and circular glasses that rested upon his thin, wrinkled face. He was extremely tall, yet slim as a rod, and moved with an energy that bespoke a youthful, lively spirit beneath his aged frame. With animated enthusiasm, he greeted us all and introduced himself. He took a seat in the two chairs at the front and center of the room.

"Thank you all for coming," he boomed fervently. "Now, before we get started, I would like to inform you all about the cacao ceremony, what it entails, and how I became connected with the Cacao Spirit." His voice signaled that he had given this spiel countless times. "Cacao is *not* a psychedelic drug, and you will *not* have wild hallucinations or anything like that. The cacao that you will be drinking today is unlike any chocolate you have probably had before. This is pure, raw cacao and is extremely bitter. Most of the chocolate that you are used to eating is highly processed and is missing over 80 percent of the natural compounds in raw cacao. This cacao significantly increases heart rate and is a vasodilator, opening blood vessels and decreasing blood pressure. It can often cause an increase in blood flow to the brain, which is when many people feel the rush and effects of the cacao. This effect can produce some powerful realizations and potential manifestations that are breathing inside of you."

I glanced at John and then toward Lauren. They both held the same expression of skepticism, excitement, and hesitation as their eyes widened and heads tilted slightly back. At least they were feeling the way I was. It seemed borderline ridiculous; yet, I optimistically willing to think that this could be powerfully transformative. Scott's helper was standing behind him preparing the blenders that were filled with a thick, brown liquid which I assumed was the cacao concoction that they had just described.

"If you really want to gain something out of this experience, you must push yourself and work your mind," Scott emphasized. "It's not a drug that is ingested and then, magically, multiple effects will arise. Cacao brings you to the door but doesn't push you through it. It is up to you to dig deep within yourself. Let the cacao be a facilitator for you to access your deepest self. It should take about thirty minutes to kick in."

Scott passed around the glasses filled with the cacao. He also passed around spicy chili peppers and leaves of an herbal plant—which apparently helped the absorption of the cacao—as well as a natural sweetener to ease the bitterness. Thinking that this was most likely going to be a once-in-a-lifetime experience, I added all three to my drink. With a spoon, I stirred the contents of my cup and felt the heat permeate through the plastic cup into my hands. The enticing smell of rich chocolate teased my nostrils as I waited for the go-ahead to sip my mystical brew.

Once Scott said we could drink, I tilted my glass to my mouth and took a sip. My taste buds spiked at the bitterness of the concoction as I felt the thick texture of the peppery cacao slide down my throat. I licked my lips, contemplating the bitter taste, which was nothing like my mind had imagined. I struggled to finish the remnants of my cup over the next ten minutes as the pungent, warm liquid didn't go down smoothly.

Over the next forty minutes, Scott went into detail about how he became connected with the "Cacao Spirit." Many years ago, after a long stint of traveling, Scott ended up in the Guatemalan highlands. He was lying on a hammock in Lake Atitlan and was contacted by the "Spirit of the Cacao." An indigenous Mayan tribe he met proclaimed they had been waiting hundreds of years for him. Scott explained that the Cacao Spirit was one of the most powerful deities in ancient Mayan cosmology and that cacao has been used for centuries as a medicinal plant. After a few years of learning about the cacao plant and its properties, he began conducting ceremonies where he would use raw cacao drinks to help people connect with their inner selves, improve access to deeply embedded emotions and traumatic experiences, communicate with their subconscious minds, and cultivate a multidimensional group energy.

A glowing, warm rush flowed in my forehead. It was a lightheaded surge as if I had just drank a double espresso. I assumed this was the rush that Scott was talking about when the cacao finally kicks in. Scott announced that we were going to do a group exercise called Glow meditation. He directed everyone to close their eyes and smile, to imagine a ball of euphoric light.

"Keep smiling until it feels real," he exclaimed. "It's okay if you fake it 'til you make it. But keep trying. Bring yourself to this beautiful abundance of positive energy and light." Before shutting my eyes, I briefly glanced around the room and observed everyone sitting squished together crisscrossed on the floor with their eyes closed. Almost all of them looked entranced in deep concentration with wide smiles painted across their faces. I closed my eyes and followed Scott's instructions as I produced a smile that was 100 percent fabricated. My cheeks bulged as if they were plastic, a result of my fake smiling. I was having trouble finding this "light" that Scott was talking about. My mind was whirling in a million directions as random thoughts bounced around. I exhaled a big gust of warm air, attempting to muster every ounce of my focus on the task at hand.

I entered the mystical world of my own imagination where an ambiguous darkness lies ever-present. My cheek muscles pulled together as my smile continued to stretch across my face. Sparklers of light and color flickered through my mind, and suddenly a blissful, warming sensation permeated my face and down the rest of my body. I had no idea if I had been smiling for ten minutes or an hour as my consciousness was fully wrapped in this heavenly warmth. An authentic, soft laughter emanated from inside of me, and I couldn't have wiped the smile off my face if I had tried. I didn't know what this glee was due to—the cacao or the power of this feeling that I so strongly desired to create. Scott's positive words of encouragement echoed in the background like comforting lyrics to the tune that was radiating from within.

"Share this light with your loved ones," he boomed. "Dig deep into that feeling that's been growing inside of you. Maybe you have neglected this feeling, but it is there. Your worth, your potential—it is always with you."

An image flashed through my mind with supernatural clarity as if I were vividly staring at my own future and absorbing each and every detail. I was standing on a Douglas-fir wooden stage wearing a white shirt, hoisting a book in my hand. It was a memoir about my journey. It was my book—I wrote it. There were many faces in the crowd, young and old. The MC handed me a microphone and introduced me, praising my inspirational book and how it inspired countless individuals to find the courage to chase their dreams.

I opened my eyes, and the bright daylight made me squint momentarily. My palms were moist, and I was breathing big, long breaths, my heart pounding rapidly inside my chest. I gained control of my body and adjusted back to my normal state. My heart's hasty beats decreased as I brought my breath to a slower, steadier rhythm. I felt renewed as if I had just woken up from a yearlong nap. I felt completely empty as if I weighed nothing and could float upward, defying gravity. But I also felt entirely whole and fully awake as if I had been recharged with a surge of tireless energy. My fingers tingled as if an electric buzz were vibrating within me. I wanted to scream to the world about this feeling, this wonderful feeling—this deep-rooted purpose to share my story with the world. I became aware of my own power and potential in a way I had never been able to before, a spark suddenly igniting into a roaring fire that had been growing inside of me since the day I had been born. Scott's words grabbed my attention as I turned my focus back to the ceremony.

"By now, you should be feeling the effects of the cacao, if you feel anything at all," Scott announced. "Certain emotions, both painful and joyous, will flow in abundance as you connect with the Higher Source. Do not fight these feelings. Let them flow naturally. Resistance will only push the problem deeper."

Scott shifted the group from the Glow meditation and began asking people how they were feeling. Everyone seemed to be sharing the sense of bliss I was feeling. As I glanced around at all the smiling faces, I could feel a warm, electric energy radiate throughout the room. I glanced at John whose eyes were wide open with excitement. This intangible vibration of connectedness was flowing through each and every person I looked at. Each person's eyes and body language conveyed a universal understanding, as if we were all on the same wavelength. No words were needed to express this energy—no words could.

Scott shifted the session from one with happy vibes to one of serious emotional release. He explained how cacao opens up the heart to allow feelings to sprout freely and openly. He directed everyone to "check in with themselves," not trying to fight off any emotions but just "accepting what is." After my wave of excitement, I was feeling slightly light-headed, like I had just gulped down a large coffee.

People were trickling out of the room as the ceremony continued on and on. Feeling ready to leave, I locked eyes with John and Lauren, and they picked up on my intention. The three of us quietly rose and left the porch. John glanced at his watch and told us we had been there for three hours! We all agreed that we were ready to leave. It was getting dark, and the three of us hungrily made our way over to a restaurant. We sat down and analyzed the details of the ceremony, laughing about Scott's interesting appearance and discussing his powerful ability to foster such strong group energy. After scarfing down our food, we headed back to the hostel.

Once showered and clean, I roamed to the hangout area of the hostel overlooking the lake, which was now enveloped in the black night sky. John and Lauren were sitting on the raised porch above the lake with a girl I recognized from the ceremony. I joined them and sat down in an empty chair. The four of us were sitting with our chairs facing each other in a circle. The calming ripples of the lake made a refreshing background noise. I was introduced to the girl—Skye. That was the second cacao ceremony she had attended.

"There was such a powerful vibration in the room," she noted with passion. John, Lauren, and I nodded in agreement. We reviewed the ceremony and shared our insights about each exercise and meditation. There was, even here at this moment, an intangible connection among the four of us that I could feel vibrating in my chest. It was an experience that was so rare and unique that the feelings we derived from it were universal in a way that drew us together instantaneously.

"Wasn't the Glow meditation incredible?" John asked in a mesmerized tone. "I felt such a strong energy! Oh boy, I don't think I've ever used the word 'energy' so many times in my life, but there's no other word to describe it!"

We all laughed. It was true. I had sometimes associated the words "energy" and "vibes" with some hippie-wacky-psychedelic connotation. But I understood it now in a different way. When people connect powerfully through feelings or emotions, there exists something that cannot be tangibly measured—only feelings, a sense of mysticism, and a force at play that cannot be explained through words. The three of them agreed with me that despite moments of powerful connection, they didn't feel able to open up in the way that some of the others did.

"Did any of you guys have any powerful realizations or moments during the ceremony?" Skye questioned.

"Yeah, I did!" I blurted out, shocking myself at how quickly I responded. "It was during the Glow meditation. At first, I thought it was cheesy. I could feel myself fake smiling, that plastic feeling in my cheeks. But as I focused deeper and deeper, I got lost in a vision." I explained how I had seen myself writing a book. I filled them in on my anxiety-ridden experience at Ohio State, coming to Guatemala alone, my time in San Andres, and meeting Arnulfo and giving stickers to the orphans. I expressed my desire to manifest my vision and write a book that would inspire people to courageously step into the direction of their dreams and realize their potential.

I was so engaged in my explanation—I could feel the passion oozing out of me—that I didn't notice their reactions until I finished my explanation. All three of them stared at me with a look of astonishment. When I uttered my last word, silence filled the room. I felt the weight of the three of them staring at me with a powerful look shimmering in their eyes. I could only hear the sound of the waves washing up on the shore. Their faces, along with the silence following my monologue, spoke louder than words could. My sense of purpose expanded.

All three of them voiced their excitement for me, revealing that they felt inspired from just hearing my story. For hours, we stayed on the porch, delving into subjects about worldly affairs and how we aspired to go after our dreams. John, in his early sixties, Lauren and Skye, in their late twenties, and me, at eighteen, talked endlessly, springing from one topic to the next, passion coursing through us all. We were the last ones in the lounge area, which had been filled with people when we arrived. We planned to meet in the morning and walk over to Los Abrazos.

When I climbed into bed that night, I couldn't close my eyes. I was pulsing with adrenaline, and sleep was the last thing on my mind. I tried falling asleep but quickly brushed off the idea, acknowledging that sleeping in my current state was near impossible. I was wide awake. A lively buzz stirred through my chest, and I lay in bed until sunrise, unable to stop thinking about the wonders of the world.

"The two most important days in your life are the day you are born and the day you find out why."

—Mark Twain

CHAPTER 26

Triumph over Tragedy

May 12, 2015

"The people who are crazy enough to think they can
change the world are the ones who do."
—Steve Jobs

My last few days in Guatemala were spent hanging with my friends at the hostel and with Arnulfo and his family. I seriously considered canceling my flight to Nicaragua and staying in San Marcos longer. My relationships with Arnulfo and my friends had grown so deep, I felt like I had known them for years. The thought of leaving them, the beauty of Lake Atitlan, and the wondrous vortex of energy in San Marcos made me sad. But I realized that this was a bittersweet component of backpacking and an inseparable part of the package. The circumstances involved in vagabonding from place to place create a dynamic for relationships to grow rapidly. That you come and leave a place in a relatively short time frame is an inevitable part of travel, but the beauty of each relationship and experience stays with you. I smiled at this realization, feeling thankful for my experiences in San Marcos, and knowing that I would carry them with me like a badge on my chest, intangibly woven into my heart.

I knew that Nicaragua held treasures for me that I would soon discover. As torn as I was to leave, I was excited about the unknown path ahead. Experiencing a new place, a new world with different people, made me feel like a child. Each new aspect of the Universe wowed me and expanded my horizon of what I thought was possible, of what existed. Like a child, I was approaching these vastly different experiences with open-mindedness. Each day brought new stimuli, new astonishing realities of the world that required my mind to be fully awake. Accepting the world as I was experiencing it revived my childlike spirit and generated an impassioned curiosity about the world and its boundless wonders.

* * * * *

In the shuttle van from Lake Atitlan to Antigua—which was a stop on the way to the airport—there was a group of six Australians. They were extremely noisy and obnoxiously loud, and they spoke as if they were yelling across the street to each other. I couldn't help but listen to their conversations. They were still drunk from the night before where they were at the "top party hostel in Lake Atitlan." They had been in Guatemala for two weeks and were heading to another party hostel in Antigua. In the first thirty minutes, they made the driver pull over to the side of the road twice. Three of the girls got out and vomited while their other friends laughed and took pictures of them. They all squealed in shock as a few pigs and chickens crossed the road, which I found surprising. *You've been here two weeks and you're honestly freaking out over pigs and chickens? Did you even leave your hostel?*

I wasn't sure what it was about these people that irritated me. Maybe it was their lack of respect for the driver or the local customs. Or maybe it was the fact that not too long ago, I too enjoyed getting hammered and partying nonstop. I didn't know why I felt both threatened and repulsed by them. I had this view of luxury travelers as pompous and ungrateful whose sole purpose was to get drunk and not even bother to experience the culture. But they were doing nothing wrong. They were simply having fun. I realized that what I was repelled by was a reflection of my past self. They resembled me in many ways and were revealing a facet of my own past that was now thousands of miles away.

I remember sitting at the kitchen table with my mom when I was nine years old hysterically crying after watching a movie that detailed extreme poverty in various parts of the world. I felt horrified and upset and sad and angry. But I also felt guilty. And this guilt crept up and stayed with me my entire life. I felt guilty that I was raised in a family who loved me. I felt guilty that I never had to worry about affording my next meal or the cost to play soccer. This guilt had eaten away at me for as long as I could remember. *It's as if I'm wrong, I'm faulted—that I don't deserve what I have because so many people have it worse. How can I have fun and enjoy these aspects of my life that are denied to millions of other people? Why me? Why am I lucky enough to be born into these resources? I never chose this, but it's my fault.*

As a child, I felt a calling, this intangible voice—not even a voice, just this message—that people needed help. It's as if I were the hope for the kids I cried for when I was nine years old sitting at the kitchen table. It's as if I had this inexplicable understanding embedded within my soul of their suffering, an empathy that existed simultaneously with my guilt. I've always believed I was put on this earth to make a difference and had the power to make an impact. I never said it aloud to anyone. It even sounded ridiculously cheesy when I said it to myself. But I felt it, this unwavering conviction that I could change the world.

I wondered if my time in San Marcos was my wake-up call, the Universe reminding me of my potential to make a difference: the power I have within me to instill hope and inspiration into the lives of those suffering and lacking the basic necessities that every human being should have.

* * * * *

Soaring through the air en route to Nicaragua, I finished Arnulfo's book, *The Light of the Soul.* As I read the final page, goose bumps formed on my arms, and hairs shot up on the back of my neck. I learned in his book that Arnulfo had grown up deaf, blind, and unable to speak for the first few years of his life. But from an early age, Arnulfo knew he had a gift unfathomable by the human imagination—a force he calls *Abuelo* or "Grandfather"—that guided him during this challenging time and showed him the light of the world.

One day, inexplicably, he awoke with the ability to see, hear, and speak. He detailed life growing up in the Guatemalan genocide and explained a brutally traumatic incident that shaped the rest of his life. When he was eight years old, he was dragged out of his home by two barbarous soldiers who threw him into a deep well along with 115 other children from his village. After having gasoline poured on them, they were left in the dark, cold well to die. Three days later, a woman pulled him out and saved him. He was the only one who made it out alive. Arnulfo transformed this tragic experience into motivation for his life mission, finding the strength and inner light to lead a revolution of justice. He has dedicated his life to helping the oppressed indigenous people, to give his love in the form of food, medicine, homes, and teaching.

I held back my tears while experiencing a flurry of emotions: confusion and inspiration, bewilderment and empowerment, sadness and hope. How could one man turn such a traumatic childhood into fuel for bringing peace and kindness to the world? How could one man sacrifice his sleep in order to use that time to feed and heal others?

Struggling is universal. We all have challenges. Yet there are some people, like Arnulfo, who can find a way to turn their suffering into a powerful, positive force. By giving meaning to our challenges and hardships, we can find the light through any darkness. Arnulfo is proof of that. I carry this lesson with me, empowered by his triumph over tragedy.

"Never to suffer would never to have been blessed."
—Edgar Allen Poe

CHAPTER 27

One with the Land

May 15, 2015

"There is pleasure in the pathless woods, there is rapture in the lonely shore, there is society where none intrudes, by the deep sea, and music in its roar; I love not Man the less, but Nature more."

—Lord Byron

After landing on the ground in Nicaragua, I grabbed a taxi to the bus station. Gabe's directions were as follows: "To get there, you take a bus from the Mercadito in Leon to Poneloya. Then you go to *la rambla* to cross in *la isla los brasiles*. On the other side, you follow the sign for the Surfing Turtle Lodge. After you pass it, you keep going for ten minutes, and you will see a Carpe Diem sign on your left side. That's pretty much it."

These directions, while seemingly straightforward, appeared ridiculously unclear to me as he rattled off a bunch of names and places I had never heard of. On top of that, I had no phone to guide me. But I knew, just as I had in my travels in Guatemala, I would get there eventually. I just didn't know exactly how.

On the way to the Mercadito bus station, we passed though the slums of Managua. Trash covered the grimy sidewalks, and rusty, wooden huts bordered the streets. The small huts were filthy on the outside, splintered and splotched in dusty grays, mucky browns, and faded blacks. Young children were running around in tattered clothing covered in dirt and stains. Despite the sewage splattered on the streets, the chipped landscapes, and grim circumstances, the children laughed and pranced around. I didn't know whether to smile or frown.

I arrived at the bus station and boarded a *colectivo* van with about ten other people, all appearing Nicaraguan. Luckily, it was only a two-hour ride to Leon, and it went by in a flash. From there, a young man practically lured me into his three-wheeled bicycle after he asked where I needed to go. I hopped in the backseat, not contemplating another possible method of transportation, and he cycled away. In less than ten minutes, we arrived at the Poneloya bus station. I thanked the bicyclist and paid him. After asking around, I was escorted to the chicken bus that would lead to the drop-off near the Surfing Turtle Lodge. No one seemed to know of Carpe Diem, but when I asked the locals about the Surfing Turtle Lodge, they nodded their heads in understanding. This reassured me.

The bus rumbled along, stopping every minute or so to drop off or pick up someone. Finally, the driver announced that we'd arrived at the last stop. I stared out the window. The paved road ended, transitioning into a dirt road with small wooden buildings and huts on the left, jungle and trees to the right. I pulled out the brochure for the Surfing Turtle Lodge that my bicycle driver had given me. I hoisted my backpack on and walked over to the bus driver. I greeted him with a wide smile, the one I always wore whenever I was lost or confused. I pointed to the brochure, and he nodded. He pointed down the road and motioned with his hand that I needed to walk from here. I thanked him and stepped off the bus.

I was smothered by a searing haze of heat the second I stepped out into the open air. The contact of my shoes on the dusty ground kicked up a whirlwind of filth, which caked onto my legs and flew into my face. Others who had left the bus were heading in the opposite direction. I really wished I had a phone or someone to help me navigate. I inhaled deeply, feeling my chest expand with worries of how the hell I would get to this place that was nowhere in sight. "Huhhhh." I exhaled, blowing out warm air while trying to release my fears as well. I started walking north in the direction the bus driver had pointed.

I've never been good with directions; in fact, I'm probably the worst person I know when it comes to having a geographical sense of direction. Considering the present circumstance, I didn't know whether this was ironic or if I were flat-out stupid for putting myself in this position. Back home, I usually relied on others for directions. I figured that since someone else was with me, that person was paying attention, and I didn't have to. When I was on my own, I often got lost, whether it was driving or walking somewhere.

Walking alone on this dirt road in the scorching heat, I started to laugh aloud. So badly did I wish to be lost in my *own* country. I actually found it hilarious how stressed I had been in the past when I had been lost in San Diego because it paled in comparison to my current situation. The sound of English teased my mind. When you're alone, you can't rely on anyone except yourself. You are forced to be fully present and alert. Your intuition is your sole guide. However, this is enough. It had to be as it was all I had as I trudged along this seemingly deserted path.

I came across a woman standing outside one of the wooden huts I passed by on the road. I greeted her cheerfully and asked if she knew where the Surfing Turtle Lodge was, fully expecting her to say no. The idea that a hostel could be out here didn't seem possible. To my surprise, she nodded yes and pointed in the direction I was walking. She signaled that the ocean was only a few hundred yards to my left and informed me that soon I would reach a restaurant where I needed to take a small boat to the peninsula where the hostel was located. I thanked her and continued marching onward.

I practically jumped for joy when I reached the restaurant with the boat. There were two young Nicaraguan kids and an older man standing by the boat. I approached them and asked if they knew of Carpe Diem. The young boy shot his hand up in acknowledgement and said he lived right next to Carpe Diem and knew everyone there. I sighed the biggest sigh of relief.

The man motioned for me to hop in, and I climbed in the small rickety, wooden boat. The boy's name was Pablo, and he was ten. He was dark, much darker than any of the people I had met in Guatemala—a merlot shade. He had thin, ink-black hair that rose to a spike in front and dense, black eyes that glistened whenever he smiled. His older sister, Michaela, was twelve and had the same skin. She had beautiful black hair that reminded me of Pocahontas. She was cheerful but firm as she managed to keep her spunky brother in check.

When we arrived on land a few minutes later, we climbed out of the boat and lifted all of the boxes out. A man with a horse and carriage was waiting, but it looked nothing like that in a *Cinderella* movie. The carriage was a faded, chipped, gray crate on beaten-down wheels. The horse was a mix between white and gray and covered in spots like polka dots. Pablo practically bounced onto the horse with no saddle. He petted the horse's mane and whispered something in its ear. Michaela and I lifted the boxes onto the crate and hopped in. The adults stepped into the boat and headed back in the direction from which we had come. Pablo directed the horse with ease. I was fascinated by how comfortable he was with this massive, elegant animal. It was completely normal to him but amazing to me. We bumbled along a dirt-paved trail surrounded by the shade of the towering trees above us. While I could hear the wisp of the waves far off to my left, a slight rise in the landscape blocked my view of the ocean. It was peculiar to me that there could be jungle so close to the sea.

We eventually came upon a large dirt opening, and I noticed a wooden sign elegantly painted with the words, "Carpe Diem: Come and Visit." A line of colorful tents shaded by trees and various other items that you would expect to find at a camping site were scattered about: water jugs, a fire pit, and clotheslines hanging from trees. A group of people sat to the right of the tents in what looked like a "hangout zone." Others sat on big, plastic, pink bags filled with hay that circled the fire pit. The bags were slightly bigger than pillows but much bulkier as they were jam-packed with hay. I walked over to the group of people to introduce myself. There were eight of them, and they all looked fatigued, covered in dirt and sweat, their faces red from exhaustion.

"Hi, I'm Jake," I announced. I could feel them all staring at me, and the group's full attention embarrassed me.

They all warmly introduced themselves, and I immediately forgot every single one of their names, except for Gabe. They had just finished the day's volunteering to help build the eco-lodge, which explained their exhaustion and mud-covered bodies. Gabe got up to show me around, escorting me to a vacant tent where I dropped off my backpack. Before coming, I told him I didn't have a tent, and he had said he had one for me. I quickly looked inside only to see a thin, raggedy-yellow matt covered in dirt and a bunch of bugs crawling around. Whoever slept there last clearly didn't zip up the tent. I took a big gulp, figuring that I would worry about what creatures were in there later.

Gabe was from Quebec and had an interesting French accent. He had thin, Havana-brown hair that rose up in the front and a small beard and mustache. His tank top revealed he was lean but strong. He had a reddish tan from the sun, and a few freckles dotted his face.

We walked over to the compost toilet, which was surrounded by a circular black tarp. It was just like the compost toilet in the Guatemalan jungle except that it had a wooden covering over the hole so a million bugs were not flying around. Gabe then escorted me to a handmade contraption that simply blew my mind. It was a makeshift shower. A large water tank rested above a handmade wooden platform twelve feet above the ground and about four feet in width and length. A green tarp covered the platform, serving as a shower curtain. A bicycle rested on the ground upside down, the front wheel missing. The back wheel had a rope attached around it that slithered up to the wooden platform, connecting to the water tank in a figure eight. Gabe pulled the rope, which went continuously in a figure-eight loop, down the bicycle wheel, and up to the water tank. He informed me that by pulling the rope, water was pumped into the faucet, which could be turned on inside the "shower." I had not the slightest idea how the mechanics of this contraption worked; nonetheless, I was awestruck by its ingenuity. He brought me to the kitchen, which was a wooden table made from thin branches and sticks. A water jug rested on it along with other utensils that hung from a wooden shelf.

After being shown around, I strolled over toward the hangout area and plopped down on one of the pink bags of hay. Pablo and Michaela were sitting there, joking and laughing with the others. They asked me in the most innocent voices if I wanted to swim in the ocean with them. I accepted the invitation and followed them as they skipped with delight. We walked west for about five minutes through marshes and brush. As we approached the vast blue sea, I practically sprinted in, salivating at the thought of the refreshing water.

The water was warm, surprisingly so. I could taste the saltiness as I swayed back and forth. Feeling rejuvenated and clean, we headed back to camp. Pablo and Michaela lived right next to our camp, and their small home had the classic tin roof that I had seen throughout Guatemala. It was obvious the way the kids joked around with Gabe that they had a strong relationship with him.

Back at camp, we all helped prepare dinner as the sun was setting. I broke up branches and put them into the fire underneath the rocket stove. After I collected enough firewood, I wandered toward the hangout area and plopped down on the couch, which was made of two bags of hay lying next to each other with a couple of bags perched up on a few wooden branches to create a backrest. I looked down and noticed a bunch of little red dots on my legs. As I looked closer, I saw tons of them along with little black flies the size of grains of sand swarming around my legs. I counted eighty bites on my left leg alone just from my toe to my knee. The other volunteers informed me they were sand flies, and that they always came out around sunset.

"They prefer to bite some people more than others," Gabe informed me. "I guess you have tasty blood."

I gulped at this notion, uneasily laughing at Gabe's comment. My mind had built up an anxious response to whenever my skin became irritated whether from bug bites or something else. The fear that it could turn into something much worse loomed large. I covered my legs in bug spray, but to no avail. The bugs finally seemed to go away after a while, but they had left their mark. My legs were covered in bites. One of the other volunteers sat next to me and showed me his arms and legs, which were also covered with bites. That eased my mind—knowing I wasn't the only one.

One of the most difficult aspects of having sensitive skin is the feeling of isolation that results from having skin irritations or reactions. My mind conjured up this notion that I was uniquely prone to this problem, that it was something only I had and no one else. It was an insecurity of mine; this feeling that only I experienced skin problems isolated me from others. Knowing I had this sensitivity made me feel inferior. But the power of *knowing* that *someone else* was going through a similar experience lifted my spirits. It reminded me that everyone has his or her own "skin problem"—whether it is in the form of a health condition, a tragic experience, an insecurity, or a struggle. Not talking about it and pretending like *only I* had this condition made me feel secluded. When I finally accepted and acknowledged that other people have similar problems, I felt my worries abate. I no longer felt alone.

We all devoured our plates of rice and vegetables as we sat around the fire. It was totally dark. My eyes were adjusting to the absence of street lamps and restaurant lights. There was nothing out here except the flames of the fire. My meager, three-inch flashlight didn't provide much light in the darkness, either. After dinner, I rose to wash up and brush my teeth. Gabe informed me that we would start working on the eco-lodge in the morning around seven, and that he would provide instructions on how to proceed. I was exhausted from the full day's journey, and everyone else looked exhausted as well.

I said good night and headed over to my tent. The tent felt like a sauna, and I was dripping in sweat. I could feel the sand and dirt on my mat seeping into my heated skin, the grains of sand sticking to my forearms and bare back. The scorching heat, along with the tingling of ants crawling on my legs and the itchy sand fly bites, made it difficult to fall asleep. I had expected the temperature to drop at night, but it seemed magnified inside my apparently heat-absorbing tent. Gabe informed us that at noon it was 39 degrees Celsius, over 102 degrees Fahrenheit.

I lay there contemplating how uncomfortable I was. The idea that I could sleep was a joke. I remembered the night I was sick in the jungle, which made me feel slightly better. Anything was better than that night. I finally drifted off into a fitful sleep.

* * * * *

The next morning, we gathered at seven to start building. Zak, one of the volunteers, showed me how to make *cob*, the material being used to construct the eco-lodge. Zak had dreadlocks and a slender frame and was a little taller than six feet. He had learned how to use cob for sustainable building at a school in Oregon. Cob is a natural building material composed of soil, sand, water, and straw. It is sturdy, has minimal environmental impact, and is very inexpensive.

Zak laid out a big blue tarp on the ground, grabbed a plastic sandbag, a bucket of soil, and showed me the correct proportions to use. He poured each onto the tarp and then added some water. He then grabbed both ends of the tarp and started walking in one direction with both ends in his hand, the mixture hot-dogged in the middle. This caused the materials to flip on top of each other. He then reversed direction in order to further mix up the sand and soil. After doing this multiple times, he pressed his feet and stomped on the muddy mixture in an effort to fully blend the materials. After stomping for a few minutes, he had me scoop up a ball of the mixture in my hands to feel the texture. Once the mixture was of this consistency, he instructed me to add straw to it, which functioned like natural glue. There was an enormous pile of straw to our left, and we both grabbed an armful, tossing it into the mixture. I joined him in stomping.

The stiff, slightly moist, muddy texture crumpled as my toes and heels pressed down, flattening it out. It was by no means soft, yet felt soothing. We then grabbed both ends of the tarp and flipped the mixture again, continuing to stomp. Finally, he had me grab the mixture again to feel the texture, signaling that it was ready. He instructed me to gather a ball the size of a bowling ball and to try to pull it apart in two pieces. The ball didn't budge. It was dense and thick and sturdy and couldn't be pulled apart. It was ready. We rolled our cob mixture into the size of about fifteen bowling balls and then brought them over to the structure of the first hut.

The base layer of the eco-hut was a large circle the size of a small hotel room stacked roughly three feet high with sandbags. Two wooden doorframes stood on each side of the circle, and cob was being put on top of the sandbags. The other volunteers were all creating their own batches of cob—dancing on the mixtures, flipping the tarp, or rolling the cob into balls. Zak called for everyone to form an assembly line to the structure. I tossed the ball to Zak, who tossed it to the next person, and so on and so forth until the ball finally reached the structure and was pressed into it.

We spent the next few hours repeating this cycle. The mud felt good on my feet, and I rubbed it over my bare chest, embracing the dirt. The sun's heavy rays beat down strongly on my shoulders and back, and the cob felt cool against my heels. I wiggled my feet in the sludgy material, feeling the grains of soil and sand gush between my toes. Feeling one with the earth beneath my feet, I stomped around, dancing in a circle. The rhythm of my stomps and each step in the cob-creation cycle became second nature to me. I found my mind wandering freely in each step, getting lost in each movement.

The hands-on—or, I should say, "feet-on"— work was oddly peaceful. Exerting physical energy and moving each limb and each finger to mold the mixture into a ball of cob infused me with a wholeness that my entire body embraced. I had become so adjusted to the efficiency of technology that the whole atmosphere of making cob and camping fostered a wakening sensation. Gathering firewood instead of using gasoline, heating food with fire and not a microwave, pumping a rope for water to shower—I was returning to my roots as a human and was being reminded of how wonderful it was to have a fully functioning body. Advancements in technology make it so easy *not to do* things. Yet *doing things* instills a sense of being alive. The action of *doing* connected me with the earth, and fully participating in nature infused me with energy.

After four hours of work, we plopped down in the hangout area and scarfed down a meal of tortillas, beans, cheese, and eggs. I lay immersed in a stack of hay covered in sticky mud from head to toe and syrupy in sweat. I now knew how the others felt the day before when I had arrived.

We sat in the hangout area unable to move. The bags of hay felt like the most comfortable cushions in the world. There was a navy-blue, old-school, acoustic guitar lying around, and one of the volunteers picked it up. He strummed and sang tunes by the Doors, the Beatles, and Bob Marley. I smiled, enjoying the calming music. The melodies resonated with me, and my chest vibrated to the guitar's jubilant frequencies. Music had become a treasure to me. Since I was traveling without a phone or an iPod, I only heard the sounds of the road, the whispering wind, and the murmurs of conversation. No radio blaring, no Pandora stations or playlists to become immersed in. This absence instilled in me a new, profound appreciation for the sounds of music.

After sitting for a few hours, we took a dip in the ocean to wash off and freshen up. I scrubbed the dried dirt off my arms, legs, chest and back. I waded out of the water and onto shore, feeling renewed.

The next two days were more or less the same. We awoke early and started working on the cob in an effort to beat the day's brutal maximum heat, which usually peaked around noon. The next two nights were no better than the first. The boiling temperature didn't abate, and I had hundreds of sand fly bites all over my legs and arms. I woke up soaked in sweat and dirt, sand glued to my back and everywhere else on my body.

As kind as everybody was, and as cool as it was making cob and camping, I couldn't ignore a hunch in my gut telling me that another adventure awaited. One of the volunteers had informed me of a cloud forest up in the mountains near a town called Matagalpa, only a three-hour bus ride from Leon. The thought of cool, misty air and breezy mountains left me yearning to explore the mysterious cloud forests and natural beauties of the Nicaraguan mountains. A feeling of independence was brewing in me—I felt confident that by listening to my intuition and keeping an open mind, exciting times lay ahead.

After four days at Carpe Diem, I said good-bye to the volunteers and thanked Gabe for having me. Leaving the small island, I felt an intangible link of connectedness with the earth coursing through my veins. My time here reminded me how wonderful it is to walk, to breathe, to move my hands and fingers and legs and toes. Instead of trying to avoid getting dirty, I learned to embrace it. Despite the scorching heat and biting flies, the external beauty of the campsite expanded my inner awareness. My interaction with the dirt and trees and sea allowed me to look inward, to accept what was in front of me, and to feel whole. I couldn't quite put my finger on what was so special about camping—whether it was the physicality of living hand in hand with nature or the mystical array of sensory detail—I did not know. What I did know is that I left with something more. I had strengthened, or maybe just uncovered, my inherent relationship with the world—that I was part of it, and it was part of me.

"In every walk with nature one receives far more than he seeks."
—John Muir

CHAPTER 28

Faith in Hitchhiking, Relinquishing Control

May 19, 2015

"Ask, and it shall be given you; seek, and ye shall find; knock, and it shall be opened into you."

—Luke 11:9

I arrived in Matagalpa in the afternoon. The temperature was much cooler than in Leon but still warm. From the bus station, I took a taxi to a hostel that the driver recommended. Eager to put my bag down and settle in, I scurried to the front desk. To my surprise, the hostel was full. Just to check if I had heard correctly, I asked again, "Wait, so there is no room?" She shook her head sideways. I asked her if she knew of any other hostels, and she told me about one a few blocks away. I thanked her and walked out, feeling defeated and confused. The volunteers at Carpe Diem had explained that Matagalpa was off the beaten trail. I hadn't considered that the hostel could be full. I had expected to walk right in, find an open bed, and strike up conversations with other travelers. I would then make a plan to go with them to explore the natural reserves that were nearby. That vision had played out beautifully in my head.

Of course, life doesn't usually play out how we think it will. The directions the woman had given me were something along the lines of, "Take a left, then walk two blocks, then hook a right, and then another left." It was about as clear to me as the perplexing graphs in my economics class. I spent the next hour roaming the town, convinced that each next turn would lead me to the hostel's front steps. I asked three people on the street for directions only to get three different answers.

My shoulders throbbed from the weight of the backpack, which was sticking to my drenched shirt. My mind was exhausted as well, probably from making so many 360-degree turns. A taxi turned the corner and skidded down the street in my direction. I shot my hand up in the air and waved him down. He pulled his car to a stop, and I asked him if he knew of any hostels close by. He lifted his hand, pointing his finger right past my head. For a second, I thought he misunderstood the question. *No, you don't understand, sir. I need to find a hostel, you know, a place to sleep? I don't speak Spanish that well. Sorry if I'm pronouncing this wrong.* I repeated my question, and he lifted his hand again, urging me to turn around. I swiveled my head around, and just ten feet to my right was a bright-orange building with the sign, "Hostal Martina's Place." I laughed out loud, thanked the driver, and joyfully trudged over toward the hostel. It's funny how the things in life we are searching for are often right in front of us. Sometimes, we're just too close to see them.

I crossed my fingers, praying there would be room for me in this hostel. I knocked on the door and waited for a response. Silence. I knocked again, this time a little harder. Each second I stood there felt like an hour. Finally, I heard someone unlock the door and swing it open. A woman stood there, and I gave her a big smile, asking if I could get a room.

"Of course!" she said in English. My heart practically melted in relief. "There are no other people staying here right now."

"Really?" I asked in a high voice, my eyebrows scrunching downward in confusion.

"Yes," she responded. "But we are happy to have you here."

"Thank you," I replied. She escorted me to a huge room filled with over twenty empty bunk beds. The blankets on each bed were in charming pastel colors in a plaid pattern, each one without a single wrinkle. I paused for a moment unsure of which bed to choose. I was overwhelmed with choices, a stark contrast to the other hostels in which I had stayed in. I set my backpack down and took a shower. It was a proper shower with a fully functioning nozzle—and hot water! I basked in the warm water, absorbing each and every drop. It had been over two months since I had taken a warm shower, and I had forgotten how pleasurable it was. I finally forced myself out of the shower and dried off, my fingers now looking like prunes.

The room was completely still—so silent that it was almost loud. My eyes gazed from one vacant bed to the next, examining the empty space. The bed that I was sitting on felt small. It was actually a nice-sized bed for a hostel. Yet the lack of movement, the lack of voices, and the lack of a presence in the room made it feel very disconnected. I craved the company of a companion, someone else to talk to, someone else to make plans with to explore the cloud forest. I thought about my family back home and wondered how my dad was doing. I wondered whether I had made the right decision to come here. I wondered if it was a sign that the other hostel was full and that I was here on my own. I wondered if I was losing my ability to embrace and enjoy being alone with only my thoughts.

I got up and walked to the front desk. I asked about the natural reserves and cloud forests that were apparently in close proximity to Matagalpa. The same lady who had let me in handed me some pamphlets that described the beautiful reserves and mountain landscapes. I couldn't peel my eyes away from one brochure that showed *Selva Negra*, a lush 300-acre cloud forest jungle with countless trees, rainbow-colored birds, and monkeys. The pictures in the pamphlet were calling out to me and the description said that anyone could come and hike the trails for free. I decided to head out in the morning to explore the wonders of the forest. The woman at the front desk gave me a schedule of the bus times and explained how to get there. Even in English, the directions she gave weren't straightforward. It wasn't that her instructions were unclear; it was that the nature of getting there was not as simple as going from point A to point B. But I wanted to go—the pictures of the stunning jungle called to me. I would go, alone, and I would make the best of it.

* * * * *

In the late morning, a taxi picked me up from the hostel and drove me to the bus station. I brought my small day pack with a water bottle, a lightweight rain jacket, a little bit of cash, and my camera. I boarded a bus that was heading to the town of Jinotega, roughly an hour away, although I planned to get off around the halfway point near the Selva Negra reserve. I showed the bus driver the Selva Negra brochure and he nodded in acknowledgement, reassuring me that he would make an announcement when we arrived there. The reserve was then just over one mile away from where the bus would stop.

People climbed aboard and piled into each seat. The musty air emitted a pervading odor of corn. Two women stepped onto the bus carrying dozens of plastic bags filled with food.

"*Queso, queso, queso!*" "*Tamale con pollo, tamale con pollo!*" They paraded up and down the aisle, blaring out the names of food they were selling and squishing people as they slid by. They reminded me of those ticket vendors portrayed in the movies, "Get your ticket here! Get your ticket here!" I had become accustomed to these vendors and to the over packed buses with people standing in the aisle, and sometimes sitting on the roof. The drivers earned money based on how many passengers they had on board, so they never turned anyone away.

As the engine roared to life, my legs vibrated, shaking my entire body. The vendors left, and the bus eased out of the station and up toward the mountains. The short, sharp streets turned into long, open roads. Buildings and people were replaced with a vast landscape of trees packed together in an endless brush of green. As we traveled up the mountains, a thick, misty fog rolled in. The cool air wisped through the window and against my face. Just as I was beginning to relax, staring out at the cloudy, mystical countryside, the bus pulled over to the side of the road.

"*Selva Negra! Selva Negra!*" the bus driver barked. I shot up, maneuvering by the people standing in the aisle, and approached the front of the bus. I looked back, my eyes meeting a sea of Nicaraguan faces. I was the only person to get up. Everyone else was apparently heading to Jinotega. I stepped onto the asphalt road, and the bus grumbled off, winding up and away from sight. A bird's far-off chirp rang clearly in my ears. I turned away from the deserted road, hearing only my shoes pivot on the ground beneath me. My eyes caught sight of a large blue banner with the words, "*Bienvenidos Selva Negra,*" or "Welcome to Selva Negra." An arrow pointed down a gravel trail, signaling the reserve was two kilometers away, roughly one mile.

I began my march toward the reserve. A wall of trees in varying shades of green bordered the trail. The fallen leaves rustled in the wind, and the freshness of misty air was a pleasant contrast to the roasting heat in Leon. I inhaled the calming aroma of bark and grass and trees and plants. Nature's company awakened me as I strolled down the trail, curiously observing the unusual curvy trees and spiky plants.

The road seemed endless; each turn revealed more gravel and greenery. I didn't mind it, though. The scenery was calming. I was alone but didn't feel so anymore. The trail finally opened up, and a wide, wooden building lay before me. Behind it, a giant lake stood completely still, not a single wave rippling on the entire surface. A stunning array of rich jungle layered beyond it, rising into the mountain with a thick, misty, mushroom ring of fog. Snow-white geese with bright-orange beaks roamed around the lake. Not even the faintest sound of a car or a person could be heard, only the soft whir of wind. I approached the wooden building and was about to walk inside when someone greeted me.

"Hi, there. Are you looking for something?" a man asked. He was dressed in a gray uniform and had a walky-talky radio hanging from his pants. I assumed he was a park ranger.

"Hello. Yes, I'd like to hike some of the trails up in the cloud forest."

"You have a few options. You can hire an experienced guide who can take you through the trails. You can pay for a horseback ride through one of the lower, flat trails. Or, if you don't want to pay, you are free to roam the trails on your own."

I contemplated my options. A guide would be nice, but I didn't have the money for what he was asking. Plus, I didn't want to limit my time to less than two hours, which is what going with the guide entailed. As much as I would have loved to ride a horse, that, too, was beyond my price range. That left going it alone.

"Do people often hike the trails alone?" I asked in a hopeful tone.

"Yes, well, sometimes," the guide responded, rising his shoulders and then shrugging. "Most people hire a guide, but we definitely have had people go explore on their own. I can give you a map of the trails if you would like to go alone."

If other people went alone, I can, too. I was silent for a moment, the gears spinning in my mind as I contemplated what to do.

"Yes, can I get a map? I think I'll go alone."

"Yes, of course." He pulled out a white sheet of paper and handed it to me. He pointed to the various trails on the map, informing me which trails were longer and more difficult and which ones were shorter and easier. "Here is the phone number of the reserve in case anything happens."

"Oh, thanks, but I'm okay. I don't have a phone," I declared matter-of-factly. He looked at me as if he were expecting me to continue. "I don't need a phone, right?"

"No, you don't need one. Just be careful. There are some poisonous snakes that live in the reserve, so be aware. And it's very slippery, especially as you get higher up. No one will be able to hear you once you're up there."

His warning rang loudly and clearly, each word magnified in my ears. *No one will be able to hear you once you're up there.* I felt my mouth drying up, and I swallowed a large gulp.

"Thank you," I replied, half wishing I hadn't heard what he had said. My burning curiosity to explore the cloud forest was now mixed with hesitation.

I began the trail wary of every step I was taking. I chose to take one of the longer trails, which was approximately a three-hour trek to the top of the cloud forest and back. I followed the signs leading toward the top. I picked up a fallen branch on the ground and used it as a walking stick to warn any snakes that might be lingering in my path. My eyes were peeled open and my senses alert. For the first few minutes, I barely lifted my head. I was so paranoid with the fear of being attacked by a snake that I wasn't absorbing the beauty around me. I pictured Cheryl Strayed hiking the Pacific Crest Trail alone, her words of wisdom ringing in my head: "Fear, to a great extent, is born of a story we tell ourselves. Fear begets fear. Power begets power."

I chose to tell myself a different story, not one of fear and snakes, but one of wonder and awe. Before long, my muscles eased up, and my tense grip on the stick lightened. I lifted my head, amazed by the scenery around me. Flowers beamed in a rainbow of color: ruby reds and amber yellows shone among the bed of green. Because it was a cloud forest, a misty fog filled the air. The green plants and trees glowed as the moisture from the clouds breathed water and life into the surrounding landscape.

The story of fear that we project in our minds can consume our full attention. It controls our thoughts and dominates our perceptions. Only when we overcome this story of fear and integrate a new story—a story of power, a story of fascination, a story of confidence—do we begin to notice the finer details that are present. Beauty resides in every picture, yet, with a perspective constructed of negative thoughts, it is easy to miss.

My senses were fully awake. Each smell stirred my fascination. Each twig of birch that brushed against my skin tickled me and reminded me of its presence. Each twitter of birds that I could hear but not see spiked my curiosity. Each shade of green—bright or light, shiny or dark—lit up in my eyes. I was not just walking in nature—nature was breathing in me. The sound of my own breath echoed, each huff and puff of oxygen resounded in the quiet air. The vibrant life thriving around me was my company. I was fulfilled by the presence of the natural elements. I couldn't grasp what it was about being in nature that was so calming. The mysticism, the authentic noises, the rainbow of color, and the enticing smells—they all created a feeling of tranquility, an assurance that everything was going to be fine. Alone or with others, morning or evening, hot or cold, it didn't matter. The forest provided answers to questions I hadn't even been aware of.

As I hiked onward, the trail began to steepen. The calming drizzle turned into a steady rain, and the ground beneath me became slippery and muddy. The fog thickened; a dense cloud was moving in, darkening the atmosphere as if the sun were setting. My ankles stiffened, and my calves flexed with each step, which now required more balance and stability. The outline of the trail was becoming more difficult to see, and branches jutted out into my path, forcing me to duck under them. Fallen logs also lay across the path; I had to focus intently as I hopped over them in order to keep from falling.

As I climbed up, squatting to avoid the porcupine of overhanging branches, my feet slipped out from under me. I slid backward a few feet, drenched in mud. I lifted myself off the ground, shocked at how quickly the ground had escaped from beneath me. My legs were brown, and my shoes were blanketed in a layer of sludge. I continued upward, more careful than ever of traversing the unpredictable ground.

After what felt like just a minute later, I slipped again. Instinctively, I extended my hands in front of me to brace my fall. I was caked in mud; the raindrops were now falling with more weight and speed, and the fog was becoming denser and the trail less clear. My muscles ached from having to keep my balance on the uneven ground. The park ranger's warning words rang in my mind: *if I hurt myself, "no one would be able to hear me," let alone help me.* The thought that I was all alone drifted into my head and I decided to head back.

I descended in the direction from which I had come. I pulled the map, which I had yet to use, out of my backpack. My muddy hands smeared the white paper, painting it with smudges of chocolate brown. The map didn't contribute any helpful information, at least to my amateur, map-orienting skills. I hadn't followed it on the way up, and I figured I would find my way back eventually. I shook my head, and felt a mixture of amusement and frustration at my inadequate sense of direction. *Just head downward. You know that is at least the right direction.* The trail started to open up again, the haze of fog lessened, and light began to slowly permeate the air. The raindrops dwindled as well, although I was already drenched and didn't mind. The familiar flowers and plants that I had passed on the way up the trail came into view.

A red bird-of-paradise grabbed my attention. It shone distinctly, a lone red flower among an abyss of green. It had three pointed spikes configured like a profound sculpture by Michelangelo. It reminded me that the people who shine the brightest are those who accept themselves as they are. Those who follow their inner voice and embrace their own true path are the red-shining flowers among a sea of green. Ralph Waldo Emerson's words stirred in my mind. *"To be yourself in a world that is constantly trying to make you something else is the greatest accomplishment."* This red flower filled me with energy and confidence. Yes, I was alone, but I was empowered. Literally and physically, I was on a path less traveled. And it felt amazing. Despite my anxiety and apprehension about how others perceived my choices, I knew that this entire journey made sense to me in my own heart. I felt a release; the weight of others' expectations dropped out of me like the falling raindrops.

I ended up back at the wooden building, which was actually a small eco-lodge. I cleaned off in the bathroom, surprised to see mud smeared on my forehead and cheeks. I ordered a burrito from the café and sat down at a table overlooking the lake. I slumped into a chair, too exhausted to move. My damp clothes stuck to me like wet laundry, and my feet tingled like jelly, wobbly from overuse. The sheer magnificence of the lake helped me overcome my fatigue. I gazed wondrously at its smooth surface and the blanket of trees beyond where I had been engulfed just an hour before. My burrito arrived, and I inhaled it in seconds; each bite was a hot pocket of pleasure. The second I finished, I wished that I had savored it. I sat still in my chair for a while, unable to get up, and continued to peer out at the vastness of the cloud forest.

Finally, I mustered the energy to rise from my seat. It was probably about time to get back to my hostel. I asked one of the eco-lodge workers for the time. He announced precisely, "3:46 p.m."

"Thank you," I replied. "And the last bus back to Matagalpa leaves at 4:30 p.m., correct?" That was the information the lady at the hostel had given me.

"No," the worker responded, his reply a mix between a question and an answer. He looked perplexed, his eyebrows scrunching downward, and his head pulled back. "The last bus leaves at 4:00 p.m."

"Seriously?" I implored.

"Yes," the worker replied, looking beyond me and apparently distracted by another task.

I quickly threw on my pack and bolted out of the building. I didn't have much money on me and couldn't afford to pay for a taxi back to the hostel. I couldn't spend the night here, either, as all of my stuff was at the hostel in Matagalpa. I had to move, and fast. It had taken me about thirty minutes to get from the road to the Selva Negra reserve. The clock read 3:48 p.m. when I glanced up as I dashed out of the building. Full of adrenaline, I didn't notice the slightest ache from any muscle or observe my surroundings as I rushed up the gravel trail back to the main road. I was solely focused on arriving in time to catch my bus.

Finally, the entrance to the road came into view, and I heaved a sigh of relief. I hadn't the slightest idea what time it was, but hoped that the bus hadn't passed yet. I rested my hands on my knees, struggling to catch my breath. The entrance to *Selva Negra* was on a rounded corner, so the road above where the bus would be coming from was obstructed from my view. I decided to walk up the road to where it opened up into a straightaway instead of on a turn.

My mind raced in a useless attempt to contemplate the time. Time was painfully slow, unmeasurable. I glanced up at the sky, noticing a thick expanse of dark gray rolling toward my direction. I had no umbrella, only my thin rain jacket. I gulped and felt a ball of saliva roll down my throat. I stared up at the looming clouds, wishfully thinking I could reverse their direction. They moved overhead at the teasing pace of a snail. *Change direction, change direction, change direction.* The rumble of a car in the distance sent a shock up my spine. The sound grew louder and louder, and finally I saw bright headlights come into view. As the vehicle got closer, I sighed in defeat as a small pickup truck zoomed by.

Each moment standing on the side of the road felt like an eternity. I had waited for many things in my life, but this was a new kind of waiting. This waiting game frustrated me—to have no control and yet hope for something to happen quickly. My period of denial finally ended when I embraced that, yes, indeed, I had missed the chicken bus. It was painstakingly clear that the bus had passed, but my mind hung onto the idea that it could still show up—an unrealistic pipedream.

I started to laugh, unable to contain myself. I was standing here completely alone on the side of a road in the middle of mountainous, jungle-filled countryside in Nicaragua without a phone or a ride. And because of that realization, all I could do was laugh. What else can you do in that situation?

The thick paste of slate-gray clouds had finally rolled in, and the drizzle turned into solid raindrops. Another car charged down the mountain, crushing my hopes yet again. Ideas racing, I searched for an alternative for how I would get out of there. A thought suddenly popped into my head. *Hitchhiking.* Just the idea of it made my palms sweat. I envisioned my dad with a stern, scowling look on his face advising me, "Jake, hitchhiking is extremely dangerous. You never know who might be picking you up." But the thought wouldn't escape my head. I didn't see any other plausible option at this point. Besides, how many people on this earth are truly out to do harm?

The grumble of a car in the distance rattled in my ears. I peered up at the approaching headlights, my heart pounding in my chest. *I'm going to do it. I'm going to do it.* The car was approaching quickly, and my hand was still by my side. *Raise your thumb, Jake. Raise your damn thumb!* The car whizzed by me, and I glued my eyes to the driver. There was a male driver with two girls next to him in the front seat of the pickup truck. Two girls were with him! Angry, I shook my head left and right, aggravated that I didn't seize the opportunity. *If only I would have known there were girls in the car before he got so close! Then I would have stuck out my thumb.* I didn't know why the idea of girls being in the car made a difference to me. It gave me a possibly false sense of security to know if girls were present, the driver wouldn't be a mass murderer/kidnapper/evildoer—what the media portrayed drivers who picked up hitchhikers.

The darkening sky was apparently just beginning its reign, and it released a heavy downpour. My fear of a dangerous driver was now contested by my cold, shivering body. The clouds began pouring buckets, and I felt like the smallest speck in the world, standing alone on the side of that rural countryside road. But as I waited for my next chance, I heard no sound of an engine, only the raindrops pelting against the asphalt road and the rustling wind. I rubbed my arms with both of my wet hands, stroking the nylon of my rain jacket continuously in an attempt to muster friction and fight my chills. My soggy clothes were compressed against my muddy skin. I wished for an umbrella. I wished for the bus to come. And a car. And someone to comfort me. And a Jacuzzi. And a teleport. And San Diego. This wishful thinking only further dampened my spirits. I knew I had to do something.

Focused intentions! The words from *My Big TOE* flashed in my mind along with Mike's explanation, "*Cultivate all of your intentions and think positively. Your intentions manifest your reality.*" I had nothing to lose and everything to gain. I closed my eyes, zoning out the showering rain and my wet shivers. I peered inward, focusing my energy on the blackness in my mind and shifting it into the image of a vehicle approaching. There was a man in the driver's seat with a woman next to him. They smiled warmly at me, kindly asking if I needed a ride. I shut my eyelids even tighter and intensified my focus, replaying this image over and over in my mind and holding onto it with every ounce of energy I could muster.

The echo of a motor in the distance interrupted my thoughts. I shot open my eyes, meeting the glaring headlights shining in my direction. A large white van was charging down the road. Without hesitating, I outstretched my hand as far as I could, my thumb on the line along with my faith. I squinted as the raindrops made my vision fuzzy.

For a split second, I thought the van had zoomed straight by me, but then, about twenty yards past me, the van pulled over to the side of the road. Its blaring-red backlights signaled that it had stopped. I wasn't hallucinating or seeing things. The van was there. It had been speeding pretty fast, so it must have taken some time to slow down after seeing me. I jogged over to the car, my pack bouncing on my back, and my heart thumping in my chest. I hadn't been able to make out what the driver looked like in the pouring rain.

As I approached the passenger side from behind the car, the front window rolled down. I turned my head toward the open window and peered inside. A man was in the driver's seat with two girls sitting next to him in the front. They all appeared to be Nicaraguan. "*Hola!*" I greeted them, smiling so wide I thought I might start laughing. I didn't know what it was about strange situations that seemed so funny to me.

"*Hola,*" the man responded in Spanish. "Where do you need to go?" he asked.

"*Matagalpa?*" I pleaded with a slight rise in my pitch, trying to conjure as much hope into that one word as possible. I held my breath waiting for a response.

"*Sí, vamos!*" or "Yes, come on!" he exclaimed. I thanked him and let out a sigh of relief. I opened up the back door, hopped in, and the van grumbled to a start and took off down the road. I started talking with the driver—Ibrahim was his name. His tone was friendly. I told him where I was from, and he filled me in on his own life. It turns out Ibrahim was an ambulance driver...and I was sitting in the back of an old ambulance! I hadn't even noticed because I was so nervous about getting in the van in the first place. I laughed inwardly at how this potentially "dangerous" man was actually someone who saved lives!

Quite the opposite of a serial killer, Ibrahim was genuine and down-to-earth, a delight to talk to. His two daughters who were in the car with him were both in their thirties. We eventually arrived in town, and he dropped me off at the central plaza. I thanked him, trying to convey my gratitude. I offered him money, which he refused. I smiled widely at Ibrahim and his daughters, waving good-bye. The van accelerated down the street and turned beyond my sight. I wondered if he would ever know the impact his kindness had on me.

I walked back to my hostel, which was only five minutes away. I stripped off my muddy, soggy clothes and skipped toward the shower. The steaming water was pure bliss as it drenched my head and dripped down my body, blanketing me in warmth. As I stood in complete satisfaction savoring every droplet of steam and water, I replayed the day's events in my head. Getting on the chicken bus, being dropped off on the side of the road at the entrance to Selva Negra, observing the mystical countryside, trekking in the cloud forest, relishing the peaceful atmosphere that nature provided, being stranded in what felt like the middle of nowhere, and hitchhiking back to town with a kind stranger. It all sounded absurd and unbelievable.

Each detail of the day amazed me—it had been a series of unpredictable events. The entire day on my own was one in which I had broken past barriers that I had built up in my mind and had never previously dared to cross. Socially, I had always felt that I needed other people to fulfill my own happiness. It was reliance, a necessity in my mind that I couldn't be happy on my own because there was some gap that required filling. But now I was happy. I had spent the entire day completely on my own and absolutely loved it. The lingering fear that I couldn't be happy being with just myself no longer existed. I enjoyed my own company and being with my own thoughts.

Throughout the day, I had been fearful in each of my endeavors to a certain extent. Yet somewhere deep inside—or maybe it resided in nature—I had an ounce of faith. I didn't know where it came from or what the notion was comprised of other than that it was an ingrained knowledge that things would work out if I believed they would. I held tightly onto this feeling, fusing it into my mind until it became a wholehearted conviction. It was as if a seed representing the unknown was sprouting within me and blossoming into a wild flower of faith...a faith that the world had a plan in store. It was a liberating relinquishment of my desire for control paired with an empowering sense of courage to change the things I could. And everything had worked out. With positive intentions and correctly aligned values, the only thing that had held me back was fear. But by taking action, that fear was dismantled, and it evaporated into thin air.

For the first time, I felt in total control of my own life. It seemed somewhat paradoxical to think this, considering many of the day's events included putting my complete faith in others. But I realized that *every human has control over his or her own life*. We cannot control the Universe—there will always be events outside of our control. But what we can control is *our own* actions. We can control the decisions we make and the direction in which we wish to take our lives. I didn't have control over the timing of the bus or the downpour of rain. They were both beyond my power. However, I did have control over how I could think and respond, how I could act and react. We all have a choice: we can either be the captain of our own ship or the passenger of another. Whether the water is calm or stormy is not up to us. What is up to us is the choice to navigate the ship or let it navigate us.

> *"Always remember, you are just one 'hearing' away from Faith,*
> *just one 'knowing' away from Peace, and just one 'action' away*
> *from total Victory."*
>
> —Rex Rouis

CHAPTER 29

The Power of Human Connection

May 27, 2015

"Accept—then act. Whatever the present moment contains, accept it as if you had chosen it. Always work with it, not against it. This will miraculously transform your whole life."

—Eckhart Tolle

Being a US citizen, I was eligible to stay in Guatemala, El Salvador, Honduras, or Nicaragua for up to ninety days. A treaty signed in 2006 allowed travelers to freely cross between borders of those countries for up to three months. I decided that I would travel south to Costa Rica when my ninety days were up. In the meantime, I still had a couple weeks left in Nicaragua. Back in San Marcos, Skye had told me about an eco-community on *Ometepe Island* called *Eden* where she had volunteered for two weeks. She raved about it and gave me the contact information for the community. I sent an e-mail to Tim, the person in charge, and he responded swiftly, welcoming me to come and volunteer.

Ometepe Island is located in the middle of Lake Nicaragua, the largest lake in Central America. The pictures I had seen of *Ometepe* were compelling and consisted of two magnificent volcanoes, stunning scenery, and rich biodiversity. I arrived at the island port of *Moyogalpa* and boarded a chicken bus for the two-hour ride to *Merida,* taking the directions on *Eden's* website intended for those "feeling adventurous." Although I was feeling somewhat "adventurous," my main reason for taking this route was that I didn't have enough money to pay for a direct and easy ride straight from the port to the eco-community, which was on the opposite side of the island and situated in the middle of the jungle.

After I arrived in Merida, the rest of the directions were hopelessly vague. The names *"Bello Horizonte"* and *"Entrada de Valencia"* didn't clarify anything, and since I had no phone to direct me, I began hiking in the direction I supposed was correct. The supposedly "30 minute, 2.4 km walk" turned out to be much more than that.

The air was heavy, and its haze of humidity emitted a fuzzy vapor that coiled around me like a snake. I was wearing flip-flops. I had figured the walk was going to be short and wanted my feet to breathe in the toasty air. Before long, my feet were caked in dust. I turned around, realizing that yet again I was completely alone on a deserted road surrounded by nothing but trees and vast jungle in the distance. Clusters of brush, fallen branches, and chaparral lined the road. Every step was a tease, inching me forward to an unknown destination.

I started singing songs aloud, belting out "Three Little Birds" by Bob Marley. This was one of the fun aspects about being alone in the middle of nowhere. I could bust out my dreadful singing voice—which is worse than my sense of direction—and pathetic imitation of a Jamaican accent. And no one could hear me. I let my voice ring out to the birds, reminding myself that "every little thing gonna be alright." The song comforted me as if the melody in my head magically lifted my spirits. I stopped "worrying 'bout a thing" and wandered down the road, strangely at peace and unconcerned with being lost. I was always lost, it seemed. But being lost was just a part of being found.

I rounded a curve in the road and discovered a few dispersed huts. Farmland stretched on perpetually in the background. I stumbled upon a teenager riding his bicycle and asked him if he knew where Eden was.

His eyes lit up, and he acknowledged that he did and pointed up the road. He biked slowly next to me, and we talked. His name was Michael, and he was fifteen. He spoke a few words in English, which he had learned in school. We approached a path that was concealed by the trees and veered off the road unexpectedly. He dropped his bike on the side of the road and directed me toward the trail as he couldn't ride along the bumpy path. We cruised down, the leaves crunching beneath our feet as we learned about each other's lives. Nothing but plants, trees and vegetation straddled both sides of the trail.

After a while, we approached a hill. As this was as far as he was going, Michael directed me to turn right and then keep straight until I reached Eden. We said good-bye, and I thanked him for his generosity and taking the time to help me. Not in a million years would I have found that trail if Michael hadn't helped me. I wandered down in the direction Michael had indicated although I still felt as if I were headed nowhere, beyond civilization.

I steadily climbed up a hill and suddenly the entire community of Eden lay before me. I had expected a rustic, underdeveloped site lacking sophistication and amenities. This was far from it. Whimsical cob buildings rose from the ground with the elegance of columns in a cathedral. Lush, vivid jungle surrounded the entire community with a breathtaking view of the volcano and the lake in the distance.

I approached one of the buildings and walked inside. The room had an earthy, modern design. Wooden tables and stools were dispersed throughout the room, and a sink and wooden countertop were elegantly placed in the center. A rocket stove and shelves lined the room's perimeter. Clusters of green and yellow bananas hung from the edges of the building's palm-leaf roof, and a ladder extended above the kitchen, leading to a compact, cozy library containing cabinets filled with books.

In the room, a man with a seemingly gentle demeanor stood straight and tall with his shoulders pulled back. His dark, dirty-blonde curls stretched down to his shoulders, and his eyes exuded a sense of calm.

"Hi, I'm Jake," I introduced. I was sweaty and exhausted. My backpack was still cemented to my back, and my shoulders were sore because of it.

"Hello, I'm Tim. Nice to meet you, Jake." His voice conveyed a sense of patience. "We're glad to have you. The volunteers are working right now, and lunch is in about thirty minutes. Let's get you settled in." Tim escorted me to a secure room where I hung up my backpack and other valuables. Apparently, in the last few weeks, there had been multiple attempted thefts. He handed me a sleeping mat, a sheet, and a pillow and directed me to only keep clothes in my tent in case someone tried to break in. A gulp of saliva rolled down my throat as he warned me of the break-ins, but he assured me that no had been harmed in any of these incidents.

A number of tents were scattered on a hill that overlooked the community about fifty yards away from the main kitchen/communal area. I hiked up the hill to a yellow tent that Tim had said was available for me. To my pleasant surprise, the tent was zipped shut and no creepy bugs were lurking inside. Relieved, I placed my mat, which was wrapped in a clean sheet, inside and propped my pillow against the far end. Compared to the last tent I had stayed in, this was luxurious.

I strolled back down to the communal kitchen where Tim introduced me to Lily, a girl from England who had a charming accent. Her blonde hair wafted down past her shoulders, and her face was neither pale nor dark—a mixture of light skin coupled with sun exposure and freckles. She had Brandeis-blue eyes and a bright smile.

She took me on a tour of Eden. We strolled past the kitchen, which had two large solar panels slanting upward toward the sun. Lily revealed that the solar panels were the primary source of energy for Eden, allowing the community to live off the grid. She also explained that each building was handcrafted using natural materials. We strolled through the exquisite edible garden, which was bursting with various colors of lettuce, chilies, pineapples, turmeric roots, and many other locally grown foods. I followed Lily's lead, picking off a wine-colored hibiscus leaf and eating it.

She escorted me to the natural pool, which glimmered with a reflection of the clear blue sky and fluffy clouds. It was easily the most spectacular pool I had ever seen. A hammock lay next to it, and beyond it, lime-green plants and trees grew abundantly and endlessly. A volcano rose in front of the pool's view, jutting out of the ground and into the heavens. The lake shimmered off to the left.

"This is the pool, as you can see," Lily reported. "There's casual nudity in the pool area," she revealed in a nonchalant manner. I wondered what the term "casual nudity" meant but figured I would find out soon. She explained that the pool had been designed to drain into the banana trees, and that the water was clean and even drinkable.

We walked down another path that led to the yoga and meditation ashram. From the outside, it looked like a circular cob structure with a palm-leaf roof. On the inside, it breathed a sense of enchantment. Handcrafted designs and swirls were inscribed onto the rich, earthy cob walls. Large wooden pillars circled the ashram, supporting the magnificent structure. The view from inside the ashram looking out was similar to the view from the pool.

"Meditation is every morning at five thirty in the ashram," Lily informed me. "Yoga is in the afternoon, usually at four." My desire to practice meditation was going to be manifested; however, this reality partially frightened me. I didn't know what to expect, and the idea of being with a group of people I didn't know and doing something so far from the realm of what was "normal" to my own experience was rattling.

"There's a board in the kitchen that displays everybody's volunteer roles. At the beginning of the week, we sign up for roles during the volunteer meeting. You will learn more tomorrow. Each person is delegated two tasks per week. They range from preparing breakfast to cleaning up for the day to a variety of other tasks. One of the main reasons we grow so close in this community is because everyone is engaged. It doesn't matter what your race, gender, or nationality is. It doesn't matter whether you stay one week or one month. The intention at Eden is to create a conscious community and live sustainably." I listened closely, absorbing Lily's words. I truly felt like I was drawn here, a place where I could delve deeper into myself, contribute to a positive and diverse community of travelers, and live in harmony with nature.

The community breathed with a supernatural, aesthetic brilliance. It seemed to me that each place I went surpassed my understanding of how beautiful a place could be. My perception of beauty was being stretched to new dimensions. I realized it wasn't so much that one place was more splendid than the next, but that I was becoming aware of the limitless nature of the earth's grandeur. The world is an unending expanse of dazzling ecological diversity, each piece of grass and sand, and each speck of leaf and bark connected to the uniqueness of a particular location. I could see thousands of trees, multiple oceans and countless lakes and still be awed.

The sound of a horn rang three times, resembling a soft trombone. Lily informed me that what we had just heard was the conch shell, which was blown to signal lunch, yoga, morning meditation, dinner, or another activity. I followed Lily back to the communal kitchen where everyone was gathering for lunch. Other than Tim, there were about ten volunteers, and they all kindly introduced themselves to me. I was welcomed immediately—the ambience was comforting and supportive. The others were from Germany, England, Switzerland, France, Australia, and Italy.

After lunch, I strolled over to the pool with the others to take a dip. I was already wearing my swim trunks, which I had changed into when I had settled in my tent. I stripped off my shirt and jumped in. The pool was ridiculously refreshing. I rose above the surface, gaping at the massive volcano before my eyes and the extravagant scenery surrounding it. A splash in the water caused me to turn around. There were two other volunteers in the pool, and a few others were about to get in. I suddenly realized that I was the only person wearing trunks. The other four guys and three girls were completely naked. I felt uneasy, not because they were naked, but because I was the only one who was not. I admired the acceptance that Eden radiated, creating an environment where people could feel free to be their natural selves, physically as well. Feeling slightly uncomfortable, I debated taking off my trunks. *Well, that would be downright weird. You hop into the pool with your trunks on and then decide to take them off? It's too late, buddy. Just keep 'em on.*

I noticed my reflection in the water and looked deep into my eyes. I wondered what the world would be like if we could all be naked and content with just being ourselves. I pondered how I would feel naked not caring what other people thought. I didn't know where my hesitation stemmed from that prevented me from going bare right then and there. I guessed it had something to do with being the only one from the United States where going nude was uncommon. But beyond that, I tried to understand *why* I felt uncomfortable. In America, society considers it taboo to show sexual body parts. Taking a step back, this seemed quite ridiculous to me—at least, in my present circumstance being surrounded by a bunch of naked Europeans. *Why can a man show his nipples but not a woman? We all have a penis or a vagina, but we act as if seeing one is a huge deal. Without those human parts, none of us would even be here. Why is it such a big deal to go naked?* As these thoughts swirled around in my head, I declared to myself that tomorrow and from then on, I would go naked in the pool.

At four, the conch sounded for yoga, and I walked over to the ashram along with the other volunteers. I was excited to practice yoga for the first time. After reading *Autobiography of a Yogi*, along with hearing testimonials from other travelers, I was eager to undertake the practice of yoga. I grabbed a green mat from the shelf in the ashram and joined the circle. Tim, who had studied yoga for six years in Southeast Asia, directed us to press our hands together above our hearts. His calming voice trickled throughout the room, emitting a sense of relaxation. "Focus on your breath," he informed us, his voice sounding like that of a wise guru.

I found my focus drifting toward the others in the room; I observed their swift and graceful movements as I awkwardly maneuvered my inflexible body. I locked focus on my breathing and moved my body slowly to Tim's instructions. We progressed into various poses, focusing on each inhaled and exhaled breath. Feeling fully engaged in each breath, I found my mind now guiding my body as if it were sending signals, and my body was responding accordingly. I fixated on maintaining my stability as I balanced on one leg, bending my spine parallel toward the earth, my hands spread wide like an eagle. The chatter and random thoughts that often plagued my mind dissipated. My brain was solely occupied on breath and movement, directed by Tim's peaceful tone.

We were all lying on our backs with our eyes closed when Tim's words awakened me. "Feel your feet and hands; slowly wiggle them and feel the motion slowly return to your senses." My mind was awake, but my body was asleep, tingling in a state of deep relaxation. I slowly wiggled my toes and fingers; they felt heavy as if they had been asleep and were finally awakened. I came to a seated position and integrated the rest of my body back to reality, feeling a blissful satisfaction. I felt as if my mind and body had taken a rejuvenating nap. At a snail's pace, I opened my eyes, viewing a world I was lost from just seconds before.

"*Namaste*," Tim uttered softly, bowing forward.

"*Namaste*," everyone repeated in a tone reflecting the tranquility breathing in all of us.

I felt a new energy, alive with the ease that nothing in the world could worry me. The conch sounded a little while later, signaling dinner. We all gathered in the kitchen and circled around the center wooden countertop, holding hands.

"Every night before dinner, we gather and go around in a circle saying what we are thankful for," Tim revealed to me. It was incredibly simple yet profound. My hands interlocked with those next to me, contributing to the connection that the positive environment was fostering. The power of being grateful was gratifying in and of itself. I had only just arrived but could sense that there was something special about Eden.

During dinner, I had a chance to connect better with some of the volunteers. Hannah was from Australia, and her carefree spirit practically poured out of her. She had short blonde curls and a smile that matched her lighthearted nature. Her steel-blue eyes glowed with optimism, and her accent was equally as charming as Lily's. Sienna and Luca were a couple in their mid-twenties from Italy. Luca had olive skin and coffee-brown hair that slicked up toward the front. Sienna was also tan with silky, smooth skin. Her dark-mocha eyes matched her hair, which cascaded down her shoulders. I was attracted to her right off the bat and couldn't help but feel disappointed that she was already in a relationship. Her personality matched her outer beauty, and I got a warming sensation in my chest whenever I talked with her. She was seven years older than me, so even if she were single, it would have been a long shot—at least, that's what I told myself. Most of the girls I met traveling were much older than me, and, for whatever reason, I felt intimidated, thinking the age disparity ruled me out. But there was something about Sienna, and my mind kept projecting romantic scenarios of how I would end up with her.

Jonas was one of those rare people whose very presence made me feel comfortable. He was bald and had a scraggly, strawberry-blonde beard. His soft-blue eyes spoke of a peace from within that animated his empathetic nature. He played guitar and sang—the music he created sent chills down my spine. Matt was also from Germany and was around my height. His thick, curly hair resembled that of a lion's mane and matched his pecan-colored beard and mustache. His direct nature fascinated me, and he was also very kind. There were some others I hadn't spoken with, and I looked forward to getting to know them better.

After dinner, I brushed my teeth and said good night to the others. I was exhausted from the day's travels. I hiked up to my tent on the hillside, which lay isolated under a tree. I squeezed inside, feeling incredibly thankful for the clean tent and mat and pillow! Yes, I even had a pillow! It didn't take long for me to drift off into a deep sleep.

"Human connection is the most vital aspect of our existence, without the sweet touch of another being we are lonely stars in an empty space waiting to shine gloriously."

—Joe Straynge

CHAPTER 30

Totally Naked, Totally Loving It

May 28, 2015

"I know of nothing more valuable, when it comes to the all-important virtue of authenticity, than simply being who you are."
—Charles R. Swindoll

Three blows of the conch echoed in the peaceful morning air. The growls of howler monkeys and the chirps of birds softly sounded in the distance. I climbed out of my tent and strolled toward the ashram. The air was crisp, and the cool breeze refreshed my waking limbs. I was the first one in the ashram other than Tim, and the others soon trickled in. Each day of the week, Tim guided a different type of meditation. Today's meditation was Five Rhythms dance, which entailed five rhythms of meditation for twelve minutes each, totaling one hour. Tim put a CD into a device that was connected with surround sound speakers in the ceiling of the ashram. The first phase entailed breathing vigorously through the nose. The second phase involved screaming out loud in order to release deeply embedded emotions. The third phase required jumping in the air with hands extended toward the sky and yelling "Who!" in a deep tone. The fourth phase entailed standing completely still with hands outstretched toward the sky. And the last phase involved dancing and flowing to music. This was drastically different from what I had envisioned meditation to be. I had pictured myself sitting still with my legs crossed and eyes closed.

The music began, and Tim's voice guided us to close our eyes and start breathing intensely through our nose. I began rapidly inhaling air up my nose and blowing out with the same force. A cacophony of huffing and puffing reverberated in the room. Tim instructed us to steer away from creating a pattern, so I wildly inhaled and exhaled in an uneven fashion, varying my length and strength of breaths. Breathing fervently was exhausting, and I was shocked at how fatigued I was so soon after beginning. I pushed past my body's tiredness, breathing intensely and moving my whole body with each breath as Tim had suggested. I tried not to think of how crazy I looked flailing my upper body up and down as I surged air out of my nostrils like a mad man with his eyes closed. But I wasn't alone. I could hear and feel the others moving with me. My mind lost track of everything except the constant flow of air rushing inconsistently in and out of my nose.

The music shifted to a new song, and Tim informed us that phase two was beginning. I was hesitant to start screaming. The idea of it just made me feel uncomfortable. Matt's loud roars vibrated in the room, and soon everybody else was releasing their own symphony of screams. *This seems ridiculous. I don't think I can take myself seriously just screaming aloud and making all sorts of noises.* My mind's internal chatter interrupted the present moment, and I focused my intention back to the meditation. The least I could do was try. After all, I was on an island in the jungle in the middle of Nicaragua.

Screams were booming left and right. I wasn't shocked anymore at the sounds of the screams but more so at the power behind some of them. I tracked my focus back and let out a bellow. "Ahhh!" I roared, my chest vibrating as the wind traveled through my belly, coursing through my throat and out my mouth. This scream was followed by another scream, and another and another, my mind no longer thinking about it. My stomach was expanding quickly; the air was pumping in rapidly and firing out. My throat burned with coarseness, and the blood vessels in my temples bulged. My body opened its floodgates, and various screams escaped. I couldn't quite decipher what they meant. It was as if a dam had been blocking the flow of a river, and suddenly, the dam evaporated, and the water poured straight through, freely and openly. The recording sounded, and the next phase began.

Tim instructed us to turn outward and face the walls of the ashram. We were directed to hold our hands above our heads, jump in the air, and chant "Who!" as we landed back on our feet. Without thinking, I delved right into it. During this exercise, I created a pattern by locking my eyes onto a spot in the wall. I leapt in the air, bellowing "Who!" as I landed back on my feet. I felt like an ape jumping up and down and grunting a low, deep sound over and over. I swayed through the movements with intense focus, my eyes glued to the spot on the wall. My throat ached from constantly barking, and my calves burned with exhaustion from the excessive leaping. Tim encouraged us to keep going, to focus on our breath and to ignore the pain.

The fourth phase began as a bell in the music signaled the next rhythm. My mind interpreted this stage as an easy one—simply keeping my hands outstretched toward the ceiling. But only minutes in, my shoulders seared in pain. I had completely underestimated the force it takes to keep your arms high above your head without moving them. A knot rolled into my shoulders, digging into every nerve. My arms pulsed in discomfort, and my face was heating like a fire. I closed my eyes in an effort to conceal my pain, praying that the throbbing would subside. I was at the point of bursting into laughter as a reaction to my body hitting its threshold of pain. The most welcoming sound I ever heard was the change in music signaling the next stage.

My arms dropped, flopping like jelly. The final stage involved us closing our eyes and simply dancing. "Flow to the music," Tim guided us in his soothing tone. My arms swayed effortlessly, feeling more like flippers than arms. I let my body take over, flowing in every direction the music beckoned. I spun around, and my arms tingled as they waved through the air. The music was directing my movements. A bell dinged, and the recording transitioned to a close. Tim softly announced the meditation was ending. I gently opened my eyes, bringing my senses back to the room. I squinted, my eyes dilating and adjusting to the brightness of the new day. I felt a smile on my face accompanied by a blissful state of tranquility.

Gradually, everyone got up and made their way to the kitchen. Nobody spoke as each morning everyone ate in silence. The purpose of this, I learned, was to allow self-reflection in order to set a positive intention for the day. For breakfast, a buffet of freshly picked fruits lay before us. Bananas ranged from sun yellows and auburn reds to grassy greens. Huge carrot-colored papayas were dotted with green spots, and there was an abundance of fresh mangoes in all shapes and rainbow colors. Sour, peachy-orange star fruits were sliced into their natural star shapes. Juicy grapefruits were bountiful, the size of softballs with burgundy flesh intermixed with seeds. There was fruit galore, and everything was grown in the community.

An herbal hibiscus tea was simmering in a pot for us all, and I filled up a mug. I sipped the infusion of steaming magenta water, an electric current of tartness awakening my taste buds. I ate my food in stillness and silence. I could hear the slow chomps of my teeth as I mindfully ate my breakfast. I usually scarfed down my food in just a few minutes. But the behavior of the others in the community, along with the calmness instilled in me from mediation, was rubbing off on me. I ate slowly, deliberately, thinking of how the mush of the banana felt on my tongue, how sweet the juice of the grapefruit tasted, how stringy the mango was.

After breakfast, the other volunteers and I gathered in the ashram for a meeting. Before the delegation of volunteering tasks began, everyone sat in a circle, holding hands with closed eyes. Matt, who was in charge of volunteer meetings, directed us all to take three deep breaths together. As I took the first breath, I pondered how peculiar this felt along with all of the other new experiences—and it hadn't even been twenty-four hours—from yoga and sharing gratitude at dinner to mediation and silent breakfast! And now this! In my past, I had never wanted or craved to experience these practices. I had always had the perception that these activities were only for a certain kind of people: hippies, shamans, and free spirits. I assumed that these things were for people who were lost or who saw the world in a strange way, and I didn't want to be a part of it. I feared being a person who spoke calmly or who was never disturbed by anything or who could find happiness in something so simple. But the experiences I was having here were dismantling the false beliefs that were built up in my mind. These activities were opening new doors into my own self that I hadn't known existed.

By the third breath, I wasn't thinking how strange it was that we were all sitting in a circle with our eyes closed taking big breaths. As we released our final exhaled breaths, I felt a connection with the others that went beyond just holding hands. It was a mutual understanding that everyone was here due to his or her own conscious decision. We were not here to express our judgments or stake our beliefs. Rather, we were here to connect, to learn, to grow.

We opened our eyes and went around the circle revealing how we felt as we prepared to start the day. From relaxed and excited, anxious or frustrated, energetic and tired, everyone chimed in on how they were feeling. No justification was needed. It was solely to express things as they were. I was breathing with a sense of calmness that invigorated me. I was feeling relaxed and eager to get moving and volunteer. I was assigned to weed the garden and help gather salad for lunch.

I spent the next three hours working in the sticky, tropical air. Sweat poured out of me as I pulled weeds from the garden with my bare hands. I crawled on my dirt-covered knees across the garden, plucking wilted plants and making way for new ones. As lunch neared, I helped Mikaela by plucking hundreds of leaves from the garden to create a salad. Mikaela was a local Nicaraguan woman who lived near Eden at one of the neighboring farms. She came during the weekdays to prepare lunch. Many other local Nicaraguans worked at Eden as well, helping to construct new cob buildings and perform other tasks with which Tim needed help. He had created jobs for the locals, and by doing so, had integrated them into the community.

When the conch sounded for lunch, everyone gathered in the kitchen. While we ate the delicious cuisine that Mikaela had prepared, I got to know some of the other volunteers. Bruno and Jeremy were from France, although they didn't travel together. A black Afro of loose curls flopped on top of Bruno's willowy, lanky frame. He had deer-brown skin and cinnamon eyes that sparkled with kindness. He didn't speak English well, and I found his French accent and mispronunciations to be hilarious. He was nineteen, and the only one close in age to me as all of the others were in their mid- to late twenties or thirties. Jeremy was also tall yet with a chiseled, muscular build. He was half-Korean and had black hair and a goatee. He had a childish spirit and was a joy to be around. Mia was from Switzerland. Her glossy, blonde hair flowed down past her shoulders, a few curls sprinkled throughout. She had piercing, aquamarine eyes and an admirable spunk about her.

After lunch, Mia announced she was hosting a voluntary dance workshop where she would be teaching *Bachata*, a Latino-style dance. I had never even heard of it, and the thought of making a complete fool of myself attempting to learn a new dance slid through my mind. But I loved to dance—and the possibility of learning a Latin American dance outweighed my fear of looking like an idiot. I meandered over to the ashram where Jeremy, Sienna, and Bruno were also waiting. It was only the four of us, and I glanced around nervously. Jeremy had spent six months living in Columbia where *Bachata* is very popular and had danced almost every day there. Sienna had also danced for years. I didn't know if Bruno had any experience with *Bachata*. I *definitely* didn't.

Mia explained the dynamics of *Bachata*. It involves a man and a woman with their left hands intertwined and the right hand of the man wrapped lightly around the woman's back in order to closely lead her. Going along with the rhythm of the beat, it entails a stepping movement along an imaginary line followed by a tap and sway of the hips on the fourth beat. Mia demonstrated and made it look ridiculously easy. In my mind, it still seemed like rocket science, and I began to regret my decision to be there. Apprehension flooded my stomach like a swarm of bees at the thought of my having to lead Mia or Sienna. *Bachata* is an intimate dance, and the woman mirrors the man's movements, creating a synchronistic flow.

Before we began, however, Mia directed an exercise for us to "loosen up." The warm-up involved us simply practicing the movements by ourselves without a partner. The music rang aloud inside the ashram, and my shoulders began to relax as I was getting the hang of the movements. One, two, three, *four*. One, two, three, *four*. Each step in the warm-up enhanced my confidence. I found myself enjoying the movements and flowing freely; my hips were swaying and my shoulders were bobbing to the tunes. I no longer cared what I looked like dancing. I was immersed in the movements and loving every second of it. Mia interjected to show another variation of the dance and advanced steps.

"Okay, let's partner up. But before we begin, Jeremy and I will do a demonstration."

She motioned for Jeremy to come forward, and they locked hands and began dancing to the music. Jeremy towered over her, yet they moved with grace, as if they were one cohesive flow of energy. Then Jeremy stood aside, as there were five of us, and he was already experienced. Mia partnered up with Bruno, and I partnered up with Sienna. The intimacy of the dance, my inexperience, and the realization that I was the one who would be leading sent a tsunami of nerves flooding through my every cell. Mia switched the music on and I locked hands with Sienna. I smiled at her, trying to prevent the palms of my already wet hands from sweating more as if I could magically stop that biological response.

The music started, and it only took a few seconds before I messed up as I tried to spin her around like Jeremy had done with ease moments before. I didn't know whether I was supposed to look her in the eyes or glance forward or hold onto her hand more loosely or move my hand on her back up an inch to the right. My nerves were blocking my ability to think straight, and the basic moves that I had performed just minutes before were now as tough as complex calculus. Luckily, she laughed lightheartedly as I probably said "sorry" thirty times, feeling like an idiot and wishing again I hadn't gone to this damn optional dance workshop. I took a deep breath, calmed my mind, and began again, this time trying to focus on the beat more than anything else. After some time, I began enjoying myself. I led with more confidence and let my body move freely, not thinking so much. I smoothly spun her around, and we continued to drift around the room, flowing with the melody.

After a break, we switched partners and took turns sitting out because there were five of us. By the time the workshop ended, I was disappointed it was over. I wanted to dance until my feet collapsed. *Bachata* was on my mind, and it was exhilarating to get a taste of it. As I walked out of the ashram, I felt an influx of emotion. The anxiety, excitement, apprehensiveness, joy, silliness, confidence, and thrill that soared through me in the past hour resulted in a wonderful feeling of satisfaction. I had crossed another boundary and entered a new door into the depths of the unknown. But leaving my comfort zone had ultimately paid off. The feeling that was now brimming inside my chest was worth every drop of sweat on my palms, every mistake I made, and every nerve that had engulfed me. Through our efforts to achieve or experience something unpredictable, a spark of empowerment is born that can ignite a torch to illuminate a new way forward.

Late afternoon was approaching, and I strolled over to the pool area where some of the other volunteers were relaxing. Just like the day before, everyone was completely naked. I was overly conscious as I stripped off my clothes—going naked in front of a bunch of people was a first for me. I lifted my shirt off and then pulled down both my shorts and my boxers. I was uncovered, open and free, yet awkward. I sensed a laugh creeping up in my stomach, but I suppressed the urge. It wasn't that I feared going fully naked, it was just strange to me. Literally and metaphorically, I felt exposed like an open book with nothing to hide.

The thought of, god forbid, getting an erection would be pretty embarrassing. I didn't know if I should look at the ladies' breasts or not, because they're just body parts, but I didn't want to be creepy, but would that be normal to not look? This was all strange to me and my thoughts were in a whirlwind. And of course, Sienna was in the pool and I wanted to look, but felt almost wrong doing so, but wow she was stunning. *Is it wrong for wanting to look? Damn it, Jake, just hop in the pool already.*

I leaped into the pool. No one looked at me differently or said anything weird to me. It seemed that I was the only one conscious of my own nakedness. As I swam around, I felt as if a weight had been lifted from my shoulders. No one here cared whether I was naked or not. At least, that's what it seemed. But more importantly, I didn't care. I climbed out of the pool and roamed over to the hammock, still fully nude. I sat down comfortably on the hammock overlooking the vast volcano. I swung back and forth, the wind sending a refreshing zephyr across my body.

Being naked, I didn't have a care in the world. Along with my clothes being stripped off, something else dematerialized as well. The physical act of being naked instilled in me a carefree sense of acceptance. A layer of self consciousness evaporated into thin air. American culture dishonored public nudity and privatized it to such an excessive extent that I felt uncomfortable being my own naked self in front of others. Nudity is simply our natural state. And after a few minutes of being naked, this overpowering wave of freedom swept through me. It seemed odd that being nude was considered such a big deal to me just a short while before. I had essentially transformed from one polar opposite to the other in a matter of minutes.

> "*You yourself, as much as anybody in the entire Universe,
> deserve your love and affection.*"
> —Buddha

CHAPTER 31

Paralyzed to Peaceful

June 2, 2015

"The oracle of breath unfolds its secrets to those who know the keys. The elements in breath are known as fire, water, earth, air, and ether."

—Swara Chinthamani

I awoke completely soaked as if I had been sleeping in a pool. The first shower of the rainy season had commenced, and my tent was apparently unprepared. Throughout the night, raindrops trickled against my tent. A puddle of water collected underneath and seeped through the nylon covering, drenching my entire body. I zipped open my tent and eagerly stepped outside, anxious to put on dry clothes. My soaked boxers stuck to the back of my thighs, and my shirt was glued to my stomach. I walked down to the kitchen and changed into dry clothes. The clock read 4:53 a.m.

I ambled into the empty ashram and rolled out a mat. I lowered onto my back, lying down in total serenity. The calming symphony of tropical birds flowed into my ears; the cooling, misty breeze refreshed my senses; the volcano, encircled in lush jungle, rested majestically before my eyes. A delicate drizzle trickled down, quietly tapping the stone floor outside. The others soon wandered into the ashram, and Tim introduced the day's meditation: Quantum Light Breath.

Quantum Light Breath is a highly focused breath meditation that involves excessive inhaling and exhaling with no pauses allowed between breaths. The continuous flow of breath provides the body with excess oxygen. In essence, Tim explained that this technique aids the body in bypassing the conscious mind in order to bring to the surface buried, painful experiences and releases negative emotions. I was curious to see what strong emotions could arise from the exercise. I had no idea what was about to happen.

Lying on my back with my knees raised off the ground and my feet planted comfortably on the mat, the musical recording began, and Tim directed us to begin breathing. "Escape any patterns," Tim directed us. "Breathe intensely, keeping the focus on your breath." I inhaled and exhaled in a rapid series of huffs and puffs with no pause between breaths. This constant sequence of intense breathing was physically exhausting. Yet, because there was no pause in breathing, my mind quickly entered the "zone"; my focus was fully directed toward my breath. "Speed up your breathing," Tim encouraged us as the pace of the music was growing faster and faster, and my breathing quickened; breaths were flying in and out of my nose and mouth with the intensity of a combustion engine rapidly whistling. A tingling sensation began percolating throughout my body, and my breathing was hasty now as I inhaled and exhaled with force, entranced in a rhythm that I was no longer aware of.

An overwhelming tingling sensation suddenly erupted over my entire body. I opened my eyes completely shocked at the electrified sensation. My arms were off the ground, and my hands were clamped shut. All of my fingers connected at one point. The tingling progressed into a stiffening sensation, capturing my every limb. An unusual feeling of an increasing and compressing density tightened in my hands, arms, legs, and chest. Simultaneously, I also felt a tickling lightness. Terrified, I tried to move and couldn't. I was still breathing deep breaths, which were gushing out of me like a waterfall. I glared at my frozen hands in fright, unable to feel my numb fingers. My hands looked like crab claws locked down and were turned inward toward me. I lowered my head back down to the ground and closed my eyes.

Gradually, I transitioned my intense breathing into a slower, steadier flow. I could hear my body's energy surging and my panting breaths escaping from my throat. As I retained focus on slowing down my breath, the warm blood began to flow back into my hands. I peeled open my eyes, now beaming at my fingers as I managed to wiggle each one. I relaxed, feeling invigorated, dazzled, shocked, and confused all at once.

The tingling sensation drifted from my limbs and out of my body. Never had I felt such relief from being able to move my fingers. I eased my knees down, stretching out my legs on the ground. A peculiar, refreshing energy pulsed through my veins. My breathing dropped to an even slower speed, slower than my normal breath. The music came to a stop, and Tim guided us in concluding the meditation.

Gingerly, I sat up, regaining my senses. I opened my eyes again, welcoming the light as I adjusted to the brightness of the rising sun. I sat motionless, staring endlessly out at the volcano. After a few minutes, I lifted myself up and rolled up my mat, energized from what had just taken place. I was also bewildered by what had happened. I had never gone through such an experience in my life nor felt such invigorating feelings. It baffled me how just through controlling my breath, I could experience such profound sensations, literally paralyzing my body.

As I ate my breakfast in silence, I attempted to contemplate what had just occurred. It was unlike anything I had ever imagined. The whole experience was paradoxical in nature—physically draining yet galvanizing. I felt completely new and unknown feelings. It was as if some force had extracted the repressed mental and emotional toxins hiding deep within me, resulting in a release, an evaporation of agony and an influx of solace. My grasp of what was possible—in the world and in my own body—extrapolated exponentially in my mind.

I had read numerous accounts from the likes of Paramahansa Yogananda and Eckhart Tolle about experiences that transcend the power of the mind and body. And finally, I could truly *understand for myself* what it was like. I had undergone a personal experience that ruptured my realm of what was possible and expanded my horizon of the unknown a thousand times over. This proliferation of worldly possibilities didn't frighten me. It fascinated me. It awakened me. My ardent curiosity about the world was breathing a new fire, a craving, a desire to learn and explore. I yearned for more of the uncertain, to discover unpaved trails of the Universe and of the mind, to continue the search for understanding the marvels of the world that can never be fully understood.

As the floodgates of my imagination poured open, a stark realization surfaced. Memories of high school arose, and I recalled blacking out at parties from drinking. It had never occurred to me up until this point why I had always felt the *need* to get plastered to the point where I had no sense of control. Yes, I had fun, and yes, there were some great times. But the underlying reason for my constant urge to be intoxicated was staring me straight in the face. Alcohol had given me a false sense of self-reliance. It was a means to suppress my self-consciousness. I was scared of being my true self, and alcohol let me escape that reality. I latched onto the label of the "happy, sociable, partying kid" because it instilled a sense of acceptance. And maybe it did in the sense that I fit a certain mold that people liked. But that mold wasn't me. Alcohol had been a medium through which I could restrain my self-doubt and anxiety and simultaneously relinquish control and feel carefree.

The oddest thing was that during that time in high school and my first semester of college, I couldn't imagine a life without drinking. I thought people who didn't party or drink just didn't get it. They didn't understand the fun I was having. I feared a life where I wouldn't party and drink. I suddenly realized that my fear stemmed from a disconnect between being me and being someone else. I had feared letting go because the idea of the unknown, a life without partying, scared me much more than my unhappiness at the time. Thich Nhat Hanh's words finally made sense to me: "People have a hard time letting go of their suffering. Out of a fear of the unknown, they prefer suffering that is familiar." Having stepped away from a life of living for the weekend, a burden had been lifted off my shoulders. The sober life I was now living was more peaceful, more comfortable, and more complete than I could ever have dreamed.

The next few days were more or less the same. Meditation continued every weekday morning with a different technique each time. I volunteered to clean the pool and work in the garden. I swam in the pool each day with the others, fully nude, not having to think twice about it anymore. I swayed effortlessly in the hammock, enjoying the breeze and the light swinging sensation as I peered out at the volcano. I indulged in scrumptious fruits, picking juicy mangoes from the trees; chewing fresh plantains and bananas; snacking on tart star fruit; squeezing fresh grapefruit juice; and slicing open coconuts with a machete, guzzling their water, and slicing out their meat to munch on. I immersed myself in Eckhart Tolle's book, *The Power of Now*, learning new ways to focus on being present and living the moment. I continued to grow closer to the volunteers and learned about their lives, feeling a kinship with each of them as if they were family. I was starting to cherish yoga more each day; my inflexible body was slowly adjusting to the unfamiliar movements, and my mind was enjoying the fruits of mindfulness. Lily taught yoga most days, and her soothing voice had calming powers. The act of verbally announcing my gratitude each night and checking in with my feelings each morning was fulfilling. It fostered a lightness and acceptance of all the wonderful things that I was experiencing.

* * * * *

Friday rolled around, and everyone awoke enthusiastic for the weekend ahead. Every Friday night, there was a cacao party, and I was excited to experience it and curious about what it entailed.

The sun was setting beyond the horizon, and we sat around a campfire outside the ashram on wooden logs, listening to Jonas play guitar and sing songs. Bruno and I grabbed Conga drums and thumped to the beat while the others chimed in as well. We sat relishing each other's company and looking out over the jungle. As darkness settled in, we gathered in the ashram and indulged in the tasty cacao balls that Hannah and Lily had prepared.

"Cheers to the weekend!" Lily toasted us in delight.

"Cheers!" we all roared back.

Tim turned on the music, and the party began. Electronic trance music vibrated the room, and everyone was dancing loosely and freely swaying to the music. I closed my eyes and let the music take over as I jumped and jived to the beat and grooved without worry or judgment. I stepped outside to take a break. A fervent fest of fireflies was twinkling in the black atmosphere. Thousands of dots were lighting up the jungle, flickering and synchronizing to the beat of the music. I stood there with my mouth hanging open, amazed at the sight before my eyes. The fireflies were dancing, too! I laughed as the sight reminded me of a rave, except that the lights were coming from flies, not people. They electrified the ecstatic atmosphere, dazzling the night, and somehow were in sync with the music. We danced into the night, and I eventually made my way to my tent and fell asleep.

> *"Self-observation brings man to the realization of the necessity of self-change. And in observing himself a man notices that self-observation itself brings about certain changes in his inner processes. He begins to understand that self-observation is an instrument of self-change, a means of awakening."*
> —George Gurdjieff

CHAPTER 32

Sharing Circle

June 10, 2015

"To share your weakness is to make yourself vulnerable; to make yourself vulnerable is to show your true strength."

—Criss Jami

My visa was set to expire soon, and I planned on heading to Costa Rica in a few days. I was interested in exploring another community-based volunteering project. With my money starting to run low, I logged onto Workaway to browse the various volunteering opportunities available in Costa Rica. As I scrolled through multiple profiles, one jumped out at me: "CHI Permaculture and Healing Community." I clicked on the profile, and the description revealed a setting surrounded by rich jungle living openly with nature; Sundays spent in silence; daily meditation; a positive community of like-minded individuals working in the garden and planting fruits, trees, plants, and vegetables.

There was a disclaimer that read, "Strict raw food diet: at CHI, we live solely on a raw fruit and plant-based diet. While this is challenging for many, please take this opportunity to experience the benefits of eating this way and see the amazing transformation that will happen to your body."

The peaceful way of life at Eden sparked my desire to continue traveling in a holistic, harmonious fashion. I had a growing fascination with how permaculture worked, and I wanted to learn the fundamentals of growing organic food. The description explained that working in the garden and planting food was a main component of the volunteer work. I had heard about the benefits of eating raw food and how it could immensely ease skin problems. Although my skin was doing much better, I still had acne breaking out on the right side of my face. I was curious to see what would happen to my body and energy level from eating and living this way. I sent the contact person an e-mail, and he responded that I could come! I planned to head out on Friday, three days before my visa was set to expire.

On Wednesday night, we all gathered in the ashram after dinner for "Sharing Circle." I sat down on the cool, hard floor and circled up with the others, sitting crisscross. Every Wednesday night at Eden was Sharing Circle. "This is an opportunity for anyone who wants to share something. It can be personal, stressful, a feeling, an event, anything. Everything that is said here remains here unless the person sharing chooses to talk about it outside the ashram. This is a sacred space, and I ask you all to please respect each other. If you wish to speak, please stand up and walk to the center of the circle so we can all see and hear you. When you are finished sharing, please sit back down. Anyone else can walk to the center and offer any advice or share a similar experience if that person is open to it."

The Sharing Circle began, and no one moved. My tailbone was rooted to the floor and apparently everyone else's was, too. The soft chirps of crickets sounded in the still, night air. My eyes moved around the circle examining the other volunteers. *I wonder who will go first? I don't feel as if I have anything to share.* I watched as their eyes slowly peered around as well, waiting as I was. Finally, Jeremy stood up from his seated position and walked into the circle. He looked up momentarily searching for the right words. His forehead wrinkled together, and he was frowning slightly, his eyes narrowed. He began sharing a personal experience, and his hands moved up and down as he talked, walking in a slow circle. His words didn't flow easily. They dribbled out of him like maple oozing down from a tree as if the emotions built up inside of him had to be gently released. After he finished talking, he emitted a large sigh of relief and sat back down.

I sat still, letting his powerful story soak in as I tried to absorb the emotions that had been clearly locked inside of him for a long time. Matt rose and eased toward the center. He addressed Jeremy and revealed a similar experience he had and offered his advice. He then sat back down. The Sharing Circle continued for another thirty minutes.

The concept of the Sharing Circle challenged my notion of what strength is. Being in a comfortable environment with accepting people allowed everyone the opportunity to reveal deep, emotionally traumatic, distressing, sensitive experiences and feelings. It was such a simple idea yet profound in its effects. As I grew up, I observed that many people, including me, became increasingly less inclined to discuss personal and emotional feelings and experiences. I always felt like I had to only show the positive aspects of my life whether through social media or in school. By expressing feelings and faults and revealing painful memories, I believed I would be perceived as weak, or worse—*be weak*. In reality, everyone has his or her own issues and problems. It's universal that we all struggle. We're humans. Pretending that we don't have issues will not erase them. In fact, it often does the opposite, and expands the problem further and deeper, affecting other areas of our lives. There is a power that stems from being open and connecting with others through a sense of vulnerability. To accept your authentic self with flaws and weaknesses and to expose yourself as you really are—no filter, no mask, nothing—is true power.

I had a flashback to the first time I was sitting in Julia's career counseling office in Ohio. Being able to confide in Julia, to simply voice my fears to her—person to person, human to human—had a magical healing power. She was simply there to listen and to understand, nothing more. I felt empty yet renewed. The action of verbally expressing my concerns, simply releasing them from my mental thoughts into spoken words, was liberating. It was as if I had a balloon strapped to me, and it had become so overstuffed with anxiety and stress that it finally released from my grip, and all the air flew out. I had waited so long that my balloon couldn't hold any more air. We all have balloons. But too often, we let our balloons become so filled with stress that they eventually burst. And this can be dangerous. *What if we all acknowledged each other's balloons? What if we could release the air from our balloons way before they burst open? What would our lives look like if we could openly talk about the deeper issues that we all experience? Would people have more empathy for each other?*

The next part of the Sharing Circle began, and we formed two circles: an inner and an outer one. I was sitting in the inner circle, facing the people in the outer circle. We were directed to connect with the person on the outer circle, telling them what we appreciated about them. Tim instructed us to scoot closer to our partners, sitting just a foot apart. I was facing Lily. He told us to spend a minute looking at each other, examining and observing without words. I peered into Lily's sea-blue eyes, which were within arm's reach. It was awkward at first, being so close to her and silently looking deeply into her eyes as she looked deeply into mine. My instinct was to say something to break the silence. But I resisted the urge and stared, mystified by her eyes.

"The person on the inner circle may begin speaking," Tim interjected. Looking at Lily straight in the eyes and with utmost sincerity, I told her what I admired about her. I told her what a great leader she was, always leading by example in the garden and assisting others in an effective and thoughtful manner. I told her how she emitted a joyous, positive energy, and that it was infectious to everyone around her. I told her how I admired her independence and strong will. I told her how I admired her passion for helping others and how I loved hearing her stories of volunteering in Africa. And I said all of this with complete honesty. I meant every word. I really did appreciate her.

Tim's voice signaled that it was time for the other person to share. It was humbling to hear the kind things she said about me, that I was brave and wise beyond my years and conscious of others. She also said something that stuck with me for the rest of my travels. "Your smile makes me want to smile. Don't stop smiling," she told me. That message really resonated with me. I never thought I had a great smile or anything. But that was beside the point. What I took away from that statement was the power I have to spread my joy. A smile can instantly change someone's day. A smile can cause a chemical change in the body. A smile can give someone else the freedom to smile.

The most rewarding part of this process was having the opportunity to express my gratitude to her. The ability to have a genuine, heart-to-heart conversation and convey my appreciation was more fulfilling than any gift in the world. And as I went around the room, I got to express my gratitude for Bruno and Hannah and Sienna and Luca. I found myself unable to control my laughter when staring into Bruno's eyes.

"I am grateful for being wiz peo-ple who are peeesful and happy," he would express every night before dinner in a genuine fashion. His strong French accent paired with his kid-like sincerity had me biting my cheeks to restrain my laughter every night as he conveyed his thankfulness. As I laughed, he laughed, too, and we both just sat there cracking up as we gazed into each other's eyes. With each sharing experience, a unique energy arose—a connection that could only be felt buzzing deep inside my chest yet was communicated by a wide smile and the look in their eyes of gratification and appreciation.

The Sharing Circle wrapped up, and we all said goodnight, the link among us woven even tighter. As I lay in my tent, that warm feeling still residing in my stomach, I wondered what it would be like if the business world adopted such a practice. I imagined once a week all the employees of a company coming in an hour earlier to work and sitting crisscross in a circle on the floor in business suits and dress shoes. I imagined what it would do to the business environment, perhaps creating a closer, tight-knit family dynamic. *Would it give people more empathy for their employees, for their boss, for their coworkers, and clients? Would they be motivated to work harder for each other? Would this tranquil, peaceful practice instill a happier work environment and lead to better teamwork? Would people be more inclined to reach the company goals? Would "work" become a word with a positive connotation instead of a negative one?* My mind ran endlessly through the possibilities that could stem from creating an open and accepting environment where people could connect beyond the surface level, delving deep past the tip of the iceberg.

> *"We cultivate love when we allow our most vulnerable and powerful selves to be deeply seen and known."*
>
> —Brené Brown

CHAPTER 33

The Gift of Giving

June 12, 2015

"Mind is ambiguous, yet heart is pure,
No mixed signals or tempting lure.
When I follow this path, I'm always free,
Not questioning life, just happy to be.
When my heart speaks, I try and listen closely,
I receive the message internally, well mostly.
Sleeping on mats, bugs my new fragrance,
Going fully bare, enjoying new places,
If my home is black, then this is white,
A contrast indeed, but the time of my life.
The last few months have shown me once again
To follow my heart, because he is my friend."

—Jake Heilbrunn (written during my stay in Eden)

I left Eden with an extra ounce of love in my heart, a new sense of peace of mind, and a feeling of tremendous self-growth in my soul. The daunting idea of practicing yoga every day and waking up at five thirty every morning for meditation became something I cherished and looked forward to. It was a challenge that pushed me to my physical, emotional, and mental limits. It was a challenge that uncovered suppressed feelings and experiences; it was a challenge that made me face who I really was; it was a challenge that reminded me of what is possible when the mind, body, and spirit work together in harmony.

Saying good-bye to everyone and leaving Eden felt odd. I didn't know what to feel. I noticed a numbing sensation as I headed out. I had grown so close to everyone and become part of the community in such a short time. I experienced feelings and sensations that I didn't know were possible. It struck me that I had both gained and lost something. New experiences and relationships had etched their way into my heart. But I had also uncovered layers that were no longer a part of me. A layer of self-criticism had peeled off, making way for the love and acceptance I held for myself, which the community helped nurture. A layer of judgment and stereotyping had crumbled, paving the way to have empathy and understanding for others and the realization that we are universal in our struggles.

I didn't want to leave Eden, but knew another adventure lay in store. Right before I was planning to head out, Tim mentioned that the last bus to Moyoglapa was at 1:45 p.m. *1:45 p.m.!! I thought the bus was at 2:15 p.m.!* Frantically, I hurried down the path that led out of Eden and into town, which was a thirty-minute hike.

I hastened down the trail surrounded by sweeping fields and luscious farmland filled with cows and horses. As I neared the end of the trail, a loud "*Beep, beep!*" blared. I knew it was the bus, and I began to sprint. I reached the asphalt and scurried toward the deserted bus stop, trying to convince myself that the bus hadn't left when I knew well that it had.

I plopped down on the empty wooden bench, defeated. The wooden beams stuck out rigidly against my back. I sat there annoyed and agitated trying to catch my breath. *I needed to catch that bus! There goes my plan. How am I going to get out of here? Why couldn't I have just made that bus! Urghh.* Missing the bus stressed me out. My mind couldn't figure out how I was to proceed. The buses on Ometepe were not always reliable and often went only once a day to the other side of the island.

I had just come from a peaceful place that had instilled a calmness and acceptance for the ways of the Universe. Yet here I was stressing over things beyond my control. I sat still on the bench breathing in the toasty afternoon air, letting my mind wander and escape my current predicament. *This, too, shall pass. This, too, shall pass.* On the bright side, I wasn't stranded on a rural mountainside in the pouring rain! After calming down, I stood up. It was time to figure out my next move.

I approached a shop nearby and greeted the vendor. He informed me that there was a *colectivo* van at 3:00 p.m. to Altagracia, another stop on the island but still far away from Moyogalpa. He didn't know if there would be a bus from there to Moyogalpa but said it would be my best shot. I thanked him and trudged back to the vacant bench. An hour later, the *colectivo* van pulled up. There were just a few others in the van, and we headed off to Altagracia. I asked the bus driver if there were any buses heading to Moyogalpa. He informed me that there was one at 5:00 p.m., and it was the final one for the day. The driver pulled to a halt on the side of the road by some concrete benches.

"This is the bus stop to Moyoglapa," the bus driver announced to me in Spanish. "It should arrive in an hour." I thanked him and stepped out. The van thundered off, spewing dust and dirt behind it as it sped into the distance.

I walked over to the uninhabited benches and sank down into a cool, uneven concrete seat. A woman and two young girls, whom I assumed were her children, approached. The kids were skipping toward the bench with glee in each of their steps and cheerful smiles painted across their faces. They all shared the same dark-mocha skin. They sat down a few feet from me, and I greeted them and said hello. The girls were swinging their feet back and forth with an animated energy. A thought popped into my head, and I suddenly remembered the stickers in my backpack. I opened up my zipper, pulled out my bag of stickers, and handed a bundle of them to the girls. Their smiles stretched even wider, and their eyes lit up as they thanked me. They explored the stickers, admiring them and examining the differences and similarities in color. The younger one burst out in laughter as she placed a sticker on her nose and looked up to show her mom.

The younger girl was named *Dulce*, which means "sweet" in Spanish, and it couldn't be a more accurate word to describe her. She bounced buoyantly, full of zest. Her hair was in pigtails, and she wore a baby-blue shirt and a long, fluorescent, flannel pink skirt that flowed past her knees. The colors of her clothes matched the enthusiasm she radiated. She was six years old. Her sister, Maria, was eleven and more reserved than her younger sister. She wore a colorful dress adorned with bright patterns and designs. She laughed with Dulce as they played with their stickers and frolicked around.

They sat next to me and began playing patty cake, high fiving each other and singing aloud. Dulce turned to me, and I started playing with her. Having grown up with two sisters, I was experienced with patty cake. We got into a rhythm, and I sped up the tempo, going so fast until Dulce messed up and exploded into a parade of giggles, burying her face in her hands.

The bus pulled up, and a group of people swarmed toward the door. I hadn't even noticed the others arrive at the bus stop. Dulce, Maria, and their mom got on before me. I climbed in and looked down the aisle to see the bus jam-packed with people. I walked toward the middle of the bus, put my backpack beneath my feet and grabbed the railing to hold on.

As the bus engine grumbled to a start, I heard my name called from behind. "Jake! Jake!" I turned around and spotted Maria and Dulce sitting a few seats back. They were sharing a seat, and their mom was behind them sitting next to another passenger. Their hands were waving in the air, motioning for me to sit down next to them. They had scooted up against the wall of the bus in order to make room for me. I gladly and gratefully accepted their offer, squeezed by a few people standing in the aisle and sat down. We started to play patty cake again. I continued to play games with Dulce and Maria, their positivity spreading through me like wild fire.

As I sat there feeling thankful to be in such joyous company and to have a seat on the crowded bus, I realized just how powerful giving truly is. It had been such a basic gesture to give them stickers at the bus stop. They were complete strangers to me—our paths had never crossed before. By simply greeting them warmly and giving them stickers, I had made friends when I least expected it. My worries about missing the bus, stressing out over my plans, and getting to Moyogalpa had vanished. My mind was occupied by the delightful presence of Maria and Dulce. Waiting for the bus didn't feel like waiting at all when I was immersed in playing games with them. I was especially touched by their offer to let me sit with them. The bus was crammed, and the hour bus ride standing in the aisle squished in between people and grasping the metal rail would have been far from comfortable. The sincerity of their offer, along with the unexpectedness of it, sent a wave of thankfulness through me. The fruits of giving are infinite—and the joy it brought me was priceless.

I said good-bye to Maria, Dulce, and their mom once we arrived in Moyogalpa. I thanked them and wished them well as we parted, feeling a piece of their lighthearted spirit etched into my own.

I checked into a cheap hostel nearby and made preparations for the next day. I was going to board the early morning ferry to Rivas and then take a bus to Peñas Blancas. From there, I would hop on a bus to the border. I would walk across the border and jump on a bus to San Jose and find a hostel there for the night. Dennis, the man in charge of the CHI permaculture volunteering, was going to be in San Jose for the weekend. He offered to pick me up in the city and take me back to CHI, which I imagined would be much more pleasant than another four-hour bus ride. CHI was located in Uvita, a vibrant beach town surrounded by jungle. The day ahead loomed large in my mind. But today had shown me that beauty often lies in the unexpected. And with that reassuring thought, I drifted off to sleep. I had no idea what I was getting myself into.

"Giving opens the way for receiving."
—Florence Scovel Shinn

CHAPTER 34

On the Road and Missing Home

June 13, 2015

"Where we love is home— home that our feet may leave,
but not our hearts."

—Oliver Wendell Holmes

The journey to San Jose was tedious. Getting to the border and going through Customs had been surprisingly smooth, but the rest of the trip strung out in slow motion. I ended up taking a bus to a city called Liberia because the bus to San Jose was full. I had expected to meet many English speakers and fellow backpackers on the bus because I thought of Costa Rica as a destination for many Westerners and travelers. I had been looking forward to meeting other travelers and conversing in English because translating everything into Spanish in my head was taxing. However, it turned out that I was the only nonlocal on my bus for the five-hour ride. The bus traversed areas that expanded my knowledge of the country. Of course, we passed through lush jungles and incredible biodiversity, but we also passed the kinds of small huts with tin roofs that I had seen in Nicaragua and Guatemala— aspects of Costa Rica that aren't often talked about. We didn't pass any exotic resorts or fancy hotels.

I tried conversing with the gentleman sitting next to me, but his words sounded like gibberish. He had a peculiar accent, and he could have been speaking French for all I knew. He soon closed his eyes, and I turned my head out the window. I was missing home. I wanted to hug my mom more than I ever had in my life and squeeze her close to me. I wanted to go out to dinner with my dad and cringe at the embarrassing jokes he kiddingly told the waiter. I wanted to catch up with my sisters and eat our favorite Breyer's chocolate ice cream. I wanted to sit by the fire pit with my best friends and laugh until my abs burned and talk about everything and nothing. I wanted my dog to jump up on me and lick my face and uncontrollably wag his tail.

An ache in my heart was widening as I thought of home more and more. I realized I needed to switch my thoughts and focus on something positive. I pulled out my journal and began reading my first few entries. I laughed inwardly as I read my first post, which I had written while sitting in the airport in Los Angeles. It seemed a million galaxies away, that day I set out on my journey. The words in my journal brought me back to the airport and the feelings that coursed through my scared, naive self. I felt the emotions I had that day as if they were as real as ever: alert and exhilarated, nervous and apprehensive, relieved and optimistic. I soaked up every word, feeling, and experience of those first few journal entries, reflecting over the transformation I had undergone in just a few months. My lips stretched into a smile, and my stresses seemed to dissipate. These writings reminded me that just beyond the corner of the unknown, a grand adventure is waiting to unfold.

The bus arrived in Liberia, and I boarded another bus for the four-hour journey to San Jose. I finally arrived late in the evening and eventually made it to the hostel. I settled in and was overjoyed to find other English speakers staying there. I hopped in the shower, and the hot water rained down with a jubilant energy. It had been almost a month since my last warm shower, and it wasn't an ounce less marvelous. I checked my e-mail and saw a message from Dennis confirming that he would pick me up the following day in the early afternoon. Exhausted and relieved, I eased into bed, eager to experience life at CHI and meet members of the community.

*   *   *   *   *

The next morning, Dennis phoned the hostel to notify me he would be arriving in the next few minutes. I grabbed my backpack and stepped out into the city. It was starkly different from anywhere I had been so far. Large buildings with glass windows replaced mountains and volcanoes. Gray-and-black asphalt streets replaced grassy trails and unpaved paths; cars and trucks replaced cows and horses; horns and sirens replaced the howls of monkeys and the chirping of birds.

I stood on the side of the street peering into each car's windshield to see if it might be Dennis. I had no idea what he looked like. For whatever reason, I imagined him to be in his early forties with a curly head of black hair and a calm demeanor like Tim. In his e-mails, he conveyed a respectful and warm personality and ended each of his e-mails with the words, "With Love and Gratitude, Dennis."

A faded, navy-blue jeep that looked like it had been through a meat grinder grumbled over to the side of the road where I was standing. It was covered in chipped paint and dents. The man in the front seat waved his arms in the air at me, motioning for me to hop in. I knew it was Dennis. I creaked open the passenger door, half-afraid I would rip the worn metal door straight off the hinges from the raspy sound it made. I tossed my backpack into the messy back seat, which was filled with clutter. And then I met Dennis.

He was shirtless and without shoes. His tan, leathered skin contrasted against the remaining grayish-white hair on his balding head. He looked to be in his fifties and was surprisingly lean—he didn't have large muscles yet was sculpted and looked to be strong. He had an ample smile and icy-blue eyes that crackled with an unusual liveliness.

"Hello, Jake," he greeted me in his German accent. Just from this brief interaction, with nothing concrete to go on, I felt there was something odd about him. A pit of uneasiness formed in my stomach despite his seemingly sincere greeting. I felt hyper alert, and not just because of his strange appearance—driving with no shirt and bare feet with the windows down in a beaten-up jeep in the middle of the city. Like I said, there was something not quite right about him. It was an intuitive notion, a gut feeling. The reviews for CHI on Workaway were all positive and said great things about Dennis—I figured that I was missing something or misinterpreting his appearance.

Other than my name, I couldn't get a word in for the next twenty minutes besides "uh-huh," "yeah," and hmm," as I nodded my head, acknowledging his whirlwind of stories. Dennis told me about how he had moved to Costa Rica twenty years ago after becoming fed up with his life in Germany. He raved about the three volunteers who were staying at CHI. "You vill love them, I just know it. They all arrived a few days ago."

Suddenly, Dennis veered off the farthest lane on the right, completely off the road. I gripped my seat, and my fingers clawed into the fabric as I recoiled and braced for impact. His car was a mere six inches away from smashing into a pickup truck as he created his own lane to the right of the paved road. My shock subsided, and I let out a sigh of relief. Dennis then swung back onto the main road. What just happened struck me as crazy, but Dennis responded in an earnest tone that he was "simply taking advantage of a situation vithout harming anyone else." And with that, the next four hours consisted of Dennis's law-breaking and breath-shortening actions of swerving around cars, creating lanes where he felt justified, and flying at extreme speeds.

We pulled over at a wooden market on the side of the road about halfway into the ride. Leaving his car door wide open, Dennis limped out of the car still barefoot and bare chested, looking like a caveman. He explained that he had gotten into an accident riding a motorcycle two months earlier, which had badly damaged his right foot.

"*Puuura viida*," he energetically greeted the vendor, hobbling into the store. "*Pura vida*" translates directly into "pure life" and holds a variety of meanings to Costa Ricans, including "hello," "good-bye," "take it easy," and "enjoy life." Dennis bought some food and put it into a bag, and we drove off again. An hour later, he pulled up to a park in a small town and limped out, leaving his door wide open again.

I didn't want to stop again. I was looking forward to getting to CHI, meeting the other volunteers, and going to bed. "Ve are stopping to eat here and zen ve vill head to Uvita," he announced, carrying the bag of food to a bench a few feet from the car. "Ahh," he sighed loudly, plopping down on the bench with a broad smile on his face. "Here ve have some carrots and cheese and tomatoes and radishes," he pulled out the colorful foods from the bag. I was surprised to see that he had bought cheese. Coming from a cow, cheese isn't a type of raw food, which I understood was the strict diet that he would be imposing on us at CHI. I chose to conceal my confusion.

He pulled out a knife and a cutting board and began slicing the food on the park bench. It was half-past eight, and few cars were driving around the park. A group of teenagers were hanging out nearby, and I could feel their glares on the back of my neck like a sunburn. I felt like a fish in the desert sitting on this bench next to half-naked Dennis, munching on vegetables and wondering how the hell I ended up here. He blabbed on about his life and beliefs and asked me an occasional question or two. Finally, he stood up from the bench, and we hopped back into the jeep and zoomed off.

We arrived at the house, which, enclosed by an abundance of trees, was hard to see in the dark. The chirps and quirky noises of animals and insects chimed into the night sky. There were two people home, and I initially assumed they were volunteers. It turned out they were a couple biking down from Mexico to Panama, and they were just spending the weekend at Dennis's home.

"Vhere are ze other volunteers?" Dennis asked with a high pitch of uncertainty in his tone.

"They left," the couple replied simultaneously.

"They left?!" Dennis cried out in confusion. "All three of them? Did they say anyfing?" A look of bewilderment was plastered on Dennis's face, and his forehead scrunched together in a wave of wrinkles.

"Yeah, they left earlier today," the man replied in a straightforward manner. "They said this just wasn't for them."

"I do not believe it," Dennis said, baffled. "Ve all enjoyed such a nice sunset before I left. Every zing seemed amazing. I do not understand zis."

Dennis had told me about how wonderful the volunteers were and how they all got along so well. Yet, he had not the slightest inclination about why they left. On the one hand, Dennis came across as gentle and loving; on the other hand, he came across as ludicrous with no sense of the world around him other than his own thoughts.

"Ahh, and zey didn't finish the plastic tarp for ze green room," Dennis voiced aloud, frustrated and perplexed. "I simply do not understand zis."

I had paid Dennis $135 for the next month to volunteer. He asked for $5 a day in exchange for four hours of work five days a week, which seemed more than reasonable to cover food costs and have a place to sleep. I thought about leaving early the next morning without telling him. His lack of awareness was unsettling and I was nervous to be alone with him—not because he posed a threat, but because he emitted an edgy aura that I didn't feel comfortable being around.

Dennis looked over at me and reassured, "Vell, zis is no problem. Ve can still get much done ze next few days. It vill be a small community of two for now," he laughed aloud. I forced a smile although I didn't find it funny and felt my stomach turning. I had expected many other volunteers to be here from the description online. I admired his ability to take the positive from the situation, but I couldn't ignore my uneasiness.

Dennis escorted me upstairs to a large open room. The entire house was constructed with almost no walls—everything was open and exposed to nature and the surrounding jungle outside. The room on the second floor had three mattresses and a few hammocks, all vacant. The couple staying the night was in the room next to me. Dennis handed me some sheets and blankets and said I could sleep on whatever mattress or hammock I liked. I thanked him and told him I was going to sleep because I was exhausted.

"No problem, my friend," he responded. "Ve can start vork vhen you avake tomorrow. No need to get up early. Zis situation is all still very strange to me. But I vish you a very good sleep." He smiled at me, and I thanked him and sat in my new bed. I wanted to ask the couple what had happened and why the volunteers left. But the lights were off in their room, and they were asleep.

Fatigued, I sprawled out on my mattress. It was comfortable beyond belief—at least, compared to my prior sleeping arrangements the last few months. I turned to view the mesh of green trees and the sleeping jungle that lay just outside the room. Despite my feelings of consternation, the house was serene, and I loved its openness to nature. The sounds of the jungle comforted me as I fell asleep.

"Life is full of confusion. Confusion of love, passion, and romance.
Confusion of family and friends. Confusion with life itself.
What path we take, what turns we make. How we roll our dice."
—Matthew Underwood

CHAPTER 35

Living with Crazy

June 15, 2015

"When dealing with people, remember you are not dealing with creatures of logic, but with creatures of emotion, creatures bristling with prejudice, and motivated by pride and vanity."

—Dale Carnegie

The next morning I awoke early, and Dennis gave me a tour of the house. It looked straight out of a fairytale. The house was constructed solely from wood and immersed in greenery, blending into the jungle surrounding it. Next to Dennis's room, which openly faced the driveway, was a small, green, wooden table with cushions and mats around it. Peaceful ponds filled with fish and lily pads and other vibrant aqua plants elegantly bordered a garden. It had the appearance of a meditation garden.

We walked around the property, and Dennis showed me an array of vegetables, fruits, and spices. Different types of lettuce were growing along with spinach, carrots, and some other plants. A huge mango tree rose from the ground in the front yard, and I scooped up over fifty mangoes and brought them inside, following Dennis's request.

We walked farther down his property and made a loop around to the backyard. Countless banana trees were growing and pineapples, ginger and turmeric roots were planted in the clay-colored soil. Lustrous flowers in vivid magentas, maroons, sun yellows and royal blues sprouted all along the house. The plants and vegetation reminded me of *Eden*.

"It is not good to have breakfast right vhen you vake up," Dennis affirmed. "The stomach is still digesting in ze morning. People are actually not hungry in ze morning but believe zhey are because society says to eat vhen you avake."

It sounded weird to me, especially because it countered everything I had been taught growing up. Breakfast was the "most important meal of the day" in my mind. But I decided that despite my hesitation in believing Dennis, I could manage to go without breakfast, at least for the day, and see how I felt. It would be a new experience, an experiment even.

A man approached, and Dennis greeted him in a friendly fashion, making it evident that they knew each other. "Jake, zis is Johnny. He has been vorking here for many years and helps me vith many zings." I shook Johnny's hand, and I found his presence comforting the moment I locked eyes with him. A native Costa Rican, he was short, a couple inches shorter than me, and had dark, deer-brown skin. He wore a cap on his head, and the bridge was curved. His hand was calloused and rough when I shook it, yet his demeanor was tranquil.

"Johnny vill show you vhat needs to be done today. You vill be chopping down ze leaves from ze trees over zhere so ve can use them for our green room vhich ve are building. Use ze vheelbarrow to take ze plants over there." Dennis handed Johnny and me a machete and a large ladder that we both carried as I followed Johnny past the mango tree.

I was relieved to get away from Dennis. Johnny and I talked for a while in Spanish, and he told me about his family and eight-year-old son. He had an admirable energy about him. My spirits lifted from being in his company and away from Dennis. I watched as Johnny maneuvered the ladder up against a huge palm tree and climbed to the top, his machete hanging in one hand. With the skills of a ninja, he chopped down large palm leaves that crackled to the ground as they fell. I began slicing down big oval leaves from the banana trees, feeling like Zorro.

Working with the machete invigorated me. It was more than simply slicing down leaves—it was an expression, a mindful exercise. We stuffed as many leaves and plants into the wheelbarrow as we could and wheeled it past the driveway, dumping them where Dennis had indicated.

The sun was ascending higher, and the humid air steamed down like a sauna. "Jake! Johnny!" Dennis belted out from inside the house. "Come here!" Johnny and I walked into the kitchen where Dennis was standing—completely naked. In the description on Workaway, I remembered seeing a sentence saying, "casual nudity." My experience at Eden had made me more comfortable around nudity, yet I still found it a little weird at first seeing Dennis fully nude. I could tell by Johnny's face and lack of reaction that this was all quite normal to him.

"I made you guys smoovies," he said. He handed us a glass containing a mixture of a thick, yellowy-orange color and a mixture of greens. "It is fresh mango juice and greens from ze garden," Dennis explained. Johnny and I thanked him and sat down at the wooden table next to the kitchen along with Dennis. The drink revitalized my taste buds; the sweet candy flavor of the mango energized me.

"Are any other volunteers coming this week?" I asked Dennis casually, trying to obscure my hopeful plea.

"Yes, an Australian girl is arriving on Friday from London, and two girls from Spain are coming on Sunday."

"Awesome!" I exclaimed. Relief surged inside of me at the thought of others arriving.

I spent two more hours in the wet heat slicing plants and wheeling them to the green room with Johnny. By the time I finished, it was almost noon, and I was worn out. The house had an outside shower, and the cooling water felt great. I strolled upstairs to the open room where my bed and the other hammocks were. I settled into one of the hammocks overlooking the scenic garden and closed my eyes.

I awoke two hours later, feeling renewed. I walked downstairs and into Dennis's room where he was sitting at his computer.

"Jake, vould you like to go to ze beach soon?" he asked. "Ve can bring some food and relax for a vhile."

"Yeah, that sounds great," I replied.

We gathered some fruit in a basket and put two hammocks in the trunk of the jeep. We rolled through town and made our way toward the beach. Uvita was a serene, charming town untouched by the tourism boom that had already reached many towns in Costa Rica. It was a tropical hamlet, and its quiet peacefulness seemed almost surreal. We drove through a loose straggle of farms, homes, and small shops on our way to the ocean. A mini jungle stood right before the shoreline, and a sign stated that a fee was necessary to enter the beach, as it was a natural reserve. Dennis rumbled through the bumpy terrain, ignoring the sign.

"I have been here for over twenty years, way before all of zhese people. I will not pay and zhey know that," he remarked, laughing aloud. An array of palm trees towered over the beach.

After hanging out at the beach for a while, we went back to the house. It struck me that I wasn't very hungry even though I had only eaten smoothies, bananas, and grapefruits the entire day. I wasn't feeling lightheaded or lacking my usual energy as I suspected might happen. I explained this to Dennis, and he definitively replied, "Of course! Zhis is how humans are supposed to eat. In nature, zhis is how our ancestors ate."

I helped Dennis in the kitchen as we prepared food for dinner. "Cut zhis broccoli into small pieces," he declared. Dennis had a way of commanding things in a domineering manner. He liked things done his way, executed efficiently and specifically. It became evident to me that this was just part of his nature, something of which he was unaware. I don't think he meant to be overbearing, but every time he directed me to do something, I became even more irritated. We sat down for dinner, enjoying a feast of uncooked vegetables: broccoli, onions, tomatoes, and greens from the garden. Dennis confidently assured me that my acne would clear up from simply eating this way.

"Vatch vhat happens to your skin. In only a veek, you vill feel ze difference," he proclaimed, a wide smile on his face. His confidence gave me hope and another reason to stay here at CHI despite my hesitations.

"Learn from the mistakes of others. You can't live long enough
to make them all yourself."
—Eleanor Roosevelt

CHAPTER 36

Releasing the World from my Shoulders

June 16, 2015

"Letting go doesn't mean that you don't care about someone anymore. It's just realizing that the only person you really have control over is yourself."

—Deborah Reber

I awoke at five thirty and started working. As commanding as Dennis was, he didn't have an organized schedule, which I had expected from his Workaway description. It had listed daily morning meditations as well, which he hadn't even mentioned up to now.

Dennis instructed me to start stapling together two 30-foot by 30-foot plastic tarps. The goal was to create one enormous tarp. It was going to hang down from the roof of the house and stretch down at an angle, essentially creating a tent so he could create a green room and grow certain vegetables during the approaching rainy season. After an hour of stapling, Dennis told me I had stapled them incorrectly because I didn't leave enough room for the tarps to overlap. He had me undo each staple, which I found frustrating, since his directions were so unclear. After another hour of stapling everything the way Dennis wanted, he announced we would head to the soccer field to prepare and stretch the tarps in order to hang them. He explained we needed to fully stretch out the tarps, and there wasn't room to do so at the house. I didn't understand exactly what he wanted and how he was going to pull this off, but I concealed my confusion and followed his directions.

We drove to an empty soccer field, where I helped Dennis lift the heavy plastic sheets from the trunk and spread them out on the field.

"Ah, ze volunteers did not do vhat I asked," Dennis moaned aloud. "You vill need to staple ze tarps like zis," he asserted. He directed me to fold the tarp and staple in a line to create a loop so a large bamboo pole could fit through. The tone of his voice and the implication of his command revealed that this would be no quick task. I was starting to become frustrated and angry with Dennis. The Workaway description had revealed nothing about this kind of work—I wanted to learn about permaculture and how to plant and grow food, not staple tarps together.

He pulled out a joint and a cigarette from his bag. "Do you want to smoke?" he asked.

I found it surprising that he had joints and cigarettes. He had described CHI as a drug-free, healing environment without mind-altering chemicals and synthetic products. Yet here he was with a pack of cigarettes and marijuana ready to light up. I had no problem with the concept of smoking. Many of the friends I had met while traveling smoked, and they were wonderful people. What bothered me were the many contradictions between Dennis's words and actions. He would spill out all of his beliefs and dogma about being healthy and following a raw food diet and then do something completely against what he said. My levels of respect and trust for him were dropping by the second.

"No, I'm good. Thanks, though," I replied.

"Have you ever smoked before?" he asked curiously.

"Yeah. I'm just happy without it, that's all," I responded.

"I don't usually smoke," he quickly retorted as if trying to justify himself solely because of my answer. "It's just that I'm stressed-out about ze volunteers leaving and all of ze vork needed to be done."

I began tediously stapling the colossal, plastic tarps the way Dennis had instructed. He sat on the grass watching, smoking and indulging in mangoes while I worked tirelessly. I kept imagining punching him in the face—the image played over and over in my mind. Staple after staple, I moved up and down the plastic sheets, pressing down on the stapler. I must have used at least a hundred staples by the time I finished the first sheet.

"You can take a break if you vant," he called out to me after about an hour, smiling widely. My blood was boiling at every little noise Dennis uttered. I walked over to him, fuming. I was doused in sweat, itchy from the grass and bug bites, exhausted from working and baking under the sun's wrath. This was not a "community," there was no "morning meditation," the work was not "permaculture," the "four hours" of volunteering were downplayed and the "natural, healing environment" was complete bullshit.

I plopped down a few feet away from him, exhausted. He was stoned, and his goofy smile was anything but funny to me. He glanced over at me and revealed, "You look very annoyed and upset. Vhat is wrong?"

I stared fiercely down at the grass. I felt a lump forming in my throat, a choking sensation that paralyzed my speech. A tsunami of frustration, anxiety, confusion, and fatigue coursed through my veins. Tears suddenly flooded out of my eyes. Dennis looked at me in horror, his demeanor instantly changing.

"Vhat is wrong?" he asked with actual sincerity in his tone. His cheeks dropped and his smile vanished. His eyebrows slanted in a narrow frown as his eyes began to water.

I poured out everything I was angry about, from the disparity of Dennis's own actions and words to the false description of what the volunteering entailed, the lack of "community," his degrading commands, how unusual this all was, and his forceful dogma. I was actually shocked at my own crying. I remembered the words from that article on solo travel: "You will cry at one point—that part is inevitable." I never believed that it would happen to me, at least not this far into my journey. And I definitely didn't imagine being here, in this field, crying, with Dennis.

To my surprise, Dennis started to cry, too. Seeing a grown man cry—and realizing my own expression of emotions had triggered his reaction—was upsetting to me. His vulnerability, which he had shielded from me until this moment, somehow seemed familiar. I couldn't quite understand why this was unsettling to me and what his crying seemed to evoke.

With sorrow in his voice, he confessed, "Zhis is unusual to me as well; I did not expect ze volunteers to leave; I have a hurt foot, and zhey left ze house in a mess. Zhis is not normal for me, either. But it is not good to come to a place vith expectations."

"But how am I supposed to know what is normal here? I just arrived," I maintained. "The description you posted online is way different than what's actually going on. If you say that something will happen on your site, then you can't blame me for expecting it to happen." I explained the discrepancies I noticed between his actions and his intentions, listing them off one by one. I chose not to talk about the cigarettes or the cheese he ate when I arrived.

"I am sorry," he apologized. "All I have is zhe best intentions for you and to make zhis a positive experience." He talked with convincing integrity, and I really felt he was being honest. "If you are unhappy, you can leave, and I vill give you your money back."

I pondered his offer and contemplated my options. I could leave, but I didn't have any idea where I would go at the moment. On the one hand, Dennis came across as sincere and truthful in his apology; on the other, there seemed to be some deeper issue he had that would not be resolved in a matter of days or weeks. My mind was in an internal battle, deciding what to do.

"I will wait a few more days and see what happens when the other volunteers arrive," I announced.

His downcast face lit up, and he wiped away his tears. I felt relieved after spilling out all of my tension. I didn't expect for the events to unfold like they did, but life seems to work out that way. I laughed inwardly at the sight of Dennis and me crying in a field and how traveling had brought me to such odd places. I wondered if the Universe had brought me to CHI and to meet Dennis—maybe there was a reason I was here, a lesson to be learned.

"Let's put ze plastic back in ze car," Dennis advised. "You are done vorking today. But please, in the future, communicate vith me if something is wrong." I nodded at him, acknowledging that I would. We folded up the huge sheets of plastic and lifted them together back into the car.

As we were driving back, I thought about Dennis's commands and how he was clearly unhappy. Something about the way he shielded his unhappiness triggered something else tucked deep within me—it reminded me of my dad's depression. My dad had always tried to shield his unhappiness from my sisters and me. He would go to the moon and back for our safety and well-being; yet, despite coming across as an invincible rock all these years, I could sense my dad's pain.

I realized now that over the past few years, I had felt it was my responsibility to save my dad from depression. The therapeutic measures he had taken hadn't seemed to help much. Like my dad, I had been trying to keep a strong face. Crying with Dennis had been a release, causing my defense—my resistance to my dad's emotional pain—to be broken. I identified with him. I could feel what he was going through. All I wanted was for him to be happy and express to me what he was feeling—whether good or bad. It struck me that in a strange way, this journey was for my dad as much as it was for me.

The dynamics of family and love are intricate. Empathy allows us to feel the emotions of other people, to understand as best as we can from our perspective what they're experiencing. I felt I had a responsibility to heal my dad and bring him out of his depression. But it started to dawn on me: what was I *really* trying to save my dad from?

Life is meant to be lived in its entirety, not filtered. We experience a rainbow of emotions, ranging from sadness and remorse to joy and laughter, which together sum up what it means to be alive. The evolution of each individual's soul takes a unique route, and despite the label and description of every individual's journey, what if each journey is perfect? Only humans label circumstances as right and wrong. Could it be possible that my dad's journey is evolving as it should be? All I can do is show him unconditional love and support. I am who I am and my dad is who he is. Coming to this realization, I felt a responsibility float off my shoulders.

Dennis pulled over to the side of the road and got out. The road was surrounded by a flush of trees and greenery. I got out as well and heard the whispering rush of a waterfall in the distance. I followed Dennis through the trees until we approached a stunning natural pool that lay in their midst. Water was trickling down from the rocks, drizzling into the turquoise pool and flowing like a smooth layer of satin fabric. The surrounding plants and trees emitted a piney, fresh scent, and the droplets of water dribbled into the pool like peaceful raindrops.

I dove in, and the water sent a shock through my body as I broke through its surface. I adjusted to the cool water, feeling refreshed and cleansed by its soothing properties. Any lingering tension drained out of me as I floated and stared up at the treetops arching overhead. I remembered that Father's Day was in a few days. I decided to write a long email to my dad when Dennis and I got back to the house, expressing my gratitude for him and the realization I had after crying with Dennis.

Dennis grabbed a bunch of leaves from a plant nearby and ground them up in his hand, forming a dark-green, oozy, liquid paste.

"Zhis plant has many natural healing properties. It is very good for your skin." He squeezed the paste into my hand, and I rubbed it onto the right side of my face. Having lived in Uvita for many years, Dennis had a wealth of knowledge about medicinal plants in the area. His interest in the well-being of my skin lightened my frustration with him. I was grateful for his generosity—it reaffirmed my belief that he had good intentions despite his stubborn, overwhelming, and dominant personality. After swimming for a little while, we grabbed a bunch of medicinal leaves and drove back home.

That afternoon, I composed a long email to my dad, pouring out the emotions and realizations that surfaced during the day. I felt that the email would have a strong impact on my dad, as I really opened up from the heart about how much he meant to me. I was eager to read his response.

*　*　*　*　*

The next day, I received a reply from my dad. He said he had read my email several times and that no words could express how much it meant to him. He expressed his admiration for my courageously pursuing a life that made me happy. Reading my dad's response, I felt a deep sense of peace. We now had both acknowledged and supported the different paths we were on—but more importantly, we accepted them without condition. By making unconventional decisions for my own well-being, perhaps I could inspire him to do the same. Yet, regardless of how my dad and others decide to act, I now knew the most important thing I could do was continue to be proactive in pursuit of my dreams.

Being alone with Dennis the next two days, I began to adjust to his inner workings—and for the most part, I chose to leave them untouched. Trying to depict what went on inside Dennis's head was way outside of my ken. It was like trying to grasp how the sun works; rather than try to understand how it exists and what elements it is made of, it made more sense to figure out when it rises and when it falls, where to be and how to adjust to its inevitable forces. I tried to the best of my ability to complete tasks as Dennis asked, but soon realized that I would never be able to complete anything exactly the way he liked.

Dennis's considerate, helpful nature could transform into forceful and degrading like the flip of a light switch.

"Vhat are you doing?" he would ask, enraged. "Do it like zhis. You are being very inefficient." There came a point where I learned to tiptoe around his commands and let certain things go instead of getting worked up about them. I finally started to laugh whenever he barked at me for doing something wrong. Laughing was my release and Dennis soon became hilarious to me. I laughed at how wacky he was and how he couldn't accept the possibility that I could complete a task in a different way than he imagined. I realized that the fault was in him, not me. I was learning how to deal with him. I was learning to navigate and live with a narrow-minded, domineering character.

"Letting go helps us to live in a more peaceful state of mind and helps restore our balance. It allows others to be responsible for themselves and for us to take our hands off situations that do not belong to us. This frees us from unnecessary stress."

—Melody Beattie

CHAPTER 37

Listen to Your Inner Voice

June 19, 2015

"Eventually everything connects—people, ideas, objects. The
quality of the connections is the key to quality per se."

—Charles Eames

In the afternoon, Dennis drove to the bus station to pick up the volunteer arriving from London. I was beyond relieved to have another person staying with us. When they arrived back at the house, Dennis introduced me to Sam. The second she walked in, I could feel her radiant charm. She had a wide smile, which revealed glistening white teeth.

"Hi, I'm Jake," I greeted her. She had hazel-green eyes that complemented her light-brown hair. Her Australian accent was like music to my ears, and I looked forward to simply listening to her speak.

After she settled in, the three of us drove to the beach where we met up with an Israeli family who were friends of Dennis. The couple seemed very kind, and they had four young boys. Sam and I swam out past the waves and got to know each other better. There was an instant connection between us as if we had known each other for years, although it had just been a few minutes.

She was twenty-one and had just arrived from London where she had been living the past two years. "When I was nineteen, I moved to

London by myself after landing a job there," she told me. "I needed to gain my independence and wanted to be on my own. I've felt this calling to travel throughout Central America. I don't know why I was drawn here, but I couldn't ignore the hunch." She sold her stuff and left London with a backpack, planning to travel for a year in Central America. She was planning to get her yoga teacher training certification in a few months.

Her free spirit inspired me. She said she was equally inspired by my story. She was the first person I had met close to my age who was ambitiously chasing her dreams, veering off the common path and following her heart.

"What do you think about Dennis?" I asked, trying to conceal any possible judgment in my tone.

"Well, he's definitely an interesting character," she revealed, laughing. I described some of the incidents that had happened. In a humorous yet reflective manner, I told her about both of us crying in the soccer field. My intention wasn't to scare her away from CHI or plant a negative seed in her mind. I wanted her to develop her own view without my biased opinion, and I was curious to see how she would interpret Dennis.

There are moments in our lives in which we feel drawn to someone, connected as if an intangible force has guided us to cross paths. These connections seem to be woven intangibly through the energy that we radiate out to the world, as if a magnetic vitality attracts us to certain people. I reflected on the fact that I was meeting such a diverse spectrum of people, many with like-minded aspirations. And I was happy that being in CHI had connected me with Sam.

We finally swam back to shore, and the three of us drove home and began to prepare a raw plant-based dinner. With the weekend approaching, there was no work to be done. I was looking forward to relaxing and enjoying the natural wonders of the Costa Rican jungle around CHI.

That weekend, I began to notice a dramatic improvement in both my energy level and my skin. At first, I was worried that without meat or lots of protein, I would feel undernourished and weak. Ironically, quite the contrary was happening, even without eating breakfast until around nine in the morning, which was unusual for me. Snacking on fruits and vegetables throughout the day, I actually felt less hungry. I was eating significantly less than I had imagined, but I didn't crave more because I was satisfied after eating such healthy, enriching food. My energy level rose, and I found that I could move around freely even right after eating, whereas I usually felt stuffed or bloated in the past. But what was most intriguing was how my skin was reacting. The acne on the right side of my face stopped breaking out after a few days of eating raw foods. The itchiness and roughness subsided, and the bumpiness was starting to smooth out as well.

Amazed by what was happening to my body, I voiced my delight to Sam and Dennis. "Of course!" Dennis replied with conviction after hearing of the changes. "Vhen you eat like zhis, you feel better! Your body is like a car. If you feed it vith quality fuel, it vill function much better."

Although I was skeptical of many of the things Dennis said, I agreed with him about this. However, I didn't need his opinion to validate what I was feeling—I was my own living proof. No one had to tell me about the positives or negatives of eating raw foods; the results—my improved skin and energy level—were all the evidence I needed.

＊　＊　＊　＊　＊

The Spanish girls—Raquel and Kenia—arrived on Sunday afternoon. I had looked forward to their arrival, which would hopefully foster more of a "community." They were both short with thick black hair and shy, kind auras. Kenia spoke almost no English, and Raquel's vocabulary was limited. The Spanish they spoke was much faster and sounded different than the Spanish spoken in Central America. I could converse with them but couldn't understand when they spoke to each other in fast-paced Spanish. Sam didn't know any Spanish, so communication was mostly nonverbal. Although very friendly, they were more reserved than Sam, and I didn't have the same connection with them that I had with her.

Monday rolled around, and the first day of volunteering for all of us was uneventful. We piled into Dennis's banged-up jeep and drove to the soccer field where we laid out the colossal plastic tarp and finished stapling it together. We all followed Dennis's orders, and his barks and imperious nature unraveled as the sun's heat intensified. Finally, the plastic tarp was finished and ready to be put up on the house. "Ve are done vorking for today. Tomorrow, ve vill put up the plastic so ve can make our green room," Dennis announced.

After we finished, we hopped back into Dennis's jeep. On the way back to the house, he took a detour. He sped onto a dirt road, and accelerated straight toward a creek which lay about twenty yards ahead of us. It was shallow, only a foot or two deep, with rocks covering the ground underneath. All of us were in total shock as Dennis unexpectedly drove straight into the creek. He stopped the car, killed the engine, swung open his door, and stripped off his shorts, exposing his fully naked body. "Ahh," he uttered as he lowered himself into the water.

The four of us were still in the jeep, unsure whether to laugh or question Dennis's brisk decision. I opened the car door and stepped into the creek. I waddled out past the car through the knee-deep water, carefully placing each foot on one slippery stone at a time. I let myself sink into the refreshing water, letting it massage my entire body. Sam and the Spanish girls did the same, and all five of us were immersed in the calming water. After sweating profusely, crawling in the grass, and stapling and folding the plastic tarp for hours, the water was heavenly. There were no other people or cars around, and the surrounding quiet heightened the serene atmosphere. It must have been an interesting sight—a jeep, a naked man, and four other people swimming in a shallow creek.

The next day, Johnny arrived early, and the six of us struggled to hoist the humongous piece of plastic onto the roof. Dennis had tied five huge poles of bamboo in a tent-like fashion onto the roof, which served as a structure on which to hang the tarp. The task looked impossible. Dennis had instructed us to staple the tarp in multiple lines, which I didn't understand at the time. Essentially, we had created loops in the plastic for the bamboo rods to slide through, which would hoist the tarp up. Despite Dennis's seemingly outlandish idea, he was brilliant. He was knowledgeable about permaculture and building. His ingenuity was remarkable, regardless of his lunacy, not to mention he had broken his foot just two months before and was climbing ladders and limping around as if he were Superman. "It is ze food," he stated, explaining that his quick recovery was a result of his healthy eating habits.

The four of us volunteers took our directed stance, holding the tarp with ropes that Dennis had tied to the roof. Johnny was on the roof with a ladder beneath him. Dennis was orchestrating us like a military commander, directing us to pull our ropes in synchronicity, which in turn would levitate the tarp off the ground. The language differences, as well as Dennis's confusing commands, made us feel as lost as polar bears in a desert.

"Vhat are you doing?!?" Dennis shouted at us. "Ahh! You are supposed to lift it like zhis together!" We scrambled to follow his instructions, and soon the tarp was halfway up. "Pull!" he shouted, and we pulled. It took about twenty minutes to finally hoist the tarp up and Dennis almost losing his voice amid a whirlwind of commands.

Even though the five of us were working together, there was no "community" feel, and there was an uncomfortable energy between us and Dennis. Raquel and Kenia's faces revealed their frustration and annoyance with Dennis's forceful demeanor, and Sam told me that this wasn't what she had expected, either. I was glad to know that I was not alone in my feelings about Dennis.

Midway through the week, Sam and I questioned Dennis at dinner about the morning meditation, which he had described online would be part of our daily routines.

"Yes, ve can do that," he agreed. Sam found it just as strange as I did that he wasn't leading us in the things he stated he would. It was supposed to be a healing community yet was anything but that.

The next morning at five thirty when we awoke, we gathered around the pond where Dennis was sitting calmly on a mat with his legs crossed. A few other colorful mats surrounded a small wooden table. Dennis rang a chime and announced we would meditate for thirty minutes. I closed my eyes and relaxed my body as the melodic drip-drop of water trickled into the pond. Birds rang out their peaceful, early morning chirps, and the jungle was awakening around us. The tranquility of CHI was truly special. My thoughts wandered like a kid at Disneyland at first as it took me a few minutes to settle into mental stillness. However, I found that I was unable to fall into the deeply relaxing, light meditative state that I had been able to experience at Eden.

There was something about being in Dennis's presence that made me feel uneasy. His overbearing demeanor projected an unfavorable energy, and it was affecting me. For the entire thirty-minute meditation, I couldn't calm my stirring thoughts. I peeled my eyes open only to notice both of the Spanish girls with their eyes wide open. It turned out they had never meditated before. Dennis didn't explain anything to them about how to meditate or what it was. I talked with Sam after, and she felt exactly the same way I did.

"I don't feel comfortable around him. He just sends out a negative vibe," she confided in me. Despite all of our dissatisfaction with the way things were going, Dennis had not the slightest inclination that anything was remotely wrong.

*   *   *   *   *

A week had passed since the Spanish girls had arrived and Dennis assigned me the task of chopping down dying plants and brush to clear the way for new plants. I grabbed the machete and began slicing away. I was absorbed in the task, chopping away as my mind zoned in and my body responded to my mental commands. After what felt like a few hours, Dennis walked over and let out a scream.

"No! Vhat have you done?!?" I peered at him in bewilderment. He was looking at me as if I had killed someone. "Vhy ze hell did you cut down my lemon tree?!?!"

"Wh…what?" I stammered in confusion.

He lifted up a small tree off the ground. "You cut down my dwarf lemon tree!" his face was red as a beet, and there was agony in his voice as if I had sliced him, not the tree.

"I…I'm…I'm sorry," I muttered. A pit formed in my stomach, and I felt genuinely bad about what I had accidently done. "I didn't mean to. I thought you said to cut…"

"I said cut down ze brush and plants and vines, not my lemon tree!" he boomed. His instructions, like usual, had been vague. I didn't recall his warning me about a tree being in the midst of it.

"I'm sorry," I said, trying to convey the sincerity I felt. "I didn't know this was a lemon tree; there are no lemons on it."

"Duh!" he piped aloud. "They are not in season."

At this point, Sam and the Spanish girls had approached to witness Dennis's outburst. I glanced up at Sam who was trying to conceal her laughter. I truly felt sympathy for Dennis. But suddenly, I felt an overwhelming urge to burst out in nervous laughter. *Dude, I'm sorry for cutting down your sacred lemon tree. Honestly, I feel really bad. But would you calm down a little? Your directions were unclear, and it was obvious that I didn't do it intentionally.* My mind had apparently shifted to humor in an attempt to cope with the stress and awkwardness of the situation. It's interesting how our minds can resort to laughter in the strangest of circumstances. Maybe humans were programmed like this as a reminder to laugh more and remember that life isn't so serious— even if you accidentally cut down someone's lemon tree.

Dennis stormed off into the house. The Spanish girls and Sam walked over to me and erupted in laughter. They all reassured me that Dennis had overreacted and that it was obviously an accident. Standing in the garden beyond where Dennis could see or hear us, we all began revealing how we felt about Dennis and CHI.

"He is not nice to me," Kenia voiced as best as she could in English.

"Yeah," Raquel revealed. "He is mean to us and says demanding things. We did not think it would be like this."

It was surprising to hear that the Spanish girls were upset with Dennis as well. Although we were all subjected to Dennis's wrath, the four of us had never collectively discussed how we felt before.

"It bothers me how he says one thing yet does something totally opposite," Sam revealed. "He preaches a natural environment yet is smoking cigarettes all of the time. I don't care if he wants to smoke, but he can't tell us this is a drug-free, holistic environment when he goes against his own word."

We all discussed Dennis's aggressive personality. Everyone agreed that the morning meditation was completely ineffective as Dennis's presence created anxiety and discomfort. He was constantly shoving his opinions down our throats and interrupting us whenever we spoke. The "healing environment" that Dennis had described online was far from our experience. The discrepancies between Dennis's actions and words were far too many to count.

That night, a thunderstorm rolled in and a huge tree fell down, knocking out the power line. In the morning, Dennis tried fixing the power while the rest of us were lounging in a natural pool nearby. However, he could not get the Wi-Fi to work.

After four days had passed without Wi-Fi, I strolled into town and went to the Wi-Fi café. I checked my e-mail, finding a message from my mom. She hadn't heard from me in a week and was worried that something might be wrong. I replied, reassuring her that I was fine and explained the Wi-Fi situation. I revealed Dennis's strange behavior, how my skin was tremendously improving and how I felt physically well despite the odd vibe that Dennis gave off. I expressed my hesitancy at being at CHI for another two weeks, but explained that things would work out one way or another. I can handle another two weeks here. At least, I thought…

"Your mind knows only some things. Your inner voice, your instinct, knows everything. If you listen to what you know instinctively, it will always lead you down the right path."
—Henry Winkler

CHAPTER 38

Stepping Stones

June 30, 2015

*"Don't wait for your feelings to change to take action.
Take the actions and your feelings will change."*

—Barbara Baron

About a week after I chopped down the lemon tree, it became clear to me that Sam and the Spanish girls were equally as fed up with Dennis as I was. Dennis had been particularly snappy, constantly interrupting us, and enforcing "his way" of doing things when our way was working perfectly fine. We were reaching the tipping point of our tolerance levels. Dennis went into town to run some errands while the rest of us were hanging at the house.

"I'm going to leave tomorrow," Sam announced.

"Really?" I responded, completely surprised. The suddenness of her statement came out of the blue.

"Yeah," she replied. "I've been thinking a lot the past few days. I came to Central America to explore positive ways of life. I want to experience and be around people who will bring out the best in me. Dennis makes me feel the opposite, and I didn't come here to feel that way."

"Where are you going to go?" I asked.

"I've been communicating with someone on Workaway. I found a hostel where I can work for three weeks."

"Yes, we want to leave, too," Raquel added. "We were thinking about going tomorrow or the next day as well."

Their words sunk in heavily. From the moment I had met Dennis, my gut triggered a warning that something didn't feel right. It suddenly hit me that I had been ignoring that warning for the past two weeks. I had settled with the idea that I would spend a certain amount of time at CHI, and this blocked my ability to *listen* to my own intuition. As the last two weeks had unfolded, the uneasiness I felt around Dennis did not subside. But because my mind was so fixed on the "plan" of staying another two weeks, I had been overlooking what was in my own best interest.

"Well, then, I guess I'm leaving, too," I announced. The wheels in my head began to spin at the thought of leaving. I had no idea where I would go or when I would leave. "When are you guys leaving?" I asked the Spanish girls.

"Probably tomorrow as well."

"There's no way I'm staying here alone with Dennis," I laughed. "I'm leaving tomorrow then, too."

I had now awakened the most powerful realization of all: I have 100 percent control over my own life. The other volunteers' decisions to leave were a wake-up call to me. Things in life rarely turn out as expected, but I had forgotten that I had the power to create my own reality. While life is unpredictable, we can always control our own response and reaction to our life's circumstances.

"Wohoo!" Sam exclaimed.

It's impossible to understand what other people are thinking if we don't express ourselves and ask questions. Likewise, others won't understand what we think unless we speak up. To forget you have a voice—or to not use your voice—is dangerous. The root of miscommunication often stems from a lack of communication in the first place.

We began discussing the conversation that none of us was looking forward to having: breaking the news to Dennis. The fact that all four of us were leaving would not sit well with him. It would require an articulate, careful selection of words to explain our decision without riling him up. It was inevitable that he would be upset. But we could do our best to figure out a plan so that he would take the news in the least personal manner possible. We decided that Sam and I would do most of the talking. Sam would drop the news at dinner, and I would back her up.

The afternoon rolled on in slow motion, and dinner finally approached. It started out as normal, and Dennis didn't have the slightest idea that anything was wrong. He was smiling his usual zany smile and talking endlessly like he did at any other dinner. The four of us stole glances at each other as we anticipated breaking the news. A swarm of butterflies fluttered in my stomach as dinner inched on. I flashed a look toward Sam, curious to see when she would start the awkward conversation. She caught my glance and turned toward Dennis.

"Dennis," Sam began, "We want to tell you something. I would really appreciate it if you would not interrupt me, and let me say my part."

Dennis nodded, his face now alert as an owl's.

"After much consideration, we have all decided we are going to leave tomorrow."

Dennis's eyes began to widen, and his eyebrows slanted downward. His face froze as if he were a statue.

"It has become evident to all of us that CHI is not like what you said it would be…"

"What do you mean?" Dennis interjected, dumbstruck.

"Please, let me finish," Sam calmly asked. "It bothers me that there is a huge difference between what you practice and what you preach. For example, you said this was a drug-free, healing environment, yet you smoke cigarettes…"

Dennis jutted in, his voice now fiery and defensive. "That is because I vas very stressed-out; I had three volunteers leave me vith no notice, and zhey didn't do vhat I asked, and my foot is not functioning like normal, and so much vork needs to be done." He argued as if he were a victim and that none of it was *his fault* but that everything had happened to *him*.

"Please, Dennis, let me finish without interrupting," Sam smoothly replied. She continued to explain all of the discrepancies between what Dennis had said on the website and what was actually happening. Dennis wanted to interrupt so badly that he looked like a kid desperately needing to use the bathroom.

He butted in again, not letting Sam finish her sentence. At this point, I was becoming annoyed at Dennis's lack of respect to let her speak.

"Dennis," I inserted. "It's not fair to keep interrupting," I tried communicating calmly.

"It's not impolite to interrupt because I am saving vasted time. If someone says something incorrect, I vill cut zhem off," Dennis argued, trying to rationalize his abrupt, narrow-minded viewpoint.

I couldn't understand how his mind worked. He was dead serious that interrupting people helped prevent "vasted time," and that there was nothing wrong with doing so. I glanced toward Sam and the Spanish girls. The look on their faces revealed the same shock that I felt.

"See, that's another example of something that we all find uncomfortable," I said. "Although you may not mean to, whenever you ask us to do something, you tend to do it in a very commanding way. Sometimes, we do things differently, and you get mad because we are not doing it your way and…"

"Vhy would I sit and vatch you do something vhen my vay is better," he cut in. None of us replied. It was pointless to try to rationalize with Dennis.

I began to realize that he would not be able to see our point of view no matter how hard we tried. Sam and I tried explaining our frustrations with him from different angles to no avail. His closed-mindedness prevented him from being able to see things from a different perspective. And yet, he was flabbergasted. For the life of him, he could not understand how he had done anything wrong.

"Okay, fine," Dennis, declared. "You can leave, I don't care." He got up and left the kitchen table, angrily storming off to his room.

In the other room, we could hear him calling other prospective volunteers. It made my stomach churn, and I genuinely felt sad for him. All seven of the volunteers who had arrived in the last three weeks had decided to leave. He still didn't think that he was doing anything wrong. He couldn't bear the idea of being alone with himself. He needed other people around to fill his own emptiness. He was an excessive talker and lacked the patience and ability to listen, which signaled to me that he was fearful of hearing anything that would challenge his viewpoint. His beliefs were as fragile as glass slippers, and the possibility of one of his viewpoints being wrong or challenged would shatter his ego.

I stood up and walked over to Dennis's room by myself. Although Dennis was clearly angry, I felt that I had emotional leverage with him from the day we had cried together in the park. "Dennis, can I talk to you for a minute?"

"Yes," he replied without looking up, his eyes glued to his computer screen.

With the utmost sincerity and no intention to hurt his feelings, I revealed, "I really think you would benefit from taking some time to be alone before you ask other volunteers to come. I believe your intentions are good, and that you've opened your home to create a positive community. But I think it would be best for you to reflect on everything we've said before other volunteers arrive."

"Thanks," he muttered. "Is zhere anyzing else you vant to say?"

"No, that's basically it. And I just wanted to thank you for everything else and for helping to heal my skin. I really appreciate it and hope everything works out for you."

I had revealed everything that was on my mind. I genuinely hoped Dennis would change although it seemed unlikely. I empathized with the loneliness that clearly afflicted him.

The next morning, I was planning on taking a bus with Sam to a town called Dominical about forty minutes from Uvita. Sam had heard of a good hostel there, and I decided I would go with her as I had no clue where else to go.

As I lay in bed for the last time at CHI, I began to reflect on my last two weeks. Overall, it had been a positive learning experience. The benefits of eating raw, organic foods had significantly improved my skin in just two weeks. I got to live in a tropical gem and was exposed to the magnificent array of biodiversity that surrounded it. But most important, I learned much more about myself and how to deal with a difficult and unreasonable person. I learned how to navigate and manage Dennis's narrow-minded, dominating persona. I learned when to let things go and when to press him, how to approach him and what tone of voice to use. He ultimately deepened the importance I placed on people practicing what they preach and sticking to their word. His lack of integrity and bossy behavior showed me what *not* to do and how *not* to treat people.

The experiences that don't go as planned are often the ones that we can learn the most from. When we are faced with obstacles, we are forced to find new ways to move forward. The unexpected is what challenges us to think in new ways, be creative, and listen to our gut. The experience reinforced the importance of following my intuition. We cannot hope for something to get better when it is clear that it will not improve. We cannot wait for life to change—we have to be that change. And we have to act in the *now*, not in the *future*. The beauty of life is experienced in the present moment. I was so caught up waiting for the next two weeks to end that I wasn't enjoying and appreciating life in the present. My mind was clinging to the future, and this signaled that something was wrong with the present and that I had to make a change.

> *"Difficulties are opportunities to better things;*
> *they are stepping-stones to greater experience...*
> *When one door closes, another always opens;*
> *as a natural law it has to, to balance."*
>
> —Brian Adams

CHAPTER 39

The Universe is in Us

June 31, 2015

"Each day holds a surprise. But only if we expect it can we see, hear, or feel it when it comes to us. Let's not be afraid to receive each day's surprise, whether it comes to us as sorrow or as joy. It will open a new place in our hearts, a place where we can welcome new friends and celebrate more fully our shared humanity."

—Henri Nouwer

On the bus to Dominical, I expected to feel happy after leaving Dennis's wrath. As Sam and I boarded the bus, she gleefully rejoiced, "Ah, we're free! I'm free! I'm free! I'm free!" I smiled at her, trying to emulate her positivity and apparent feelings of freedom. But I couldn't—even as hard as I tried. Not knowing where I would go next made me feel uneasy. Sam was planning to leave Dominical the day after tomorrow and head toward another town to work in a hostel for a few weeks. I had absolutely no idea what my next move was going to be, and this concerned me. I had settled on the idea that my journey was going to end after spending a wonderful month in CHI—I had not expected my plans to fall through. Despite having faced the unexpected multiple times on my travels, I was downcast. I began to stress out over the details of what to do. My money was running low, and I was going to be alone after Sam left.

We arrived in Dominical and approached a hostel. After we checked in, Sam informed me that she was going to do some yoga on the beach and spend some time on her own. After taking a shower and getting my stuff settled, I walked into the main hangout area of the hostel. There were a couple of guys and a girl talking excitedly as they were putting on their socks and shoes. I smiled over at them, and one of the girls greeted me.

"Hi! Did you just arrive?" she asked.

"Hey," I responded. "Yes, I just got in a few minutes ago."

"Oh, cool!" she exclaimed. She oozed positivity. "I just got in this morning as well. We heard there is an amaaazzzinngg hike to a waterfall, and we are going now if you want to come."

"You know...I..." I paused for a moment. I was searching for a nice way to say "no." My spirits were dampened, and for whatever reason, I was feeling close-minded. I didn't know any of these people, and the thought of a long hike sounded exhausting.

In the split second that I was contemplating my decision and searching for a justification for not going, she interjected again. "Come on! It will be a blast. We've heard from like everybody that the hike is sooo worth it!"

"You know what, yeah. Yeah, I'll go. Why not?" I blurted out before I had a chance to process what I agreed to.

"Wohoo!" she cheered. "Okay, we're leaving in two minutes, so go grab some hiking shoes and whatever else you need!"

I scrambled into my room and threw on a pair of swim trunks and my hiking shoes. I met them back in the hangout area, and we all walked outside to board a van that was going to take us to the waterfall—the Nuayaca Waterfall it was called, one of the biggest in Costa Rica.

There were five of us including me. Kim was the one who had greeted me and convinced me to come. She had glistening, hazelnut skin that shone just as much as her buoyant energy. She was bald and looked unlike most of the travelers I had met. I liked Kim immediately; her optimistic nature made her a delight to be around. She was a yoga teacher from Brooklyn and was visiting Costa Rica to prepare for a yoga retreat. Joakim and Jun were two friends from Norway. They were spending a month surfing up and down the coast. Joakim had long, strawberry hair that hung down to his neck. He had facial hair to match and light, pale skin beneath it. He was the definition of an adventure seeker. He had spent a year sailing around the world, and I loved hearing his stories. Jun had fair, blonde hair and light-blue eyes. He and I connected instantly over soccer, and I enjoyed being around his easygoing, curious persona. Amanda was peppy, yet not in the same way as Kim. She had grown up in Costa Rica, and her spontaneous attitude was about as free-spirited as one could possibly be. She had been to the waterfall before and had convinced everyone else to come. Amanda had long, dirty-blonde hair with a hint of red that swayed with a carefree kick to it.

The van dropped us off, and we began the hike to the waterfall. The clayish trail was wide and encompassed a vast canopy of ivy trees and emerald leaves. Bamboo trees sprung out of the ground like densely packed bundles of asparagus. A patchwork of green hills roamed endlessly throughout the tropical rainforest. Time seemed nonexistent as we hiked toward the waterfall, engaged in each other's storytelling. The whisper of falling water was getting louder and louder, and a pervasive cooling mist countered the humid air. We followed a staircase down toward the sound of rushing water, which became more amplified the farther we descended.

As I reached the bottom and turned a corner, I was struck by the pure magnificence before my eyes. Extending out from the trees lay a massive cliff towering 150 feet above a bed of rocks. Water cascaded down the face of the rocky, mossy cliff. A refreshing mist soared outward as droplets of water evaporated from the falls into thin air. It was a force of nature both profound and mesmerizing.

We followed the trail farther down to the next waterfall, which had a natural pool. This waterfall was just over 60 feet tall, and mossy ferns and plants were embedded in the rock wall. The water gushed down as if sliding down steps of a staircase, with a hissing noise that drowned out everything except the wondrous nature of its being.

The five of us eagerly submerged ourselves in the pool. I swam towards the cliff where water was flowing downward like a silky curtain. I hoisted myself up onto a rocky platform, sitting beneath the falling water. The water gushed down onto my head and shoulders, flooding me in a shower of endless energy. The loud rush of water stormed my ears, and I became immersed in the waterfall.

Sitting under this abundance of water, I couldn't help but smile at how things had worked out the last few weeks. The abrupt ending in Uvita had left me feeling anxious for the unknown path ahead. Just as I was beginning to feel lonely, an opportunity surfaced that led to this magical place. Dennis's door slammed shut, but my reconsidered, second decision to say "yes" to an invitation by a stranger had led me through a new door—and what a door it was!

When we truly align with our deepest selves and follow our intuition, the Universe has a mysterious way of working with us, not against us. The rough moments in life bring us down only so we can realize how far up we can climb from there. It's when things go down and don't work out like we planned that the brightest opportunities arise.

I spent the next week in Dominical with the amazing new group of friends I had made. I said goodbye to Sam and wished her well on the rest of her travels. We laughed about the whirlwind of events at CHI and how everything worked out. We promised to stay in touch as we moved forward on our own journeys.

On my last night, I sat on the beach with Kim and Joakim peering out at the shining crescent of a moon in the dark night sky. A few bolts of lightning flashed in the distance, illuminating the horizon. The waves were calmly rolling to shore, and the palm leaves swayed in the wind. We alternated from insightful conversations to stillness and zoning out in our own thoughts as we looked out into the endless sky and absorbed the scenery around us.

A light, tickling sensation enveloped me as I sat in complete peace on the sand. Being honest with myself and projecting a positive energy had consistently drawn me to meet like-minded, inspiring people from all over the world. My body relaxed as if I were releasing every ounce of energy that was in conflict with who I was—who I had become. I glowed with a sensation of complete self-acceptance like the sun expanding its light infinitely outward.

In that moment, I was convinced that some higher force—God, the Center of Nature, Oneness, spirit, Allah, or whatever one wishes to call it—was present all around me and within me. My entire being was connected as if by a magnet to this ever-present sensation of wholeness. Every question that I had ever had—trying to understand depression and hardships and passion and life and death—none of it mattered. My mind had broken down into simple terms what life meant to me. I finally accepted it without question, not wondering why, but just accepting.

Life is an endless journey. Every experience that we have is simply a lesson in the grand scheme of things. There is no right or wrong. It's up to us to determine the purpose of our lives and to live in accordance with what fulfills our soul. My time in Dominical had provided me with answers I didn't know I was seeking. Now, I was ready to come home. There was just one more thing that I wanted to do.

"Peace comes within the souls of men when they realize their oneness with the Universe, when they realize it is really everywhere, it is within each of us."
—Black Elk

CHAPTER 40

A Leap of Faith

July 9, 2015

*"Sometimes you find yourself in the middle of nowhere,
and sometimes, in the middle of nowhere, you find yourself."*
—Unknown

The highest bungee jump in Central America lay amid the cloud forests of Monteverde. I stepped into the red cart overlooking the vast, beautiful valley. The cart, attached to the lone cables above, began moving slowly toward the center of the misty jungle ahead, 470 feet above the ground. A blanket of clouds filled the sky, and the wind whipped against my body as the cooling air awakened my senses. The cart shook slightly in the flapping wind as it approached the center of the cables. I gazed down at the cloud forest, which, from my vantage point, looked like a tie-dye of green swirls.

Raul, the worker on the cart with me, strapped me into a vest and attached my feet and waist to the bungee line harness. He double-checked everything and exclaimed above the sound of the wind, "I'm going to count down from five. On one, you jump. Are you ready?" he shouted.

"Yeah!" I yelled back. My heart began beating harder and faster in my chest like a locomotive train gaining speed. As I neared the edge of the cart, warm blood surged through my veins like an electrical current.

"Five, four, three..." Raul's voice rang out as I peered over the edge, gaping at the green patterns below. The variety of shades and textures looked psychedelic. My feet were on the very edge and there was nothing I could say or think to control the drumming inside my chest.

"Two, one!"

I bent my knees and launched myself forward like an eagle, extending my arms and legs out wide. My stomach dropped so quickly I couldn't prepare for the emotions and screams of exhilaration that poured out of me. A million thoughts flashed through my head, all surrendering to a bolt of adrenaline. The wind fanned fiercely against my face and concealed every sound except the rush of air in my ears. I felt weightless, my body simply a source of lightness, plunging toward the green floor beneath me. The swirls of green trees were becoming bigger and bigger, and I finally felt a sudden resistance that halted my free fall. I bounced back toward the sky, my head and body spinning like a merry-go-round, and the world a blur of greens.

When I finally stopped spinning, I hung upside down, viewing the world in a way I had never seen it before. Blood rushed to my head, and wooziness set in due to my loss of equilibrium. I felt so alive, so invigorated—so free. After a couple more bounces and swings, I crunched my abs together to hoist myself up. Raul dropped down a rope, which I caught and hooked onto my vest. Slowly, he pulled me back up toward the cart. I peered out at the sweeping forest, examining the shape and size of trees which only seconds before had appeared as green swirls.

The refreshing air swam through my nose, filling me with well-needed heaps of clean oxygen. As I rose to the top and stepped into the cart, I was buzzing with inexplicable energy. My smile was so wide that my cheeks were scrunching up into my eyes, blocking my vision. I felt on top of the world.

Every emotion I had experienced in the past year flashed through my mind. I recalled the memories of waking up in my dorm room every day—confused and itchy and anxious and depressed. I remembered sitting alone in the staircase of my dorm every week in tears— ravaged with self-doubt and uncertainty, enslaved by my own mind. I had set out on this journey from a dark place searching for proof—proof that there isn't just one way to live; proof that we can create our own special and unique reality by taking action that aligns with our truest desires; proof that by going beyond what the mind deems as possible, we can understand how truly powerful we are. And I had found that proof; I had answered my questions.

When I started my travels, I thought the journey would be about finding myself. And maybe it was. But maybe it was more about *uncovering* myself. Maybe it was about peeling back layers that had built up over time from external influences and opinions and stigmas and beliefs. Traveling had opened my perception to a world of infinite possibilities, unlocking doors and revealing new facets of life that awoke my inner being.

When we are kids, we have a unique fascination with the world. Every flash of color, every minute detail, every invigorating smell, every baffling sound, every new face—they captivate and enthrall us, filling us with desire to experience and take in the boundless pieces of the puzzle we call life. These fresh elements arouse our growing curiosity of the realm before our eyes. We aren't concerned about being right or wrong, rich or poor, democratic or republican, boy or girl, black or white. We just accept the kaleidoscope and influx of emotions and sensory detail that is life. We simply are. We are beautiful, breathing balls of energy and love. And we still are.

Traveling had a way of reminding me of that—providing me with a set of newborn eyes to view the world. It brought me back to the essence of being a child, breathing anew—once again optimistic, open-minded, and adventurous.

But the journey really wasn't about leaving school or traveling or arriving at a "destination." It was more about the *process*—about listening to my inner voice and following my intuition.

Epilogue

Since returning home to San Diego, I've enjoyed spending time with family and friends, surfing, practicing yoga, reading and writing.

The day after returning home, I started writing this book and got a job bussing tables at a restaurant in the evenings. In the meantime, I created a blog "Eyes Fully Open" (www.jakeheilbrunn.com/blog) where every week I share my insights on living life fully aware and topics related to human nature and motivation. I've also been creating inspirational videos and messages on Facebook, YouTube and other social media platforms. If you want to read my articles, watch my videos and see my messages, please visit www.jakeheilbrunn.com and subscribe to stay updated.

I had the privilege of speaking to 2,000 students at Torrey Pines High School—the school I graduated from—where I shared my story and the lessons I learned from my journey. My wish is to speak at other schools and venues to inspire people to have the courage to listen to their intuition, pursue a meaningful life and venture off the beaten trail.

I've stayed in touch with many of the people I met traveling, including Arnulfo. I've joined forces with him and his NGO *Amor,* which is dedicated to providing aid to the indigenous communities of Guatemala devastated by genocide and extreme poverty. A percentage of the proceeds from each book I sell will go directly towards supporting AMOR. If you wish to be a part of Arnulfo's mission and get involved, please visit www.amorguatemala.org.

Aside from writing, speaking, and continuing to take steps to get my book out into the world, I'm not sure exactly what my future holds. I do know that I will continue to pursue my goal of inspiring others to take the actions that will help them lead a fulfilling, purposeful life.

Thank you for being a part of this journey with me. I would love to hear about your own thoughts, plans and dreams. Feel free to email me at jake@jakeheilbrunn.com.

Acknowledgements

Grateful and humbled. Words can only convey so much, but these two embody how I feel when I think about trying to thank all of the people who helped me create this book.

To my dad, for the countless hours spent helping me with edits. Your dedication to my book means the world to me.

To my mom, Nikki and Bella, for your continuous love and support in my life, my book, and my dreams.

To Nana, Poppy, and Opa Chuck: you've given me the opportunity to live a life pursuing what makes me happy. You've instilled in me the foundation of what it means to be conscious and respectful, and your guidance is something I cherish.

I'm indebted to Martha Bullen (coach) for counseling me and Madalyn Stone (editor) for all of your help and patience. A huge thank you to all my beta readers for your invaluable feedback (you know who you are!) A special thanks to Barbara Swovelin, Kevin Haselhorst, Hilary Kraft and Paul Coleman for your feedback, advice and assistance. Thank you to Jake Ducey for inspiring me to forge my own path and being a role model.

I'm deeply grateful to my Kickstarter community (all 154 of you!) for raising the funds to make this book a reality. A special shout out to: Charles, Greg, Judy, Erica and Jason Heilbrunn, Walter Greene, Jacob Neeley, Jake Scornavocco, the Schubach family, Phyllis and Jerry Rogovin, the Pittard family, Bill and Tina Hall, the Roussos family, David Milward, the Patrick family, Graceful Departures LLC, the Pearlman family, John Vallas and Swell Coffee Co, the Perkins family, Mitchell King, the Goldberg family, Martin Goodman, the Quigg family and Barbara Swovelin.

Nothing but love for Chandler, Elliot, Jacob, John, Peter and Eli for having my back through thick and thin.

Thank you to Workaway for providing cultural exchange and making the world a better place. To all of the generous people I met on my travels who enriched my life and made this journey what it was—I'm so grateful for your help.

And to all the unnamed who helped me along the way, I give you my deepest thanks.

CPSIA information can be obtained
at www.ICGtesting.com
Printed in the USA
FSOW01n0430070916
24665FS

9 780997 761207